DOING ETHICS
IN
BUSINESS

DOING ETHICS IN BUSINESS

New Ventures in Management Development

Edited by
Donald G. Jones
Drew University

Oelgeschlager, Gunn & Hain, Publishers, Inc.
Cambridge, Massachusetts

International Standard Book Number: 0-89946-159-x (cloth)
0-89946-167-0 (paper)

Library of Congress Catalog Card Number: 82-8294

Printed in West Germany

Library of Congress Cataloging in Publication Data
Main entry under title:

Doing ethics in business.

  Bibliography: p.
  Includes index.
  1. Business ethics—Addresses, essays, lectures.
I. Jones, Donald G.
HF5387.D64   1982   174'.4   82-8294
ISBN 0-89946-159-x
ISBN 0-89946-167-0 (pbk.)

Contents

Preface

Acknowledgments

v

Preface

This book is about applied business ethics, reporting on unusual new management development programs in ethics training and discussing other means of applying ethics to business. Designed primarily for executives responsible for human resource development in corporations, teachers and students of ethics, business educators, and for culture critics who follow developments in business, this volume tries to strike a balance between practice and theory. For someone interested in setting up a training program in management ethics, this book can serve as a practical guide. As an introduction to applied ethics, it is a primer that tries to speak in plain language while maintaining intellectual integrity.

The central theme that ties all of the chapters together is the integration of ethics into management practice. Programs are described in which this goal is the basic objective. Conceptual frameworks and models of decisionmaking showing how ethics can be integrated into business are also presented. And practices, procedures, and cultures of management are scrutinized with a view to showing the possibilities of such an integration and the perils of failing to do so.

The purposes of the book are fourfold: (1) to present a state-of-the-art analysis of select new training programs for ethical management; (2) to provide an introduction to applied business ethics; (3) to explore new ways business ethics can be taught and integrated into management practice; and (4) to encourage the further development of business ethics as a collaborative enterprise of professional managers and educators.

Because of the uniqueness of this volume, a comment about its genesis is in order. In the summer of 1980 Drew University sponsored a workshop conference, "The Teaching and Application of Ethics in Industry," which was funded by the Allied Corporation Foundation and held at the Allied Training Center in New Jersey. Twenty-four participants, evenly divided between executives and professors, read papers and discussed what was going on and what ought to be going on in relating ethics to corporations. All of the contributors to this volume attended the workshop except for Douglas Sturm. Chapters in this book are revisions of the initial presentations in light of the workshop discussions, further reflections, and new experiences. While Laura Nash attended the conference, her chapter, "Ethics Without the Sermon," represents fresh work and is related only indirectly to the Drew conference.

Divided into three parts, the ten chapters in this book all address the question, "how can you teach ethics and how otherwise can ethics be institutionalized in corporations?" Part I contains reports from five major corporations. Three are reports on unusual experiments in management ethics training at the Allied Corporation, Cummins Engine Company, and Lockheed–California Company. Each includes a rationale and evaluation. Chapter 4 reports on the unique venture of combining policy formation and planning with ethics training at Northwestern National Bank of Minneapolis. Chapter 5 in this section presents the results of an ethical impact analysis done at Sun Company.

All of the essays in Part I provide an introduction to the new field of business ethics. To read them is a little like looking over the shoulders of ethics teachers as they try to apply their craft to the world of business.

Part II contains two chapters, both of which introduce the new discipline of business ethics to readers who might be confused or doubtful about such a discipline. Chapter 6, "Ethics Without the Sermon," offers a practical procedure of ethical inquiry consisting of twelve questions. The author's aim is to present this process of ethical inquiry so as to be comprehensive and immediately available to business executives. Chapter 7, which is on teaching business ethics, provides a definition of business ethics with proposals as to objectives and methods appropriate to teaching ethics to managers and students of business.

Part III emphasizes the "doing of ethics." One chapter is by a former executive concerned with the question of what constitutes the "essentials of an ethical corporate climate." Another essay centers on a case study as a means of testing an ethical method, while another employs an empirical method in "assessing government regulation vs. self-regulation of marketing ethics."

As the editor of this volume, I confess to a certain exhilaration in being acquainted with a group of authors who can write on business ethics without defending or attacking business and who can come out of more comfortable chairs of theory into the ambiguities of the real world without sacrificing scholarship. The exhilaration I feel arises out of a conviction that scholarship is best done when ideological bias is minimized and when theory is tested in the real world. This has characterized our attempt as we have explored new frontiers of business ethics.

If this book makes more understandable the meaning of ethics and its relation to business, it will have succeeded.

D. J.
The Darden School of Business
Charlottesville, Virginia
April 1982

Acknowledgments

My debt of gratitude to the Allied Corporation is great. Because of a grant from the Allied Foundation in 1980, Drew University was able to host an innovative conference on the "Teaching of Ethics in Industry," and the papers and discussion from that conference led to this book. In addition to the initial grant, Allied made their training center available as the location of the conference.

Particular thanks go to Mr. Alan Painter, Corporate Vice President and Executive Director of the Allied Foundation, for his professional guidance and interest throughout the project.

Gratitude is due the Ethics Resource Center of Washington, D.C., and Mr. Gary Edwards, Executive Director, for a grant that helped defray expenses and provide support for the project in less tangible ways. During the final stages of preparation, The Center for the Study of Applied Ethics at the Darden School of Business provided essential support including the expert secretarial help of Joanne Gaydos, to whom I am especially grateful.

Gerald E. Ottoson, a contributor to this book, and my former team teacher in the Allied Business Ethics Seminar, deserves special thanks. This book would not have been possible without his pioneering efforts in management ethics training. I owe thanks to Charles Bischoff, Jr., Director of Management Resources, for his continued support of my work and Arnold J. Frigeri, Director of Management Development, and Daniel A. McElwreath, Manager of Management Development, for their collaborative efforts in team teaching the Business Ethics Seminar at Allied. A special thanks also goes to Bruce Grob who provided logistic and psychological support throughout. Finally, I want to thank my son David, who designed the cover of this book and who at thirteen seems as ethical as he is a Rubik's cube expert.

PART I

Applied Ethics in Five Corporations

Chapter 1

A Business Ethics Seminar for Executives at Allied Corporation

Donald G. Jones

Is it possible to get busy corporate executives to think, read, and talk about ethics? Can pragmatic managers benefit from reflection on rights and duties, conflicting values, and competing stakeholder claims? Managers at Allied Corporation tried to find answers to these questions in the spring of 1973, in a "Business Ethics Seminar" for upper-level managers. Insofar as the enterprise of ethics aims to minimize human harm and promote human welfare, the objective of the seminar was to help managers learn to integrate a concern for human welfare into managerial practice.

The answers came in. Yes, ethics was a subject that evoked intense conversation, head-on debates, sober reflection, and considerable good humor. Yes, discussing the ethical aspects of practical management was so interesting to these pioneering participants that they recommended almost unanimously that the seminars be continued. By 1982, over 300 managers had attended Allied's Business Ethics Seminar, which had become one of the high-prestige seminars among the firm's in-house development programs.

I was a team teacher with Gerald E. Ottoson, Director of Training and Development for Allied, in the seminar's pilot program. This chapter is an interpretive report on this unique venture in developing managerial resources. I describe the seminar's rationale and content in order to introduce readers to the concept of business ethics. My not-so-hidden agenda, however, is to promote the teaching of ethics to managers and managers-to-be.

GENESIS OF THE BUSINESS ETHICS SEMINAR

Allied, a diversified transnational corporation, has been a major producer of specialty and industrial chemicals, fibers, and energy products. In 1982 it ranked fifty-fifth among *Fortune's* 500 largest industrial corporations. It comprises over 200 plants, quarries, research labs, and other facilities and employs more than 58,000 persons in the United States and overseas.

Allied's history over the past decade has been interesting, dramatic, and at times even tumultuous, and the Business Ethics Seminar has been a continuing forum for analysis of this history. The first major changes came when John T. Connor, Secretary of Commerce under former President Lyndon Johnson, became chairman in 1968. Connor streamlined operations and hired a host of new professional managers—many of whom were young managers with high potential and who are now in top positions in the company. Connor also instigated fresh approaches to strategic planning, including a version of "management by objectives" called "the action plan" that involved all salaried employees in goal setting and strategic planning. A new professionalism marked by creativity, flexibility, and innovation was introduced.

John T. Connor brought something else to the company that seemed to fit the changing market and macroenvironments of business. Allied had been proud of its community relations and basic market morality. Connor, known as a good corporate statesman, enhanced that pride by providing a vision and a style of leadership that encouraged the company to be a "good corporate citizen." Connor's in-house policy directives, public speeches, and managerial style communicated his commitment to ethics and corporate responsibility.

This is not to say that Allied was a paragon of corporate virtue, for there was no evidence that the concept of social responsibility and corporate ethics was systematically integrated into managerial practice. Nevertheless, it is fair to say that Allied's employees, especially under the leadership of Connor, had a strong feeling for ethics and the concept of social responsibility.

In 1973 the declarations of social responsibility by American corporations were challenged by the unveiling of the "Watergate" scandals. Week after week in the spring and summer of 1973 headlines proclaimed the illegal political contributions of corporations to the Committee to Re-elect the President. Allied's experience was unusual. On the same day that front-page stories announced large illegal contributions by American Airlines and Gulf Oil, the business sections of various papers reported that John T. Connor, Chief Executive Officer of Allied, had been contacted directly by Maurice

Stans, then Chairman of the Committee to Re-elect the President, and asked to make a corporate cash contribution of $50,000. The *New York Times* reported that

> Connor rejected the request, noting "that Mr. Stans had suggested that the Allied gift should be made early—before the new Federal disclosure requirement covering contributions took effect."[1]

As Allied managers remember it, the sense of pride and relief that followed was accompanied by both informal and formal expressions of concern about business ethics, and in this upbeat atmosphere the first gesture toward institutionalizing the study of ethics was made. The vice-president of corporate affairs sent a memo to the director of training and development suggesting that he consider including a business ethics module in the management development program. This suggestion from one of the most powerful executives in the company was received as a mandate.

After many conversations with his counterparts in other companies, members of the clergy, professors of ethics, and business school teachers, Gerald E. Ottoson—on whom this mandate fell—was convinced that no one knew very much about business ethics as a formal discipline. Moreover, no one had heard of any sustained efforts to integrate ethics into managerial practices. Undaunted, Ottoson continued to educate himself by reading and conversing about business ethics.

This background to Allied's ethics seminar is instructive for two reasons. First, a senior manager gave a precise directive to develop a program in business ethics. Following this directive, an upper-middle manager educated himself and became committed to the project. These factors are two essential ingredients in the development of an in-house program in business ethics—clear and strong support from the top and a manager who is a "believer" and reasonably knowledgeable about the subject. Without these elements, managerial participants are not likely to commit themselves to such programs.

Based on the Allied experience I suggest a third prerequisite for success—the program must be relevant to managers' needs, in form as well as content. Effective teaching techniques for managers—who are problem solvers, decisionmakers, and sometimes professional talkers—include discussions, simulations, and stand-up presentations. Similarly, the executive training programs must include management problems from real life. To ensure that the subject matter was relevant to the managers' needs, Ottoson tried out various short case studies in the seminar, thus discovering which issues were relevant and which were not. In addition, each candidate was asked to submit a very brief study, only a few paragraphs long, describing an ethical dilemma that he or she had encountered in a managerial setting. Because many of these cases may represent highly sensitive issues, participants were encouraged to maintain anonymity and to protect confidences. These case studies were discussed during the seminar.

Ethics became increasingly relevant to Allied managers in the summer of 1975 when the Kepone story came out in the media. All of the details about this issue and how it was resolved are far too complicated to discuss here in detail. Briefly, however, Kepone was a pesticide originally developed by Allied and was manufactured in small quantities for Allied by other companies. Between 1966 and 1973 it was produced at an Allied plant in Hopewell, Virginia, without any problems of worker safety or health. In 1974 Allied signed a "tolling" contract with a small company called Life Sciences Products, headed by two former Allied managers. Life Sciences Products was to manufacture Kepone for Allied, as other firms had in the past. As it turned out, LSP was a shoddy operation that was eventually convicted of willful OSHA violations and criminal environmental violations. The Justice Department brought a criminal indictment of 1097 counts against Allied, charging that Allied had conspired to set up Life Sciences to evade federal water-pollution-control regulations and that it previously had polluted the James River.[2]

Allied was eventually cleared on all counts of this indictment relating to LSP. However, Allied was convicted of illegally discharging Kepone and another nontoxic waste into the James River during the period when it manufactured Kepone itself in Hopewell. The repercussions were staggering. Allied faced numerous lawsuits, a highly charged political environment, and harmful publicity. Some managers at Allied complained that customers and suppliers were becoming chary of business relations with Allied. *Smithsonian* magazine refused to run an Allied advertisement, citing the Kepone affair as the reason. By 1980 Allied had paid more than $15 million in fines, donations, and claim payments.[3] One executive explained, "We were the good guys one day and the next day we were the bad guys." Allied's Chairman Connor said that he had believed that Allied was a "leader in adopting the new environmental rules." He called the Kepone affair "the most shocking experience of my business career."[4]

Within a short time, Allied plunged from ethical self-confidence to self-doubt. The corporation, meanwhile, continued its ethics seminar, where the Kepone case and related issues received critical attention, where some of the key actors in the case became seminar participants, and where the question "how can we avoid problems like this?" was treated seriously.

In May 1979 Connor retired and Edward L. Hennessy, Jr., became President and Chief Executive Officer. A financial man with a reputation for fast, aggressive, and decisive leadership, Hennessy made three decisive moves within less than seven months on the job. He sold or closed old plants and losing operations, writing off $139 million; he made a major acquisition, paying $589 million in cash for the Eltra Corporation; and he terminated the jobs of 700 salaried employees. According to the 1980 Annual Report, "Net income rose to a record $8.15 a share, 37 percent higher than 1979's. . . . Sales increased . . . to a new record of $5.5 billion."

Hennessy's stated goals of "increased profitability and growth" were unmistakably clear to Allied's employees. At the same time, fearing that some employees might misinterpret this strong financial emphasis as a relinquishment of the commitment to corporate responsibility, Hennessy reissued Allied's policy statement on "Proper Business Practices." He also created the "Proper Business Practices Committee" as an internal mechanism to advise managers and to interpret the policy statement. His sixteen-page statement outlining his view of ethical business practices was reinforced by other formal and informal communications, all of which made it clear that the new CEO at Allied intended to achieve his financial objectives in conformity with the highest ethical standards. In declaring his management philosophy and corporate objectives and strategies, Hennessy indicated that:

> No Allied manager should ever acquiesce in any action he believes is illegal, unethical, or dishonorable. This is both a moral principle and a matter of good business. No corporation can expect to prosper long on the basis of improper or unethical dealing.[5]

This directive on business ethics as well as others refer specifically to Allied's commitment to environmental excellence, product and worker safety, equal hiring and promotional opportunities, and ethical personnel management. To reiterate his ethical concerns, Hennessy sent an article from *The Wall Street Journal,* "Some Middle Managers Cut Corners to Achieve High Corporate Goals," to his managers along with the following pungent memorandum:

Gentlemen:

As we concentrate on our "stretch" objectives for 1980 and beyond let's remember that how we achieve them is just as important as the results themselves.

One of our strengths at Allied is our strong commitment to business ethics, supported by imaginative programs to ensure understanding and compliance. The attached article . . . is a jolting reminder of what happened in several major corporations when some people mistakenly thought that the ends justified the means.[6]

The Business Ethics Seminar is an "imaginative program" at Allied to help managers understand their responsibilities.

THE BUSINESS ETHICS SEMINAR: TEACHING METHODS

The seminar is intended for upper-level managers "whose business decisions have significant effects on the corporation's reputation as well as its profitability."[7] Initially, the seminar was aimed at the top tier of managers, on the theory that the concept of business ethics would gain credibility throughout the organization if subordinates saw that Allied was so serious about the subject that it gave its best people training in ethics. As senior managers improved their practices, it was reasoned that they would become better role models, reinforcing their subordinates' own efforts at ethical management.

A few years after the program began, enough corporate and divisional executives had taken the course to allow room for managers at the next level down. It was decided that the best time to give ethics training to senior managers is before they become senior executives. By including people in key decisionmaking positions today, they believed they would be reaching the people who would be running the company tomorrow, and after eight years this goal has been achieved. The president of The Chemicals Company, the corporate vice president of planning and development, the chief financial officer, and the associate general counsel are among the alumni of the Business Ethics Seminar.

The seminars are cross-functional and interregional, with a typical seminar being made up of fifteen to twenty-five managers from marketing, finance, research and development, law, and so forth, representing facilities from Canada to Mexico. This rich mixture has been regarded as an important feature of the seminar's effectiveness. In fact one of the unintended benefits of the program, according to alumni evaluations, is that participants gain knowledge about the company's operations and insight into other functional areas.

How do we reach these busy, experienced managers? Four assumptions about adult learning guide our approach. First, the students' active participation is essential, which is especially true for professional managers who are highly independent and require a teaching methodology that honors their independence. Our format includes simulations, small-group activities, and short stand-up presentations. Second, adults—and particularly managers—are problem solvers. Hence many of the materials are case studies of real-life problems; our conceptual tools are drawn from discussions of such problems or are applied directly to these problems. Third, adults learn better and more quickly when the subject matter is related to their own experience. This is why we ask each participant to submit a real-life case study involving an ethical dilemma that he or she has faced or is currently facing. Fourth, adult learning is achieved most effectively when personal developmental needs are met. In midlife, we feel, people have two fundamental needs: to accomplish something and (at the later stages) to accomplish with integrity something that is of value. The Business Ethics Seminar helps managers to fulfill the professional need to become a better manager as well as the personal need to feel that their life work is worthwhile.

The seminar is designed to elicit the utmost concentration from participants. It takes place at a well-appointed corporate training center and lasts for three days. The off-site location permits concentrated, intensive involvement. The three-day time span is in part a concession to managers' busy agendas. Three days sound like too short a time to cover business ethics adequately. And of course it is. However, adults can learn quickly in a short period. Furthermore, the amount of classroom time—twenty-four hours— is equal to the time spent in a half-semester course at a university. Participants also do a night of homework plus reading and writing before the seminar. These reading materials may include such familiar titles from the *Harvard Business Review* as "Can the Best Corporations Be Moral," "Can an Executive Afford a Conscience?," "Is Business Bluffing Ethical?" as well as more current titles such as "Ethics Without a Sermon." In addition, participants read a few minicase studies that illustrate typical ethical dilemmas in a managerial context and which serve as models for the participants' own case studies.

The seminar continues to be team taught with strong in-house direction from Arnold J. Frigeri, Director of Management Development and Daniel McElwreath, Manager of Management Development.

THE BUSINESS ETHICS SEMINAR:
TEACHING OBJECTIVES

The course material is organized into an introductory section and three modules. The introduction helps participants to become more sensitive to ethical dilemmas and to define for themselves the meaning of ethics. Each participant shares with the other students an ethical dilemma encountered in his or her functional area, and participants discuss these problems as well as the written cases already submitted.

The three modules deal with three types of obligatory relationships. We believe that a good starting point for this kind of training program is a careful assessment of the ethical implications of the employment contract. Hence module one looks at the "obligations of employees to the firm" and module two attends to the "firm's obligations to employees." The final module treats the "firm's obligations to others"—the ethical implications of the social contracts that business has with the marketplace and with society at large. (The agenda of a recent seminar appears in Appendix 1A.)

The program as a whole has four objectives:

1. To enhance managers' ability to perceive and to analyze ethical problems in management.
2. To improve managers' capacity for ethical decisionmaking.
3. To help managers understand the corporation's stated policies concerning proscribed activities as well as its policies concerning the firm's voluntary social responsibilities.
4. To help managers learn how ethics can be incorporated into corporate planning and organizational change.

As the agenda in Appendix 1A suggests, the program is organized so that we can meet these objectives sequentially. Nevertheless, the objectives are interrelated. In our work on each ethical problem we try to move from the particular to the general case; from reactive to proactive resolutions. For example, one dilemma faced by a purchasing manager was the question of whether or not to purchase from a small supplier that failed to comply with equal opportunity guidelines. Without the contract, the supplier might have to lay off half its workers and might even go under.

First we raised concrete questions about the problem. What are the relevant facts and business pressures? Who should make this kind of decision? What are the EEOC guidelines? What are the competing values and stakeholder claims? Moving from these narrow issues to larger issues, one manager raised the question of paternalism. "What right do we have to coerce a small company concerning an internal matter?" Another manager responded, "But this is an issue of social justice. Equal opportunity is a social value in this nation and it is the responsibility of large companies like ours to make that value a reality in the marketplace." Following this discussion we moved to the still larger issue of business social responsibility. To what extent is a corporation an agent of social change? Are there limits to the social responsibility of a business? Finally, the case discussion ended with the issue of anticipatory management. If we come up with an appropriate ethical response to this dilemma in a reactive way should we then not move toward a consistent universal policy? By anticipating ethical dilemmas, managers can integrate ethics into corporate planning, policy formation, and proposed organizational changes.

This movement from specific to general, reactive to proactive, informs our discussion of each case study as well as our progress throughout the three-day seminar. To give a clearer picture of our means of achieving the four objectives, I describe each objective in turn.

1. Perceiving and Analyzing Ethical Problems

Our first step is to heighten managers' awareness of the ethical dimension of the ends and means of business. As Daniel Callahan notes in his discussion of "Important Goals on the Teaching of Ethics," one must "stimulate the moral imagination" by drawing on students' affective capabilities—"empathy, feeling, caring, sensibility."[8] The second step is to move beyond sensibility to sense: to help students recognize ethical issues intellectually.

Ethics is a rational discipline. To "do ethics" well, it is necessary to learn conceptual tools of the trade and to use them coherently and consistently. The seminar emphasizes analytic skills for two reasons. First, managers constrained by orderly procedures use their time more efficiently than managers who operate randomly. Second, learning analytic techniques puts managers on notice that ethics is more than a "knee-jerk" activity.

We have developed three frameworks that managers may use to analyze ethical dilemmas. Any ethical problem may be recognized as:

1. A conflict among values.
2. A conflict among duties.
3. A conflict among desired outcomes.

These categories overlap, for most ethical problems involve all three types of conflicts. We have found, however, that using these frameworks helps managers to define all aspects of a given ethical problem.

Values. In promotion or job termination cases, for example, the conflict may be among the value of rewarding or punishing individual performance, the need for remedial justice (affirmative action), and the value of rewarding seniority. Or the conflict may be a simple clash between short-term efficiency and long-term human resource development.

In buyer–seller relations, market ethics has usually honored "parity" and "truthful representations" as governing values. Where there is great disparity by reason of size, economic advantage, unfair access to information, unfair marketing opportunities, or blatant dishonesty, we would quickly spot an actual or potential ethical problem.

A common issue that arises again and again in managerial ethics training programs is the perceived conflict between personal values and institutional values and duties. Starting with value analysis can lead to a greater appreciation of the implicit and explicit corporate values that shape managerial behavior. An example of a clash between personal values and institutional obligations was given by a marketing manager in a major pharmaceutical company. He related that he was on a "marketing strategy team," which included a large advertising firm. The advertising agency recommended placing full-page ads in certain sex-oriented magazines that he found disgusting from the point of view of sexual morality and because of the magazine's blatant exploitation of women. He asked, "Do I dare express my personal convictions or do I treat this as just another bottom-line problem?" This kind of exercise in knowing where to draw the line when personal integrity competes with management values seems to serve a genuine need.

Obligations. A concern common to all ethical theories is the social interdependence of human life, an interdependence that implies reciprocal obligations. At the core of many ethical problems in management are competing claims of the persons and organizations to which a person is obligated. The starting point in ethical analysis of such a problem is to identify all interested parties or stakeholders. (By "stakeholder" I mean all agents or agencies that may be affected by the decision.)

A typical example of a managerial obligation conflict is a case of forced performance-grading quotas. A vice president tells a general manager that she should have two more "grade fours" among her subordinates. (Grade 4 is the lowest on a scale of 1 to 4.) The general manager is convinced that the lowest possible grade for any of her twelve subordinates is 3.5. What complicates the matter further is that one of the 3.5 subordinates is a close friend. Giving a grade 4 means firing the employee. Here is a clear and simple case of conflicting duties to a superior, to subordinates, to the firm, to a friend, and to oneself.

In more complex cases, managers may find themselves caught between competing duties to suppliers and shareholders, host countries and home countries, hourly workers and senior management, consumers and distributors. Helping managers to look beyond technical and functional concerns to perceive these competing stakeholders' interests is an important aim of the seminar.

Outcomes. A central question in any kind of ethical analysis is "Who is getting hurt?" Going directly to this question by assessing predictable harms and benefits is, in the language of classical ethical theory, to adopt a "utilitarian" approach. This straightforward method of looking at alternative courses of action and determining their probable consequences is probably more compatible with managers' mental habits than are other approaches. In fact, this approach makes use of traditional managerial modes of analysis such as "decision-tree theory" and "cost–benefit analysis."

A plant manager commented after one of the seminars that the most valuable outcome was his own increased sensitivity to the ethical complexities of plant management. He then declared that in business meetings he now frequently poses problems with hidden, ethical dimensions, just to see if his people can recognize them. He reported that to his chagrin the most common response has been to treat the case as strictly a technical business problem, offering the refrain, "we can get around this problem by doing this or that." When the plant manager raises the question, "but should we?" the subordinate is usually shocked to discover that an executive would even think this way. Encouraging and training managers to think about the consequences of their actions in human terms is the most important objective of the program. Aside from the intrinsic moral justification for this objective, I am convinced that learning to count the human costs will make managers more effective as well. This seems to be one of the lessons we are learning from Japanese managers.[9]

2. Ethical Decisionmaking

We cover a minimal amount of ethical theory and some relevant historical and cultural material, but managers have little time and less tolerance for academic presentations about deontological, tele-

ological, egoistic, and so on, ethical theories. Their goal is application. To achieve this goal we provide rational models of ethical
decisionmaking. Sometimes these models are used in a highly structured way, going through the reasoning process step by step. At
other times, by using the models in free-form commonsense discussions, these models help the participants ask the right questions
in solving the problem.

The analytic techniques just described lead naturally to one model
of rational decisionmaking. Having identified conflicting values
and duties, the manager can rank them in order of importance.
Then the manager can outline alternative courses of action and
determine their probable consequences, again ranking outcomes
according to their beneficial or harmful effects. Finally, the manager can make a decision. The resolution may favor one particular
benefit, value, or claim. Or the resolution may strike a balance
among opposing claims or benefits. (Appendix 1B contains a model
used in the seminar that describes this reasoning process in a step-
by-step fashion.)

The decisionmaking process just described is most appropriate in
situations that are complex, subtle, and full of ambiguities. What
about the hard cases, when a decision involves a "regrettable"
means of achieving a necessary end, or when the end brings human
injury? Such situations include pending plant closings, whistle-
blowing, preferential treatment, bribery, and deception. To reach
decisions in such cases, we have found useful a model deriving
from the just-war theory, one of the most refined and profound
studies of ethical decisionmaking in Western thought. When, if
ever, is it justifiable to use deadly force? And what are the limits
to the use of such force? Analysis of the ethics of war *(jus ad bellum)*
and of ethical conduct in war *(jus in bello)* has given rise to the following set of principles that may be used to determine whether
draconian measures are justified in particular situations:

1. Just Cause. Are there overriding reasons for ever considering this course of action?
2. Just Aim. Are the intended objectives and motives justifiable?
3. Last Resort. Have all other means been exhausted?
4. Reasonable Chance of Success. In a pragmatic sense can we
   expect to achieve the objectives?
5. Legitimate Authority. Who should decide? Is the action being carried out by the most appropriate authority?
6. Proper Announcement. Is there an appropriate record or
   declaration of intent?

7. Proportionality. Will the good to be gained be proportionate or outweigh the harmful effects? (This question calls for a calculus of human costs and benefits.)
8. Just Means. Do the strategies and tactics employ only necessary measures? Are they discriminating and designed to mitigate harm?

This model does not guarantee any right answers. Reasonable people of goodwill may disagree as they apply these principles, but the model does help people to organize their thinking so that interested parties can engage in a reasonable discussion. At the very minimum readers will be able to identify more precisely points of disagreement. At the maximum, this model might help managers achieve a consensus.

3. Understanding Current Ethical Policies

Our third objective is for managers to understand the corporation's current policies and guidelines concerning proscribed activities as well as voluntary social responsibilities. Our treatment reflects the two basic principles of ethics: to avoid harm and to promote human welfare. In this case, avoiding harm means simply refraining from Allied's proscribed activities. The company's guidelines for these kinds of activities cover such sensitive aspects of business practice as questionable payments, business entertainment, political contributions, conflict of interest, insider information, financial accounting, and billing practices. Reference is made to laws, to governmental regulations and guidelines, and to Allied's general policies articulated in the "Proper Business Practices" statement.

When a given ethical problem is black and white (e.g., can you make a domestic payoff to get the contract?), our task is to clarify company policy and relevant law. When the ethical problem is ambiguous (e.g., what is reasonable business entertainment when you have a potential windfall sale?), our task is to draw lines, define terms, and clarify concepts, all the while staying as close as possible to the letter and spirit of the law and company policy. To help us achieve this goal we invite key senior officers and members of Allied's Proper Business Practices Committee to join the seminar to present a corporate point of view on certain ambiguous cases.

Virtually all of the ethical guidance on the Allied policy statement—similar to the policy statements of most other firms—centers on the task of profit making. Hence the guidelines offer a starting point, not a final goal for ethical conduct. Allied's expressed concern for social responsibility, on the other hand, is an open-ended mandate, requiring not only avoidance of harm but also active promotion of human welfare.

Allied encourages employees to take part in community affairs and politics. The Allied Foundation distributes large sums of money. Marketing managers may cut prices for certain nonprofit organizations, such as hospitals or religious organizations, under special circumstances. These and other examples of social responsibility are discussed and reinforced in the seminar. We also treat hard questions, where there are painful tradeoffs between social good and the bottom line. An example is a marketing manager on allocation during a period of short oil supply who has to reduce his product by 25 percent. If customer A is a hospital, (already receiving a 20 percent discount), customer B a small plant facing layoff problems, and customer C a hot-shot broker who buys in large volumes, what does he do? In the interest of good and responsible management, such questions are seriously considered in the seminar.

4. Shaping Ethical Policies

Our fourth objective is to help managers think about how ethics may be integrated with corporate planning, policymaking, and organizational change. We have two reasons for adopting this goal.

The first is our conviction that most corporate misdeeds result more from poor management and faulty institutional arrangements than from individual maleficence. Because of our strong individualism most Americans tend to think of ethics merely in terms of individual conscience. A manager is either a good apple or a bad apple, and we all know that it is "the bad apple that spoils the cart." This kind of moralism pays little heed to the organizational context that may be either supportive or inimical to good ethical conduct.

We believe, rather, that ethical behavior is a social phenomenon. It is constituted to a large extent by purposes and expectations of social roles; by explicit policies and rules; by systems of rewards and punishments; by shared values. Thus we believe business ethics should not be left to the individual conscience. A basic aim of business ethics is to reform and improve institutions in order to improve individual managerial practices. A rough paraphrase of a Talmudic saying sums up this point: "It is not so much the rat as it is the rat hole that is the culprit." The course description of Allied's Business Ethics Seminar puts it yet another way: "Bad management is both a cause and consequence of bad ethics. Good management is both a necessary precondition and consequence of good ethics."

The second reason why we stress incorporating ethics into corporate planning and organizational change is that the best time to handle an ethical issue is before it becomes an issue. This is a variation of Thomas Jefferson's dictum: "The time to guard against corruption and tyranny is before they shall have gotten hold of us." Some of the questions we have used to prod managers into creative anticipatory thinking are as follows:

1. What are three or four of the most critical ethical issues that you have confronted or observed while working for Allied?
2. Which of these issues have been resolved or have become a thing of the past? Which remain of ethical concern for Allied?
3. Can you define a managerial policy or organizational change that would have helped you to deal with this issue or would have kept it from becoming a problem?
4. Are there any policies, systems, or practices that encourage good ethical behavior at Allied and that you find praiseworthy?
5. Are there any policies, systems, or practices that, from an ethical point of view, should be reexamined and perhaps reformulated?

Illustrating the importance of incorporating ethics into managerial forms and policies are the changes made at Allied since the Kepone scandal. The *New York Times* described these changes in an unusual editorial accolade:

> ... Sinners can repent and old dogs learn new tricks: it is a pleasure to report that Allied seems to have been converted into an environmental good guy.... Allied has overhauled its safety and environmental programs. A high corporate officer is now in charge. Plant managers are rewarded for good safety records and replaced if they can't handle their new responsibilities. A committee of experts assesses the potential hazards of everything Allied produces; several risky products have been abandoned or delayed.

> ... The Environmental Protection Agency praises the caliber of Allied's new safety managers and the company's cooperative spirit. The agency even touts Allied's committee for risk assessment as a model for other companies.[10]

But it is not enough to incorporate current ethical concerns into organizational changes and strategic planning. Managers must also try to anticipate future social values. During the past decade, the failure of American business to take seriously problems of dwindling energy and environmental resources, product safety,

worker health, and equal opportunity brought harsh personal and '
social injury and invited massive governmental regulation. I am
quite sure if this essay had been written in 1962, the words "energy"
and "environment" would not appear. Question: What words soon
to come from the lips of managers are being overlooked today?

The ethics seminar at Allied deals with this question. We break
up into small groups for what we call "social–ethical forecasting."
Participants are asked to imagine what issues coming at them
down the road could, in the next generation, be considered serious
social and ethical problems and may invite new regulations if not
addressed voluntarily. We then ask them to recommend anticipatory management procedures. What are appropriate mechanisms
of accountability? What new information and monitoring systems
need to be established? Are new codes or policy guidelines in order?
How should managerial style be altered? We may not be able to
solve problems before they appear, but at least we can learn to think
far enough ahead so that problems will no longer take us by surprise.

BENEFITS OF PROGRAMS IN BUSINESS ETHICS

What are the benefits of a management development program in ethics to a company like Allied? My skeletal answer is
based in part on surmise and in part on observation and evaluation. It also assumes long-term and cumulative benefit rather than
the short-term benefit accruing from a single seminar.

Over the long run the program builds *cohesiveness of managerial
character*. Persons from a wide range of specialties share ethical
problems and work together to resolve them. A concern for ethics
at the top can be a profound influence shaping managerial character among middle managers and hourly employees alike.

Even partial achievement of the program objectives can bring
the benefits of a good reputation. A reputation for integrity makes
doing business in a "social accountability oriented society" much
easier. In the marketplace, integrity is a business asset equal to
capital assets. In terms of long-term business survival, growth, and
profitability, a record of fairness, honesty, and goodwill is just as important as competitive prices, product quality, and efficient service.

Avoidance of costly lawsuits and of the attending costs of lost
time and energy is an important benefit expected from this program. Obviously, a management development program in ethics
cannot create moral perfection. But if the program plays a role in

reducing corporate venalities and thoughtless costly mistakes, it more than pays its way by giving the legal department more time to spend on preventive management and less time in courtrooms.

The program leads to *more professional management.* Because ethics education is training in analysis of problems, practical judgment, and rational decisionmaking, it can improve managers' competence across the board. Moreover, we feel that solving every weighty managerial problem requires trading off conflicting human values. Managers who attend to the ethical aspects of their decisions will be working with a broader, more realistic data base and a wider range of alternatives.

Finally, training in ethics gives managers *a strong dose of realism.* Peter Drucker has said that most managers live "in a sea of abstraction." Using technical, pragmatic, and legal language often enough can create the fantasy that management is a world of numbers, systems, agencies, production units, and *persona ficta* corporations. An aphorism of the poet Wallace Stevens is poignantly relevant: "We do not live in the place itself; we live in the description of the place." By using the austere language of economics and management science, managers run the danger of viewing business as a cold profit-making machine. By using the language of ethical discourse we are reminded that business is, after all, a human activity fraught with ambiguity, compromises, and sometimes uneasy consciences. A forum to come clean with these existential realities experienced by every thoughtful manager has the beneficial effect of rooting management practice in the real world of people relating to people, with all of the concomitant ethical obligations implied.

NOTES

1. Ben A. Franklin, "Inquiries Into Nixon's Re-election Funds Turning Up a Pattern of High Pressure," *The New York Times* (July 15, 1973), Section I, p. 36.
2. Marvin H. Zim, "Allied Chemical's $20-Million Ordeal With Kepone," *Fortune* (September 11, 1978), p. 85.
3. Ibid., p. 83.
4. Ibid. The author of the article notes that John Connor, "a devout Catholic," felt so deeply about the injury caused to Life Science Workers and the cleanup problem around the plant posing a hazard to the neighborhood, that he said it was Allied's moral responsibility to do something. "Whether or not we had legal responsibilities, we at least had the moral responsibility to resolve the damages and to help the people who had been injured," he said. Allied's response to the Kepone case has been exemplary in many ways including the establishment of

an internal environmental and safety program receiving commendation from many sources, including the EPA.

5. This quote is from an in-house presentation by Edward L. Hennessy, Jr., at the first "management meeting" after becoming the CEO at Allied. It is on page 14 of his printed speech, October 3, 1979. In this presentation Hennessy reinforced the new posture on social responsibility by affirming a "commitment to environmental excellence," and affirming Allied's duty to "make jobs and promotional opportunities equally available to all persons regardless of race, creed, sex or age," (pp. 14–15).

6. Internal Memorandum, November 27, 1979. The article referred to, "Some Middle Managers Cut Corners to Achieve High Corporate Goals," is by George Getschow, *The Wall Street Journal* (November 8, 1979).

7. From the description of the "Course #139—Business Ethics Seminar," under the category, "Special Interest Programs," in the *1980 Management Development Programs* catalogue, p. 11.

8. Daniel Callahan and Sissela Bok, *Ethics Teaching in Higher Education* (New York: Plenum Press, 1980), p. 69.

9. Richard Tanner Pascale and Anthony G. Athos, *The Art of Japanese Management* (New York: Simon and Schuster, 1981), pp. 49–52, and Chapter 4.

10. "Praise for an Ex-Polluter," *The New York Times* (January 28, 1980), Section A, p. 16.

APPENDIX 1A

Agenda, Business Ethics Seminar
Allied Corporation

Team Teachers
Arnold J. Frigeri, Daniel A. McElwreath, Donald G. Jones

Wednesday

Introduction **What is Business Ethics?**

8:30– 8:45 A.M.	Orientation and preview
8:45–10:00 A.M.	*Typical Ethical Dilemmas* Confronted by AC Managers (Participants share ethical concerns)
10:00–10:15 A.M.	Break
10:15–11:00 A.M.	*What is Business Ethics?* ...Presentation: The Meaning of Ethics ...Case Study Illustrations ...A Model: How to Perceive Ethical Issues
11:00–12:00 P.M.	*Changing Business Environment and Ethical Issues* ...Presentation ...Discussion (Managers reflect on changing markets and macrosocial environments)
12:00– 1:00 P.M.	Lunch

Module One **A. Obligations of Employees to the Firm**
B. Ethics as Integrity and Rational Decision-Making
Reading: Allied Corporation—Proper Business Practices Policy.

1:00– 2:15 P.M.	Small Group Case Studies
2:15– 3:00 P.M.	*Issues Centering on Basic Business Conduct* (Conflicts of Interest, personal use of corporate assets, honesty, loyalty, insider information, secrecy, etc.). ...Cases ...Discussion
3:00– 3:15 P.M.	Break
3:15– 4:15 P.M.	*A Model of Decision Making:* Ethics of Allowable Exceptions ...Whistle-Blowing Case Study ...Census-Reduction Case Study

4:15– 4:45 P.M.	*Employee Obligations:* Sensitive and Gray Areas ... Free Form Discussion
4:45– 5:00 P.M.	Small-Group Assignments
5:00– 6:00 P.M.	Social Hour and Free Time
6:00– 7:00 P.M.	Dinner
7:00	Case Study Work
	Free Time Crisis of Conscience at Quasar Cumberland Gasket Allied Chemical, A., B., and C.

Thursday

Module Two   A. Obligation of the Firm to Employees
B. Management Ethics: Contextual or Universal

8:30– 8:45 A.M.	Review and Transition
8:45–10:00 A.M.	*Issues Centering on Employee Relations* (Hiring, promoting, firing, performance evaluation, internal placement, women and minority opportunities, wages, worklife quality, right of privacy, etc.) ... Case Studies from Allied Managers ... *A Model of Decisionmaking* for Resolving Dilemmas ... Attention Given to Issue of Competing Obligations and Stakeholder Claims
10:00–10:15 A.M.	Break
10:15–11:00 A.M.	*Reflection on Organizational Culture and Values at Allied* ... Small Group Exercise ... Plenary Discussion
11:00–12:00 P.M.	*System Sensitive Ethics and the Role of Management* ... Presentation: Tensions Between Conscience and Organizational Responsibilities ... Group Discussion on Resolving Value Conflicts
12:00– 1:00 P.M.	Lunch
1:00– 3:00 P.M.	Case Reports
3:00– 3:15 P.M.	Break
3:15– 4:15 P.M.	*Ethics and the Art of Japanese Management*
4:15– 5:00 P.M.	Film: *Machiavelli—Man and the State.* ... Discussion on Uses and Abuses of Power ... Discussion on Ethics and Managerial Leadership

5:00- 5:30 P.M. Free
5:30- 6:30 P.M. Social Hour
6:30- 7:30 P.M. Dinner
7:30- 8:30 P.M. Guest Speaker and Discussion

Friday

Module Three **A. Obligation of the Firm to Others**
                          B. Integrating Ethics into Planning,
                              Policy, Codes and Organizational
                              Structures

8:30- 8:45 A.M. Review and Transition
8:45-10:00 A.M. *Issues Centering on Market Relations and Outside Publics* (Competitive bidding, pricing, purchasing, marketing, bribery, disparagement,
discounts, rebates, product responsibility, government relations, shareholder interests, corporate social responsibility, etc.)
    ... Case Studies from Allied Managers on Market
        Behavior
    ... Presentation: The Relevance of Certain Ethi-
        cal Values on Market Behavior (Honesty,
        equality, freedom, promise-keeping, sanctity
        of life, gratitude, justice as reparation)
10:00-10:15 A.M. Break
10:15-11:15 A.M. *Corporate Codes and Policy Guides of Conduct*
Film: *On Corporate Codes.*
    ... Discussion of Allied's "Proper Business
        Practices" policy
    ... Discussion of Questionnaire passed out to
        participants (including an analysis of the
        responses)
11:15-12:30 P.M. **Fallen Image of Business and Social**
Responsibility
    ... Presentation: The Credibility Crisis of Cor-
        porations (How it happened, what it means,
        what the appropriate response is)
    ... Reflections on the Doctrine of "Social
        Responsibility"
12:30- 1:30 P.M. Lunch
1:30- 3:00 P.M. **Anticipating Ethical Issues and Preventive**
Management
    ... Small Group Exercise: Identifying Ethical
        Issues on the Horizon
    ... Report back on Implications for Management

3:00- 3:30 P.M. **The Integration of Ethics into Management Processes**
... Presentation: The Role of Ethics in Planning, Policy, and Organizational Reformulation
... Short Case Illustration on Product Responsibility
3:30- 3:45 P.M. **Why Business Ethics**
... Summary and Challenge
3:45- 4:00 P.M.   Wrap-up and Evaluations

* * *

APPENDIX 1B

A Rational Model of Ethical Analysis and Decisionmaking

This model helps one to develop orderly procedures for identifying ethical problems, resolving them, and forming policies to help prevent their recurrence.

Step *One*   *State the ethical dilemma in plain language.*
An ethical problem almost always falls under the following headings:
a. Competing values.
b. Conflicting obligations.
c. Cost-benefit trade-offs in predicting outcomes.

Step *Two*   *Identifying relevant facts, ranking them in order of significance.*
This step assumes the importance of *empirical* analysis.

Step *Three*   *Identify Relevant Values.*
Values may be reduced to one term such as, "informed consent," "minority justice," "honest," "sanctity of life," or "loyalty."
Values may also be put in declarative sentences such as "humans have a right to life" or, "the public good must be served."

Step *Four*

List alternative courses of action.
A warning is in order here. Human beings have a tendency to restrict the options to as few as possible. We all seem to want to avoid or deny perplexity. One way of doing that effectively is to perceive issues in an either/or fashion, which is strategy to avoid complexity and ambiguity. *All* options *must* be considered.

Step *Five*

a. *Rank values in preferential scale.*
b. *Rank predictable consequences in terms of certain harmful or beneficial effects.*
c. *Make your decision.*

Step *Six*

Adopt a proactive posture and propose a policy or institutional arrangement for preventing this kind of ethical dilemma from reoccuring.

This is the issue of anticipatory ethics.

Chapter 2

Training for Ethical Management at Cummins Engine

Michael R. Rion

Some years ago a *New Yorker* cartoon featured several somber businessmen clustered around the chief executive's desk, consternation reflected on their faces. The executive presses the intercom to say, "Miss Dugan, will you send someone in here who can distinguish right from wrong?" Too frequently, this vignette symbolizes the perception of managers that ethics is someone else's business, not necessarily irrelevant to management decisions but certainly not part of the manager's competence. But ethics cannot be integrated effectively into management decisions unless line managers accept responsibility for the moral dimension of their decisions as well as economic features. Ms. Dugan ought no more to send in someone who can tell right from wrong than she should someone who can tell a profitable sale from an unprofitable one. To that end, in-house training in ethics and management is an important strategy. This chapter discusses one such program, recently developed at Cummins Engine Company, Inc.

BACKGROUND

Cummins is a major worldwide designer and manufacturer of diesel engines, with annual sales of nearly $2 billion and nearly 23,000 employees worldwide. A successful producer, whose engines are widely acclaimed in the industry, the company also has a strong tradition of social responsibility. Top management, from the founding of the company, committed the firm to ethical business practices, support for the local community, and respect for all stakeholders whose lives or interests are affected by company action. Like any increasingly complex organization, Cummins does not meet its goals with perfect accuracy and the problems of sustaining and implementing ethical management arise regularly. Nevertheless, the company has a deserved reputation as a leader in socially responsible ethical business management.

A staff group devoted to responsibility concerns is one manifestation of Cummins' effort to sustain its commitment to ethical management.' Currently, a public affairs group includes government and community relations, environmental management, and corporate responsibility. The mission of the corporate responsibility department is, broadly conceived, to support the company's efforts to make ethically responsible decisions. This means many things: development of ethical practice policies; staff support for top management; *ad hoc* and more regular consultation with line managers on particular issues they raise; and monitoring of certain policies already in place.

Those efforts convinced staff members a few years ago that further effort was necessary to emphasize line manager responsibility for the ethical dimensions of decisions. No staff support can possibly cover the array of issues managers face daily, and the department's role is conceived as support *to* line managers, *not* their conscience. A call from Ms. (or Mr.) Dugan occasionally is understandable, but corporate responsibility could never, and should never, replace the responsibility of line managers. Accordingly, a pilot training project was inaugurated as one effort to strengthen the capacity of managers to resolve ethical issues in their work. This context is important to understanding the project since it has programmatic as well as educational goals. More specifically, the project aims:

To increase the confidence and competence of individual managers dealing with ethical issues.
To develop a network of managers who, over time, can be mutually supportive in strengthening the ethical dimension of managerial decisions.
To expand or "leverage" the resources of the corporate responsibility department through greater interaction with line managers and their issues.

A PILOT PROJECT

Since December 1979, four groups of managers each attended a pilot series of three day-long workshops on ethics and management. Evaluations of the program were encouraging, and it is being continued on a regular basis. A brief description follows.

Groups of eighteen to twenty-four managers were selected from middle and upper management. Concerns in selecting the initial groups included finding interested individuals, providing diversity of organizational functions in each group, and avoiding participation by subordinates and their supervisors in the same group. Participation was entirely voluntary and enthusiastic. Indeed, numerous managers inquired about the program along the way, and there will be little difficulty in recruiting participants for future series.

Each group attended three day-long workshops, spread over approximately six months. The interim periods between the sessions were used for individual meetings with the instructor and for development of case material for succeeding workshops. Staggering the series also enabled the experience from each session of a series to be used in revising the subsequent series.

The structure of the three workshops is based upon its stated learning goals:

1. To increase recognition of ethical dimensions in management decisions.
2. To acquire concepts and methods for ordering and analysis of ethical issues.
3. To strengthen the capacity for resolution of ethical issues in management decisions.

These goals represent the process of ethical judgment, and the entire process is experienced with cases in each session. The emphasis, however, is sequential: the first session focuses upon recognition, the second upon ordering and analysis, the third upon judgment. Although some of the normative ethical content of the workshop is discussed below, a brief summary of the sessions may be helpful here. Session 1 includes development of an adequate definition of ethics; discussion of the goals, successes, and failures of ethical management at Cummins; exploration of the sources of moral disagreement, and assessment of Cummins' explicit policies on ethical practices. Session 2 is devoted largely to apprehending and applying a conceptual framework for ordering and analyzing moral responsibility. Finally, Session 3 is devoted exclusively to analysis of several participant cases; the aim is both to hone judgment skills and to explore in greater depth certain moral concepts relevant to the cases selected.

The style throughout the sessions is participative and inductive. Definitions and concepts are developed in relation to case discussions with a minimum of freestanding didactic presentation. Handouts covering the conceptual material are provided after each session to assist in understanding and recall. Thus, the resources employed primarily comprise the experience of participants, some Cummins documents, and the input of the instructor. There are no assigned readings from published literature.

Before turning to some pedagogical assumptions underlying this design, a further word about next steps is important. In addition to repeating the series for additional managers, other activities are planned to sustain the network of persons who have completed the workshops. Most notably, periodic "alumni/ae" sessions are planned for participants of the earlier groups to gather to share concerns and explore in depth a current issue in the company. In addition, the instructor, who also heads the Corporate Responsibility department, maintains regular contact with past participants and calls upon their assistance when issues arise in their areas. These efforts beyond the initial training are essential to the programmatic goals discussed earlier.

PEDAGOGICAL ASSUMPTIONS

Two assumptions are especially important in the pedagogical choices leading to the workshop series design. First, participants are busy managers whose day-to-day responsibilities are sufficiently consuming to make difficult any focus on learning ethics outside the actual workshop sessions. Thus, the sessions do not depend upon participant reading, although suggestions are made for interested individuals and the handouts do provide some conceptual material to which one can return after a workshop. Instead, the workshops depend very much upon the participants themselves as the crucial resource. Their knowledge of the company and its "culture" and their daily managerial experience provide both an initial point of interest for them and the rich fabric of case materials that form the basis for much of the discussion. The importance of tapping participant experience cannot be overstated, for an in-house training effort must inevitably relate to the particular characteristics of the "house."

A second assumption is that working adults learn new material best in increments over time rather than through intensive, one-time doses. The cumulative acquisition of clearer views of ethics and some conceptual "tools" works better if one has opportunity to digest some material before more is added. This is why the workshop series is designed to include interim periods rather than being given in a single three-day program. Not only do participants have the space to absorb new material, but they are also able to assess what they are learning in light of day-to-day management experience. Contacts with the instructor during the interim periods and the post-workshop activities described earlier likewise contribute to this ongoing learning.

NORMATIVE CONTENT

The description to this point explains the purpose and skeletal design of the ethics and management training program at Cummins. Instructors with differing approaches might well adapt the design to their own perspective. What follows now is the author's own normative approach that is incorporated into the training design.[1] Comments are necessary at three levels: social–economic structure, institutional ethical commitments, and individual ethical judgment in managerial roles.

1. The Social Context of Management Ethics

Contemporary concern for management ethics arises from an anomaly in traditional democratic capitalist social theory. Large-scale organizations impinge upon individuals and societies in ways that theory fails to explain. Public policy and its administration are not necessarily the representative voice of the people or a broader vision of the public interest, while market mechanisms often fail to control the impact of business decisions. Much debate in contemporary society, as well as much of the literature frequently appearing in many undergraduate and professional courses, is focused at this level. Ranging from critiques of the capitalist system and constructive alternative economic theories to various proposals to control and reform corporate economic structure, these debates encompass a range of significant questions. They are not, however, the key questions for management ethics.

Managers wield significant power affecting the lives of various "stakeholders"—employees, customers, suppliers, stockholders, governments, and communities. To say that managers should simply maximize profits as agents of shareholders presumes that the market dynamics are effective and relatively quick to respond. If so, it is *possible* that competitive pressure would prevent the worst abuses. The truth, however, is that this assumption is invalid for a whole range of corporate decisions. And, when the assumption is false, the injunction becomes dangerous. If managers are ignoring realms of corporate impact removed from market constraints, immense injury can occur to employees, customers, communities, and the public interest. There is no ready theory as refined as the free-market model to take its place, but in corporate offices the reality of managerial discretion and influence is evident.

Management ethics, and particularly management training in ethics, must take as its immediate base the realities of managerial discretion and seek to provide ethically sound and practically helpful guidance in exercising that discretion with sensitivity to human dignity and human values. The underlying assumption is that, without a clear social theory or public policy to provide more adequate accountability for corporate power, business corporations hold a kind of public trust—society requires business enterprise for human well-being, and individual corporations derive their power ultimately from society's consent that the business is fulfilling its public trust. Part of this task is learning how to avoid harm and respect stakeholders.

This point does not diminish the importance of the broader issues of appropriate political–economic structures. Managers, as citizens and as corporate representatives, must engage in discussions of these issues as our society searches for more adequate models. In the meantime, corporate managers should not be harming people, and in its simplest terms, that is the narrow task that management ethics sets for itself within the larger debate.

2. Institutional Ethics and Ethos

The institutional context for the exercise of managerial judgment is a critical feature of ethical management, and one not readily affected by training. Although much research is needed on the institutional requisites for an ethically responsible corporation, a number of elements seem essential. Firm and visible top management commitment, and especially a history of such commitment, is essential to keeping ethical dimensions of management on the agenda of operating managers. Staff support is useful, and policies and codes of conduct have a place, as does recruitment policy. Management ethics training is a single component, ineffective without a supportive institutional context. Such training needs to examine the peculiar context of an institution, but its focus will be upon equipping managers better to fulfill institutional goals if those goals include ethical management. If not, the training may help individuals, but its impact will be lost unless it is part of a wider strategy to reshape an unfavorable ethos.

3. Ethical Judgment in Management

Understanding the managerial role and the kinds of decisions that face managers is essential to teaching ethics for management. As Charles Powers and David Vogel point out, management, unlike other professions, finds its *raison detre* in organizational purposes and needs rather than in independently inspiring goals such as health or justice.[2] The manager's role responsibility is essentially a formal one, receiving content only through the particular goals and directions of a specific organization; hence the importance of the particular institutional ethos. But individual character and judgment are not thereby imprisoned in organizational conformity. At the extremes, individual and corporate identity can diverge to the point of resignation, perhaps in protest, or converge in deadening acquiescence, but most managers find sufficient compatibility with corporate goals to carry on *and* sufficient ambiguity and leeway in corporate policies to allow for creative individual judgment. Parallels between ethics and business judgment may be instructive.

Corporate goals determine the general direction and criteria of business judgments—what markets deserve priority, whether pricing is premium or competitive, what standards by which to judge potential return on investment, and so on. The manager must effectively integrate these criteria with the complexity and detail of specific decisions, and here his or her education, ingenuity, and common sense determine the outcome. The same holds true for the ethical dimension of managerial judgment. Corporate goals and policy may set general expectations and even some specific guidance, but individual understanding of concepts such as fairness and honesty will be decisive in the manager's decision to select a particular supplier or to discuss certain issues in a negotiation.

Few managers have frequent opportunity to pass judgment on major corporate goals and strategies, but all managers deal both with specific details and with precedent-setting policy decisions at their own level. Ethical considerations are nearly always present. In the "big issues," such as investment in South Africa or closing a plant, they are most clearly on the agenda; in the routine decisions of individual managers fulfilling their particular organizational roles, ethical issues likewise abound but are not as often recognized. When they are recognized, the ethical dimensions may confound the decisionmaker because the legitimacy and conceptual tools of ethics are not as readily accepted as are those of finance or marketing or production. Ethics may seem relative, vague, or irrelevant.

The managers have a decision to make, with pressures from all sides, and without any formal education in the field, ethical considerations will enter the decision only through implicit dimensions of character and generalized feelings of what is fair or right.

If ethics is to be taught effectively to managers, these characteristics must be taken into account—managerial role responsibilities in the institutional context, continual pressure for decisions, and the frequent lack of clarity about ethical reasoning. Ethics, understood as the principles and process of reasoning about moral responsibility, must be taught in ways that link clearly to institutional roles and to the particularities of business decisions and in ways that encourage a sense of confidence and competence on the part of the individual manager.

Before presenting substantive ethical principles, it is helpful to clear away some obstacles to understanding by clarifying the definition of ethics and confronting the implications of moral disagreement. Different instructors would approach this problem in various ways. In summary, the approach used here is to generate a definition of ethics out of the participants' own experience, indicating that the essential features are respect for persons rooted in human community; consistency and universality; and special authority and action guidance. Moral disagreement is addressed through case discussion and an effort to locate sources of disagreement using two conceptual perspectives. The first suggests that there may be ethical agreement at the level of principles but disagreement in application, with a strong analogy to similar disagreements in applying business principles to particular cases.[3] The other perspective offers a way to sort out disagreements rooted in different assessments of the situation, in different personal loyalties or basic beliefs, as well as in different ways of moral reasoning.[4] The point throughout the discussion is to understand the source for moral disagreement without paralyzing moral analysis and to argue that managers can reason together in sorting out their ethical responsibilities.

Recognition of ethical issues and the possibility of ethical reasoning in managerial decisions opens the way to understanding substantive ethical principles as they relate to business decisions. Most of the available textbooks for business ethics begin this process with such traditional categories in ethics as teleology and deontology, and egalitarian, libertarian, and meritarian conceptions of justice. Whatever its merits in other arenas, this approach appears misguided in light of the manager's needs and initial unfamiliarity with ethics. These concepts come across either as too abstract for "the real world" or as terribly blunt weapons by which the enthusiastic novice too readily divides the world and judges decisions. When utilitarian and formalist theories significantly overlap in their practical conclusions, an approach to practical ethics may do well to look elsewhere for an initial framework.[5] The most pressing questions a manager faces—in ways questions of *role* responsibility—are *whether* he or she is indeed responsible for a particular issue, and if so, *what* does that responsibility entail? What may be most useful is a framework for reasoning through these questions, a framework that determines the relevance of substantive principles and enables their application in concrete circumstances. The framework used here is as follows.[6]

NEGATIVE AND AFFIRMATIVE RESPONSIBILITIES

A distinction between negative and affirmative responsibilities offers initial guidance in determining one's moral responsibility. Simply put, the responsibility not to harm others is more stringent than the responsibility positively to help others. Virtually all ethical systems, even in different cultures, acknowledge a moral minimum that prohibits doing injury to another person and, as a corollary, requires corrective action when harm is inflicted.

The distinction applies to corporate action. Much of the debate and criticism surrounding the notion of "corporate social responsibility" has focused on affirmative responsibilities such as corporate contributions to charitable programs, extra costs to enhance architectural beauty or employee well-being, or "donation" of executives' time for community groups. These actions may be laudable and can certainly be conceived as moral responsibilities rooted in respect for persons. But they do represent affirmative choices open to debate depending upon the circumstances and one's view of morality and the role of corporations. In contrast, there are fewer disputes that corporations should not knowingly market unsafe products (the definition of "unsafe," of course, occasions significant debate).

A first "cut" in applying ethics, then, is the simple injunction: do no harm. What does this enjoin? While a precise definition will lead to disagreements about human nature and needs, a reasonably specific range of considerations offers a core definition despite inevitable ambiguities at the edges. The harm that can be done to persons and to institutions includes the following:

1. Material injury, including direct assault; impairment of health; deprivation of food, clothes, and shelter; economic loss.
2. Deprivation of freedom, including political rights and personal choices.
3. Violation of certain moral principles such as promise-keeping, truth-telling, and justice.

In undergraduate and graduate courses, this definition would spark debates leading into the theories of Rawls and Nozick and a whole range of social philosophical issues. As a framework for managers reasoning through problems, however, the definition provides sufficient material to assist the analysis.

To recapitulate, a fundamental moral principle is to avoid injuring others, and understanding "injury" often requires careful analysis. Furthermore, we are obliged to correct or compensate for injury that we have caused. But even if we are scrupulous in avoiding injury, we do not exhaust the range of moral action, for there are occasions when we ought to prevent or correct injury caused by others, and there are also numerous affirmative responsibilities.

Responding to Injury Caused by Others: The "Kew Gardens Principle"

The distinction between negative and affirmative responsibilities is meant to indicate that certain responsibilities ("do no harm") are more stringent and of higher priority than others ("help others"). An important middle step between the two are instances where we have the opportunity to prevent or correct harm that others inflict. We do not violate the "do no harm" principle if we fail to act, but in the face of clear need, it sometimes seems that offering aid is more than mere generosity.

What is at stake here is how to determine when an agent is responsible to act. It has been said already that one is responsible to act to correct self-caused injury. A set of considerations known collectively as the "Kew Gardens Principle" helps to decide when one is likewise responsible to act in the circumstances like those described above (i.e., where the injury is not self-caused). The principle takes its name from a murder in the Kew Gardens section of New York that was witnessed by thirty to forty bystanders, none of whom so much as screamed or called police. The principle seeks to clarify why we would ordinarily believe that rendering assistance under such circumstances is morally obligatory.

The Kew Gardens Principle

To the degree that each of the four factors below holds, the agent has an increased moral obligation to aid another:

1. *Need*   There is a clear need for aid; (for example, a harm has been or is about to be done).

2. *Proximity*   The agent is "close" to the situation, not necessarily in space but certainly in terms of notice; that is, he or she knows of the need or could reasonably be held responsible for knowing of it.

3. *Capability*   The agent has some means by which to aid the person in need without undue risk to the agent.

4. *Last Resort*   No one else is likely to help. The first three factors create a presumption to aid the person in need. This presumption is strengthened to the degree that the agent is likely to be the only one who will render help. Given our propensity to fail to act on the false assumption that others will do so, it is important both to assess this consideration carefully and to give the other three factors greater weight.

The Kew Gardens principle is generally applicable in managerial decisions as a "rough and ready" tool to guide considerations about moral responsibility. When claims are pressed upon managers by various stakeholders, the four considerations outlined may be useful in sorting through whether the managers are obliged to act (there may be affirmative responsibilities that lead them to act, but here the question is whether they have a more stringent obligation to respond). An example would be a call for a company to provide free day care to the preschool children of company employees. Such an enterprise might be justified as a good and generous corporate program. But to establish that the corporation is more clearly morally obligated to provided day care, it would be necessary to assess the need, the company's capacity (financially and otherwise) to meet this claim alongside others, and the likelihood or possibility of available alternatives. Disagreements are bound to arise here, but the Kew Gardens principle at least provides a framework for working through the issues. Over a whole range of managerial questions, the principle may prove helpful in limiting and defining managerial moral responsibility.

AFFIRMATIVE MORAL RESPONSIBILITY

The preceding discussion focuses upon the most stringent moral obligations that embody respect for persons: avoidance of harm, correcting self-caused injury, and coming to the aid of those harmed by others. These are the most stringent precisely because they are minimal; without adherence to these obligations, more generous deeds would be of no avail. But general compliance with negative injunctions does not exhaust moral responsibility, for respect for persons yields principles of doing good as well as not doing evil. Where there is human need, or the opportunity for human growth, ethical concern rooted in respect for persons can call forth response. Negative injunctions focus narrowly upon human needs bound up directly with the agent's actions and define a generally realizable set of obligations. In contrast, affirmative responsibilities extend to all human needs and open up a range of actions beyond the resources and capacities of the individual agent.

Beyond negative responsibilities, then, people must choose the moral commitments they intend to pursue and those that they cannot or do not wish to pursue. A simple example is personal charitable giving. From among the numerous solicitations received each year from worthy organizations, donors must choose the organizations to which to devote their limited funds. This choice need not reflect negatively on the worth of the charities declined, for it follows from the donors' limited resources and their commitments and interests. So it is with the full range of possible affirmative moral responsibilities. Individuals choose from among a multitude of potential projects and charitable acts limited patterns of commitment that express both their moral sensitivities and their unique identities. Individuals might argue about the appropriateness of particular choices. Unlike negative injunctions where there are some clear ways to understand individual responsibility, affirmative responsibilities cover such a wide range and relate as much to the agents' values and personal identity as to independent considerations that resolution of such disputes is difficult.

There are parallels here to the affirmative moral responsibilities of corporations and, thus, of their managerial decisionmakers. Here, as well, negative injunctions are more clear while affirmative responsibilities can unfold a range of actions that, if vigorously pursued, could pull the corporation away from its primary task and exhaust its resources. Like individuals, corporations have limited resources and distinctive identities that are reflected in their limited affirmative moral commitments. The amount and nature of corporate charitable contributions, extra fringe benefits for employees, and corporate championing of particular social causes illustrate the variety of such commitments. Resolving disagreements about a corporation's commitments is as difficult as it is for individuals, for again it is a matter of corporate values and role as much as one of independent assessment of the options.

The point is not to discount affirmative responsibilities because of their extent and the difficulty of determining which ones are appropriate. These considerations actually underscore the importance of going beyond negative injunctions to embody fully moral commitments. But these same considerations also indicate the necessity to view particular affirmative responsibilities as less stringent than negative injunctions.

SPECIFIC MORAL PRINCIPLES

The discussion to this point outlines a way of understanding moral responsibility. Within that framework, specific moral principles give further definition to particular responsibilities. A reasonably thorough list of moral principles includes:

Promise-keeping
Truth-telling
Reparation (compensating for previous wrongful acts)
Gratitude
Justice
Beneficence (doing good, preventing or removing evil)
Nonmaleficence (refraining from doing evil)
Morally virtuous self-development

The relationship of these substantive principles to the responsibility framework is sketched in Table 1. Development of specific principles can take place within this context.

Once this general framework is apprehended, the most fruitful learning—for both practical and theoretical purposes—comes from working through cases and parsing the meaning of relevant concepts. In this way, links between ethical theory and concrete problems can be built that illumine both practice and principle. Consider the following example.

Table 1. Moral Responsibilities

	Negative Responsibilities		Affirmative Responsibilities
Correcting Self-caused Injury	Avoiding Injury	Correcting Injury caused by Others	
Reparation	Do no harm (nonmaleficence)	Beneficence as preventing or removing harm	Beneficence as doing good Developing moral virtue
	Compliance with promise-keeping truth-telling gratitude justice		
	(Concept of responsibilities to stakeholders in most relevant here)	Kew Gardens principle aids in determining responsibility	

⟵——————————————————————————
Increasing stringency of Obligation

A CASE OF FAIRNESS AND HONESTY

Company A's product may have a list price and a standard warranty, and yet competitive conditions might encourage discounts or extended warranties in some purchase contracts. For example, the customer says, "Company B will provide a better warranty; how about you?" If the customer's business is sufficiently important and this condition has become the key competitive factor, Company A may match the warranty. The circumstance can puzzle conscientious managers. To be sure, the concessions are direct responses to competitive pressure, but is it right to treat customers differently just because one asks for special treatment and the other doesn't? Furthermore, is it right not to tell the other buyer about this possibility? After all, the manager knows both buyers well and sees them frequently. Is it nevertheless acceptable to maintain a different, and unstated, way of dealing with the two buyers?

These questions are natural anxieties in day-to-day marketing management, reflecting some sense of fairness and honesty. Although relatively simple, the issues described offer a rich opportunity for exploring more fully the meaning of fairness and honesty

in ways that illuminate both this case and the more general application of these concepts. Although the following discussion is by
no means definitive, it illustrates how linking ethical concepts to
cases within the framework outlined can yield genuinely helpful
and ethically sound conclusions.

First, has Company A harmed those who do not receive and do
not know about the extended warranty given certain customers?
Assuming the product meets appropriate quality and reliability
levels, the customer receives nothing deficient—the product is pur-
chased at a reasonable price with a warranty that is standard for
the industry. In fact, the customer might even be able to buy extra
warranty protection. At a minimal level, then, no customers receive
less than adequate terms simply because others receive more. But
the notion of harm goes beyond material problems. Given the central role of ethical principles in sustaining community, the customer *is* harmed *if* the different treatment is deemed unfair, *if* the
company owes disclosure to that customer, or both.

The essence of fair treatment is treating like things alike, and the
traditional dilemma in defining justice is to determine which categories are relevant, and which are not, for differential treatment.
In the distribution of goods, for instance, familiar dispositions include "to each according to merit," or "to entitlement," or "to need,"
or, even, "to each the same thing." One's view of the morally appropriate distinction depends upon deep assumptions about justice
and society, and conflicting theories are well known to those familiar with social philosophy and ethics.

In the differential warranty case, the issue is not distribution but
what constitutes relevant differences in commercial exchange relationships. Fairness in this case is treating customers alike according to commercially relevant differences. Favored treatment in
return for a bribe, for instance, would be unfair because the willingness and capacity to provide bribes are not a commercially relevant
distinction. Rather, it sets the individual interests of those involved
against their commercial role responsibilities. On the other hand, a
volume-based discount is certainly commercially relevant if the
volume realizes genuine cost savings for the seller. In the hypo-
thetical case at hand, the question is whether a differential warranty is offered simply because a customer asks and is favored or
because the seller's judgment of the marketplace is that this exten-
sion is competitively necessary to make the sale. That is, does the
request reflect marketplace conditions that make extra warranties
a commercially important variable?

Resolution of this question requires specific judgments about
marketplace conditions, company and industry practice, and legal

constraints. But the discussion to this point illustrates how the fairness concept can help to order analysis of the company's responsibility. If the product and warranty offered to all customers meet certain common standards and if the marketplace is a dynamic one where sales are lost or made under ever-changing circumstances, a differential warranty provided in response to tough customer negotiations may not be unfair.

But even if the marketing manager reaches this judgment, the manager may still feel troubled about not revealing this special deal for one customer when meeting frequently with another. Here the question of truth-telling in negotiations arises. In negotiations between a purchaser and a seller, each party seeks to protect its own self-interest and each has something the other desires (money in exchange for a product). In order to enter negotiations at all, each party surely must reveal certain facts: the seller ought not to mislead the customer about product nature, quality, and reliability, while the buyer must provide appropriate proof of creditworthiness. That is, an exchange depends upon reasonable knowledge about the items to be exchanged, namely, financial resources and the desired product. But self-interested parties are not ordinarily expected to reveal their respective "bottom line," that is, the specific limits that guide their negotiations.

In the actual course of negotiations, an important distinction arises regarding information one party rightfully wants to withhold from the other, a distinction between protection and deception. Truth-telling and lying can be envisioned as a spectrum ranging from complete openness to reticence to active deception. Deception is clearly a violation of the principle of truth-telling, although in certain circumstances that principle might be overridden (the Jew in the basement, Nazi at the door problem). But where along the line from reticence to openness a particular case falls varies with the circumstances. In negotiations, the argument is that some basic information must be revealed but that a variety of relevant details and tactics can rightfully be protected; to refuse to reveal them is not a violation of truth-telling, but actively deceiving the other party by purposefully misleading and false statements would be.

In the case at hand, it is conceivable that the marketing manager appropriately withholds information about the differential warranty as a bargaining chip, and, so long as the manager does not deceive the buyer about possibilities, he or she has not violated the basic principle of truth-telling. Of course, the specific discussions can become complicated, and the "rules of the game" could even make putatively false statements—"that's my final offer"—acceptable if both parties clearly understand that this statement *means,*

"I'm still trying to negotiate harder than you are." Likewise, if a naive party does not seem to know the "game," we ought not to take advantage of this party by excessive protection of relevant information. Specific judgments, then, would depend upon the circumstances, but an understanding of the negotiating process and the distinction between protecting information and deceiving someone can aid the conscientious manager.

A final note on this example concerns the role responsibility of managers. Even if the marketing person in this case determines that differential warranties are not unfair and that no relevation of one deal is owed to another customer, the manager's general relationship of trust with that customer's representative will still create some tension. But the tension stems from complexity of role responsibilities, because each person must represent different interests in their corporate roles and yet as persons and business associates they have very cordial relationships.

This case illustrates in cursory fashion how particular moral concepts can be elucidated in ways that are helpful to resolving managerial decisions. Specific cases are helped by, and serve to illustrate, different principles, and a set of well-chosen issues can bring to bear all the familiar principles. The utilitarian–deontological distinction, avoided at the outset, can also be introduced in appropriate ways at this stage. The challenge to ethics as applied to management is to build these links between important concepts and actual decisions, a challenge still largely unmet in many of the recent publications in the field. Training experiences such as the model described here offer one avenue not only for imparting ethics to managers, but also for exploring the intellectual frontiers of management ethics.

NOTES

1. I am indebted to Charles Powers and to Jon Gunneman, whose contribution to my understanding of management ethics is far greater than subsequent footnoted references could suggest.
2. Charles W. Powers and David Vogel, *Ethics in the Education of Business Managers* (Hastings-on-Hudson, N.Y.: Institute of Society, Ethics, and the Life Sciences, The Hastings Center, 1980), pp. 2–4.
3. The perspective offered is an adaptation of the levels of moral discourse in Henry David Aiken, "The Levels of Moral Discourse," in his *Reason and Conduct* (New York: Knopf, 1962), pp. 65–87.
4. The model here is borrowed from Ralph B. Potter, *War and Moral Discourse* (Richmond, Va.: John Knox Press, 1969), pp. 23–29.
5. See, for example, Robert M. Veatch, "When Ethical Paths Converge," *Hastings Center Report,* August 1979, p. 48. Veatch notes the considerable overlap in prac-

tical ethics reached by co-authors of a medical ethics text, one an avowed utilitarian, the other a formalist.

6. The approach described is clearly more formalist than consequential, and this normative "bias" is made clear to participants in the course of the program. The framework owes much to the discussion in John G. Simon; Charles W. Powers; and Jon P. Gunnemann, *The Ethical Investor* (New Haven: Yale University Press, 1972), Chapter 2.

Chapter 3

Applied Management Ethics Training at Lockheed–California Company

Robert C. Batchelder

The Lockheed–California Company, headquartered in Burbank, California, is one of the major operating companies in the Lockheed Corporation. Employing about 24,000 persons, the Lockheed–California Company (Calac) manufactures the L-1011 Tristar wide-bodies commercial aircraft and the P-3C anti-submarine patrol aircraft for the U.S. Navy and several foreign nations. It also is producing updated versions of the U-2 high-altitude reconnaissance aircraft, and is carrying out extensive research and development in advanced aerospace technology.

In 1979 Calac launched a large-scale training effort designed to upgrade the basic managerial skills of its first-line supervisors and middle managers. "Applied Management Ethics" is taught as an integral part of this ongoing Management Workshop program which, during the ensuing two and a half years, has provided training to 2000 supervisors and managers at Calac.

This chapter first describes the Management Workshop program in order to delineate the context within which the teaching of ethics takes place at Calac. Next the content and method of teaching are outlined. The final section of the chapter attempts to evaluate the strengths, weaknesses, and impact of teaching ethics at this level of management in a large manufacturing enterprise.

THE CORPORATE CONTEXT

Background

Early in the 1970s the Lockheed Corporation suffered a series of devastating economic setbacks. The financial effects of these reversals—when combined with the huge development costs associated with the design and manufacture of the L-1011 Tristar, Lockheed's entry in the wide-bodied commercial aircraft field—left the corporation facing stringent financial constraints throughout the decade of the 1970s. Consequently, all expenditures that could possibly be eliminated or postponed were cut back.

One activity suffering such cuts was management training and development. In Calac the staff responsible for this function was reduced to a single person. In-house management training activity was minimal, and no supervisory training was done for more than six years.

Beginning in 1978, however, orders for the L-1011 began to rise, and a corresponding buildup of production at Calac was initiated. Laid-off workers were recalled and many new employees were hired. By mid-1980, 40 percent of the workforce had seniority of less than two years. A growing workforce implied increased demands for first-line supervisors*—at the very time when the supply of supervisory talent was diminishing. Many experienced supervisors (and long-term skilled employees), from whose ranks new supervisors would logically have been drawn, had joined Lockheed during World War II, and by the late 1970s were retiring in increasing numbers. This swelling demand for supervisors combined with a decline in their supply resulted in a rapid influx of inexperienced persons into the supervisory ranks. A familiar scenario was repeated many times: on Friday, a person would be working on a machine or shooting rivets into an aircraft assembly; on Monday, this person was a supervisor. Little or no training or other resource was provided to help the person make this sudden transition into management. The programs from earlier years that would have been helpful had been eliminated—victims of the budget crunch. Turnover among new supervisors began to rise sharply. Some quit; others were fired; and others voluntarily returned to hourly status. Management realized that the situation was self-defeating. Something had to be done to provide training, especially for new supervisors, in the skills of supervision and management. The decision was made to add staff to the Management Development Group,

---

*At Lockheed a person in the first level of management, equivalent to a foreman in other industries, is called a supervisor.

and this staff was charged with the responsibility of providing adequate training programs to meet the needs of new first-line supervisors. The result was Management Workshop I. Begun in April 1979, it has become the standard training program for supervisors at Calac.

Management Workshop I

Initially designed to meet the needs of new supervisors as well as hourly workers who were identified as potential supervisors, Management Workshop I has progressively been made available to all supervisors regardless of seniority. The workshop runs for two weeks, providing 80 hours of classroom training. The sessions are held a short distance from the plant in pleasant surroundings, and lunch is provided for the participants, who typically number 20 to 25 per class.

The focus of Management Workshop I is on interpersonal and management skills. Approximately 60 percent of the original program was devoted to these topics. Twenty percent was devoted to introducing supervisors to various support functions within Calac that can aid the supervisor in accomplishing assignments: Labor Relations, Medical, Group Insurance, Safety, and so on. The remaining 20 percent was devoted to technical modules that provided knowledge about specific paperwork and procedures required of supervisors. As the workshop has developed over time, the percentage of instructional time devoted to management skills has increased while the time devoted to technical and procedural topics has decreased.

Instruction for most of the core subjects within the interpersonal and management skills area is provided by Calac's management training staff. Faculty from nearby universities are engaged to teach certain other management topics. All the modules on technical subjects and on Lockheed support organizations are taught by Lockheed personnel.

When Management Workshop I was launched in 1979, the initial estimate of the target population was 750 supervisors, primarily from Manufacturing, Quality Assurance, and Product Support. The immediate response to the workshop was highly enthusiastic. Demands for seats in the classes began to grow as it became obvious that a critical need was being met. It soon became necessary to double the number of workshops originally planned. Thus, during the first year of the program, a new workshop began every week, and two workshops ran simultaneously at all times. By the end of the first year, over 900 supervisors had been trained—but the waiting list continued to grow as other branches within Calac (Engineering, Finance, Computer Services) heard of the workshop and asked to send their supervisors to be trained. Workshop sessions continued throughout 1980 and 1981, with the number of supervisors trained passing 1500. For 1982 classes are projected to continue throughout the year, although at a slower rate.

Management Workshop II

One of the first comments that senior management began to hear from participants in the Management Workshop I went something like this: "What we have learned is exciting and valuable. However, we cannot begin to implement it without the support of upper management. Why don't you provide the same kind of training for our bosses?" This message was repeated with such frequency and intensity that senior management soon authorized the development of a Management Workshop II for the next two levels of management: department managers and division managers.

The first session of Management Workshop II was held late in 1979. It provided one week of training focused exclusively on interpersonal skills and management skills. Although pitched at a somewhat different level, so as to be appropriate to the responsibilities of managers, the content of the new workshop is consistent with the material being presented to the supervisors—and indeed, several of the topics are taught by the same instructors.

The response to Management Workshop II has also been enthusiastic, with nearly 500 managers completing the 40-hour course during the first two years. The workshop will continue to be offered throughout 1982 in response to continuing demand.

TEACHING "APPLIED MANAGEMENT ETHICS"

In both Management Workshop I and Management Workshop II, four hours are devoted to teaching "Applied Management Ethics." We turn now to a description of the content and approach used in presenting this subject.

The Instructor

The instructor is a member of Calac's Management Development staff. He earned a doctorate in ethics from a major university, and has taught at both the undergraduate and graduate levels. Prior to joining Lockheed, he had gained broad experience exploring with persons at all levels of business and industry the ethical issues arising in their work within the corporate setting.

The Participants

The participants in Management Workshop I are supervisors, the first line of Calac management. Who are they? What are their characteristics?

The heaviest concentration within each class is from Manufacturing. The typical production supervisor has had little or no formal education beyond high school. This person typically graduated from high school, went to work in the factory, proved to be effective at doing his or her assigned work, began to demonstrate some superiority in intelligence, energy, and leadership—and was promoted to supervisor. Apart from their edge in intelligence, drive, or experience, supervisors tend to reflect the whole spectrum of people doing factory work in Southern California.

Each class also includes supervisors from operations other than Manufacturing—such as Engineering, Finance, and Data Processing. Supervisors from these areas may have had some college education—or may even have graduate degrees, although they would be in a minority.

What the participants have in common is a high level of technical skill—whether mechanical, scientific, or financial. They tend to have fewer people-oriented skills. In general, the intent of the workshop is to meet this deficiency by focusing on the interpersonal and management skills that all managers need, regardless of their sphere of technical competence.

The workshop classes reflect the broad mixture of people who make up Calac. Every class includes significant numbers of minority persons—Blacks, Americans, Chicanos, and to a lesser degree, Orientals. Most classes also include women, although usually less than 20 percent.

The managers who attend Management Workshop II tend to parallel the supervisors in background. Production managers most frequently have themselves come up from the ranks of supervision after having started as mechanics. A somewhat broader diversity of background and experience (Engineering, Finance, Publications, etc.) is represented in the management groups. Each class includes a mixture of college graduates and noncollege people. In Management Workshop II, minorities are usually present, but in much smaller numbers than in the supervisors' classes. Only an occasional female manager is present, reflecting the general scarcity of women in management throughout the company.

The Approach

The approach to teaching management ethics to this diverse group of management personnel is based on a series of assumptions or guidelines:

1. Given the time limit of four hours and the educational mix in the class, the decision was made not to attempt a systematic presentation of alternative ethical theories.
2. The class has been structured so as to maximize discussion and involvement by participants; each class session is broken for part of the period into subgroups for analysis of cases.
3. The decision was made to focus on issues not only pertinent to the level of responsibility of the participants but also emerging from their sharing of problems and concerns. (This is in contrast to many texts and cases in management ethics that tend to focus on issues and decisions facing a corporation president—such as the social impact of closing an obsolete plant.)
4. The instructor assumes that a commitment to moral values and the possession of considerable moral insight already exist within the participants. The role of the instructor is not so much to "instruct" as to serve as a catalyst to provoke discussion and provide opportunity for participants to articulate their value commitments, to reflect on them, and to sharpen their moral reasoning through practice.
5. The instructor seeks to provide insight from ethical theory as it is pertinent to the cases and examples raised by participants.
6. The intent is to stimulate participants to "do ethics"—that is, to engage in reflection upon values they hold, and also upon the values that do prevail and ought to prevail within the organizational context of their work.
7. It is assumed that it is fruitful to focus reflection both at the level of personal value commitments and also on the values operating within the corporate context.

Content of the Sessions

The first of the two two-hour sessions in "Applied Management Ethics" begins by defining ethics as a process of reflection upon the values, obligations, and commitments that guide our decisions and actions. The instructor briefly outlines the results flowing from ethical reflection (clarity, consistency, and heightened commitment)—and their importance for the integrity of the individual and of the community.

Class members are then asked to reflect briefly about their work, and to identify individually the values, obligations, and ethical commitments that they see as central to performing the job of supervisor as they personally feel it ought to be done. These items are listed on the blackboard. A general discussion follows, in which some items are questioned, and the relation between such concepts as fairness, honesty, efficiency, and respect for persons is explored.

Next, the class is divided into small groups to discuss one or two brief case studies incorporating moral dilemmas that might be encountered by supervisors in their daily work. Participants are asked not only to decide what action they would take in the situation presented by the case but also to articulate the moral reasoning leading to their decision. Their conclusions are shared with the whole class.

The session concludes with the instructor illustrating a series of five points from the discussion to be considered seriously when making a responsible decision about any difficult moral choice:

Goal A definition of the good to be pursued or enhanced.

Rules Identifying existing rules, policies, or laws that apply, and to which obedience is owed.

Issue Defining clearly the central ethical issue at the core of the situation being considered—and seeking others' perspectives as a correction to one's own bias.

Persons Identifying all persons or groups affected by the decision about to be made, and their rights or interests that ought to be respected.

Alternatives Seeking to expand the range of alternative actions that are available.

The second two-hour session of the workshop begins with a brief lecture and discussion on the nature of "responsibility" as an ethical category. Main points include:

Responsibility as responsiveness.

Responsibility as accountability.

Responsibility as obligations arising in particular roles and relationships.

Responsibility as accepting the consequences flowing from one's own actions.

Responsibility as active, involving initiative.
Responsibility of managers for the actions of others.
Responsibility of managers for the health of the organization.

A case study discussed in small groups provides an opportunity to explore how these dimensions of responsibility apply in a specific decision.

The idea of the manager's responsibility for maintaining the health and effectiveness of the organization itself becomes a transition point in which the focus of managerial ethics shifts from difficult personal choices made by individual managers to the network of values, obligations, and commitments that prevail—and ought to prevail—within the corporation viewed as a community. A list of "values essential to the health of the organization" is discussed as implying managerial commitment to such values as quality, efficiency, truthful communication, trust, teamwork, fairness, respect for and development of people, and delegation.

Finally, the supervisors and managers are reminded that their ethical responsibility includes the establishment and maintenance of a climate within their department that encourages all employees to behave in accordance with values that promote the well-being of the organization and its people. A brief checklist to aid in doing this is provided.

Ethical Issues Raised

Several of the central issues that emerge from discussions of ethics among Lockheed managers and supervisors revolve around the theme of communication, as it is affected by the use and abuse of power in the management of people within the company. In certain branches of the organization, an approach that supervisors characterize as "management by fear" had become in recent years a dominant mode of running the company. Within such an atmosphere of fear, where there was also very strong pressure to meet production schedules and stay within established budgets, many supervisors and lower-level managers felt that in order to "survive" they could not tell the truth about their operations to higher management. If, in a production review meeting with the boss, a subordinate manager reported truthfully that the department was having problems getting a job completed on schedule, or was running over budget, this manager risked being castigated and humiliated before his or her peers, or even being demoted or fired. Having experienced or witnessed such treatment once or twice, most managers quickly learned to do what was necessary to survive. When the implicit or explicit message of certain powerful bosses was "Reports of behind schedule condition are unacceptable," many subordinates became very skillful at manipulating figures and charts in order to "tell the boss what the boss wants to hear."

There is a broad consensus in the workshops that feeling forced to "cheat and lie" has caused a great deal of moral anguish and also cynicism among individual Lockheed employees. Moreover, such a climate has been destructive for the company as a whole, since it deprives top management of the accurate information it needs for making major policy decisions.

Even though there is general agreement—and gratitude—that currently Lockheed's senior management is moving strongly to reverse this pattern, and is committed to honest and accurate reporting at all levels, the painful experience of having lived through the former regime causes the moral issue of "honesty and truth-telling" to be one of the issues discussed must intensely within the modules on management ethics. The commitment to honesty, as understood by supervisors and managers, is multifaceted. It involves not only truthful reporting of facts and numbers, but also such dimensions of good communication as openly giving employees information about higher management decisions that affect their work; being open to hear the concerns of employees; letting employees "know where they stand" by being explicit about the standards and expectations by which their performance is judged; giving frequent feedback to employees on both the strengths and weaknesses of their performance; encouraging the development of a relationship of credibility and trust with one's superior as well as with subordinates; and finally, the obligation of each manager to make explicit the expectation that employees are to report accurately on problems as they emerge, rather than tell the manager what they think he or she wants to hear.

Another moral issue that is frequently raised in discussion—even though not many managers and supervisors confront it in their regular work—is the issue of payments made to foreign officials in connection with the marketing of Lockheed's products overseas. Many who were embarrassed by the disclosure some years ago that Lockheed had made such payments express satisfaction that the company now has stringent policies and regulations that ensure strict adherence to the Foreign Corrupt Practices Act passed by Congress in 1977. Others still feel outraged that Lockheed received undue bad publicity for doing what was legal at the time it was done as well as being practiced by many other companies as a customary way of doing business in certain parts of the world. Indeed, these managers question the propriety of the U.S. Congress seeking by legislation to outlaw business practices that are legal and customary in other nations—particularly since strict adherence to the 1977 law puts U.S. companies at a competitive disadvantage in relation to their European competitors who are free to engage in such practices without restraint. Discussion on this issue within the limited time available in the workshops serves to clarify certain dimensions of the problem, although it seldom resolves the basic conflict, which has its roots in the difficult ethical problem of varying moral norms in different cultures.

A moral standard on which there is strong consensus is quality. Given the nature of Lockheed's products and the overriding commitment to passenger safety, there is a strong and universal commitment to building the highest possible quality into the aircraft "before it flies over the fence" to the customer.

There is also widespread understanding of the importance of fairness as a standard for treatment of employees. Ironically, adherence to this value causes considerable anguish for managers of salaried employees at Lockheed. Two factors in the environment of the company tend strongly to produce salary inequities: (1) a cost of living clause in the union contract that in a period of high inflation keeps pushing hourly wages higher; and (2) the market forces that permit a newly graduated engineering student to command a starting salary higher than that received by a seasoned engineer who has been working at Lockheed for several years. Managers are acutely aware of the inequities that these forces introduce into Calac's salary structure. But the continuing annual operating losses of the California Company (which offset the profits of Lockheed's other operating companies) mean that the dollars needed to correct these inequities are simply not available. Hence managers are in the painful position of having to administer a situation that includes unfairness they are powerless to correct.

A further ethical issue arising in the work of managers that is frequently discussed is the responsibility of the manager for developing his or her subordinates. This norm has long been a commitment at Lockheed, with its tradition of providing training to continually enhance the technical competence of its employees. However, the emphasis upon technical excellence has in the past tended to overshadow the importance of developing managerial and interpersonal skills that persons need to manage effectively. The very existence of the management workshops is seen by participants as a sign of an emerging commitment by the company—which they are obligated to further—to give conscious attention to the broad-guage development of subordinates' capabilities, both for the subordinates' good and for the long-term good of the company. Learning how to delegate responsibility effectively to one's subordinates thus emerges as one of the key responsibilities of the manager.

AN ATTEMPT AT EVALUATION

Participants' Evaluations

A precise measure of the participants' evaluation of Management Workshop I is available, because 90 days after the conclusion of the workshop, supervisors are invited to return for a day's followup session. At this time, each supervisor fills out a written evaluation form that assesses the value of each module in the original workshop in terms of its usefulness on the job. For Applied Management Ethics, the figures are as follows:

23.2% Immediately useful (Gave me skills I am now using on the job).
50.4% Generally useful (For improved understanding of my job).
18.2% Interesting (But not sure how I can use in my job).
6.5% Marginally useful (Time could have been better spent on other topics).
1.7% Not useful (Should be dropped from the workshop).

The significant point of these figures is that three months after returning to their normal work routine, three-fourths of the supervisors found Applied Management Ethics either immediately or generally useful in carrying out their jobs. (This level of appreciation was typical for most of the modules having to do with management skills and interpersonal skills.)

Evaluations from managers participating in Management Workshop II also indicate a moderately high level of appreciation for the ethics module—lower than certain popular modules but higher than others. In both the managers' and supervisors' workshops the dominant feeling seems to be one of genuine appreciation that the subject is treated—which is taken as a sign of senior management's concern to improve the ethical standards by which the company operates. This appreciation is tempered by a certain degree of skepticism about whether top management's concern is serious enough to significantly and permanently change some of the lingering questionable practices and attitudes that are most troubling to those at the lower and middle levels of management.

Strengths and Weaknesses

Certain obvious weaknesses of the workshop flow from the inherent limitations of the four-hour format. Indeed what is attempted within these limits can hardly be called the teaching of ethics, but instead only the opening of the subject—an underlining of the importance of ethical norms for any community or organization; an identification of some of the places within the work of Lockheed where ethical issues may arise; and a stimulus to participants to raise to consciousness the values, obligations, and commitments that are already operative for themselves personally and for the company as a whole. Profound issues are raised, but frequently there is inadequate time to deal with them systematically and rigorously. There is insufficient time to lay out a clear theoretical framework that would be helpful to participants in bringing some order and consensus out of the often bewildering variety of ethical norms brought to the workshop (and the workplace) by supervisors from widely diverse backgrounds.

If it is assumed that one objective of teaching management ethics is to influence the moral climate of the whole organization, then questions may be raised about the effectiveness of starting the training process with supervisors, who are at the bottom of the managerial pyramid. Would it not be more effective to begin at the top with executives who have the power to set the direction for the company? Viewed from one perspective, this question is valid. In a hierarchical organization, leadership comes from the top downward, and there are severe limits to what a supervisor can do to change the organization's policies and practices without the leadership and encouragement of higher levels of management. Ideally, it would have been better to begin with top management. But in the real world, however, a person starts where it is possible to start. In Calac, there was a recognized need to provide training for supervisors, and so that is where the teaching of management ethics began.

Viewed from another perspective, however, this is not entirely a weakness. The first-line supervisor is in a pivotal position in the company. Taken collectively, supervisors have a profound impact, because they are in daily face-to-face contact with the overwhelming majority of all of Calac's 24,000 employees—hourly, technical, and professional. If a significant proportion of the 1500 supervisors who have completed Management Workshop I were to clearly and consistently articulate to their employees the importance of maintaining high ethical standards in the daily work of the company, the long-term impact on the organization and its climate would indeed be powerful.

It seems evident that there are certain strengths in the current effort to teach ethics within the context of Calac's Management Workshop series. First, ethics is treated as an integral part of management training. The implication is that seriousness about the ethical dimension of work is, and ought to be, a normal concern of supervisors and managers. The discussion of ethical issues involves all managers and supervisors—not only the select few who might choose to attend the workshop if ethics were offered as a special topic for those especially interested.

Probably the most important strength of teaching Applied Management Ethics is that it provides legitimacy and an occasion for the surfacing of ethical concerns and the sharing of insights on perceived moral problems arising in the life of the company. It has wisely been said that large numbers of business managers, individually, are ethically sensitive and committed persons but that the way modern corporations are organized provides no structure wherein this sensitivity can be exercised and commitment expressed in relation to moral issues arising in corporate life. In some ways, Applied Management Ethics provides such a structure. Persons can express their concerns without appearing to be malcontents. They can share insights and learn from the experience of others; they can learn that others share many of their own concerns and commitments. And the process of sharing and discussion may contribute to the building of an explicit consensus on moral issues that was previously covert and inchoate. By allowing ethical concerns to surface, the sessions may contribute to building a consensus about what is wrong in the company and what can and ought to be done to correct it. It is too early to say, but it may be possible that the management workshops, including their modules on ethics, are playing a significant consensus-building role in changing the basic management philosophy and practice of a major corporation.

Chapter 4

Learning Ethics by "Doing" Ethics at Northwestern National

Douglas Wallace and Janet Dudrow

Charles W. Powers and David Vogel, in *Ethics and the Education of Business Managers,* describe six capacities on which moral judgment depends: moral imagination, moral identification and ordering, moral evaluation, tolerating moral disagreement and ambiguity, integrating managerial competence with moral competence, and a sense of moral obligation.[1] Powers and Vogel emphasize that the goal of business ethics training is "to develop the *capabilities* to put managerial situations under ethical discipline." This emphasis on capabilities is comforting and welcome, for it suggests that moral reasoning is not a talent but a collection of skills that can, to a greater extent than often supposed, be taught and learned. The authors' description provides a much-needed theoretical framework from which to develop a better understanding of the necessary elements in the educational process and challenges us to develop tools and techniques.

During the past year, we have been implementing a program of employee task forces at Northwestern National Bank of Minneapolis, designed to address social and ethical issues affecting or affected by the bank. The intent is twofold: to develop policy recommendations that will be well researched and thoughtfully considered in a participatory manner to enhance their legitimacy, and to provide bank employees with practical experience in working through complex ethical issues. As an educational process, the task force program is unusual. Most ethics education processes—even in a management setting—consist of a set of training or workshop sessions in which particular concepts are discussed and applied to institutional situations. The task force process, by contrast, is learning by doing: Members of the task forces work through ethical considerations in order to develop *real* policy recommendations with *real* consequences. There is considerable evidence that such experience-based learning is not only more profound but also more lasting.

The design of the task force program at Northwestern Bank was a result of previous experience, observation, and a considerable amount of intuition. Yet we find that it does, in fact, develop each of the six capacities enumerated by Powers and Vogel, which likely accounts for a good deal of the program's success as an educational venture. This chapter describes in detail the task force process, illustrates how the process develops the six capacities, and suggests subjects for further study.

The Process

Two of the issues to be addressed by the task forces were selected by the Bank's Management Policy Committee (MPC)—the top policymaking body composed of six senior officers—from results of a modified Delphi study. The study, which involved fifty people who had been identified as alert and sensitive to social issues, consisted of a multistage identification and prioritizing process. The top ten social issues that were chosen by the study were presented to the MPC, who then selected two issues—privacy and constituent rights—for study by the task forces. In addition, another topic to be studied by a task force—The Role of the Bank in Community Development—was identified by a committee of employees and also adopted by the MPC.

An internal public relations and recruitment program was launched to attract volunteers to the program. Task force membership was selected from among those who had volunteered by a screening committee. Each task force was made up of fifteen interested employees from a variety of operating areas and levels of authority although, by design, none of the task force members was a member of senior management.

An intensive, day-long orientation program was conducted for the task force members. The program included a practical session on how to work in small groups, an overview of Dr. Robert Terry's analysis of perspectives on social issues, introductory speaker presentations on the task force subjects, and enough unstructured time for the task force members to begin to get to know each other.

The task force operation itself is modeled after the Citizen's League, a Minneapolis nonprofit, public policy, research organization. The process includes a six- to eight-week testimony phase, in which experts on various aspects of the issue under study are invited to speak to the group. These presentations have been made by national, as well as local and regional, experts. Following the testimony phase, the task force members develop findings, conclusions, and recommendations for bank action. The final report is presented to the MPC at a meeting of the MPC and task force. After a deliberation period (four to six weeks), the MPC meets again with the task force members to explain which recommendations will be implemented, which will not be implemented, and, perhaps most important, the reasons for rejecting any of the recommendations.

The recommendations the MPC decides to adopt are then drafted into assignments to department managers either for immediate implementation or for inclusion in the corporate planning process. Six months after the conclusion of the task force, the task force members are given a progress report on their recommendations.

We decided to employ a task force process because we believed such a process would, over time, develop a critical mass of people committed to engaging in ethical analysis and would, therefore, alter the climate and reward system—the cultural ethos—of the corporation. In addition, we believed that such a process would result in better corporate policies because complicated social and ethical issues would be tackled in an anticipatory, rather than a crisis-oriented, manner.

Education happens as a result of the *project;* therefore the content of what is learned varies from topic to topic. Nevertheless, the six capacities, or elements, of moral judgment appear to be developed among the task force members as a result of the *process,* regardless of the topic under study.

The Elements of Moral Judgment

Moral Imagination: The first capacity that Powers and Vogel describe is:

> ... the ability to perceive that a web of competing economic claims is, simultaneously, a web of moral relationships. A person with moral imagination is not only sensitive to, but hunts out, the hidden dimen-

sions of where people are likely to get hurt; a person who anticipates being thrust into situations where the managerial choice will be intolerable and imagines how the events leading to such a choice could be avoided.

The first component of moral imagination is the need, not for some sort of "conversion," but for an ability to broaden the base of information upon which decisions are made—for including ethical analysis *along with* economic analysis. This is not an easy task for, as Powers and Vogel note, "many of the moral factors attendant—and consequent—to business decisions are remote and distant from the decisionmaker." In addition, they point out that most people will not acknowledge their power to make decisions that affect the lives of others, and thus, they tend to "rationalize away their ability to make self-conscious, moral choices."

The second component of moral imagination calls for an anticipatory and incremental application of Rawls's "veil of ignorance": In any given situation (present or future) where the decisionmakers assume they do not know which individual in the situation they will ultimately be, they will tend to develop solutions with an eye toward the welfare of the least fortunate individual.

Thus, to stimulate moral imagination in managers, we need an educational process that, first, makes the moral factors less remote from them; second, confronts them with evidence of their own power to affect people's lives; and, third, develops an ability to anticipate the effects of a decision on the least fortunate individual.

The process of soliciting testimony from people knowledgeable about the problem under study brings immediacy to the issue and provides the participants with evidence of the effect of corporate actions on individuals, by having those who have directly or indirectly experienced those effects address the issues. The Constituent Rights Task Force, for example, heard Paul Donnelly, a Detroit public interest lawyer, talk about individuals who have taken complaints about perceived employee rights violations to court. The Community Development Task Force heard about the issue of urban displacement. In addition, the testimony by guest speakers almost invariably touched on the question of how crises can be, or could have been, avoided. Donnelly, for example, emphasized continually that "if a company is socially oriented, fair, and treats people decently, it won't get sued."

The process of stimulating moral imagination among the task force members, in most cases, was not difficult. Because the members of the task forces are nonsenior management people, they often felt a keen identification with the ethical issues under consideration. For example, the moral ramifications of urban displacement are likely to be more immediate to nonexempt workers (who are more likely to live in the central city) than to senior executives (who typically live in suburbs and affluent parts of the city). It is not difficult for these participants to ask themselves, "If it were I who was going to be displaced by a condominium conversion, how would I react?", because, for several of them, displacement is a real possibility.

Moral Identification and Ordering: The second capacity on which moral judgment depends, according to Powers and Vogel, is moral identification and ordering, which is defined as:

> ... the ability to see which of the moral claims being made are relevant or irrelevant, clearly distinguished or chaotically asserted; to determine when the moral language that is being introduced by others is merely rhetorical or accurately states a real moral problem. It is also the ability to see behind the seemingly "merely descriptive" or amoral language in which managerial problems are typically described to the issues where human welfare is at stake.

The way a person casts an issue implies certain assumptions; no set of circumstances is termed "a problem" without some presumption about why they are perplexing. Powers and Vogel point out that we need to develop tools of analysis to uncover value or ethical assumptions implicit in claims and arguments, along with a set of signals that alert the person that the tools need to be employed. Several conceptual tools were introduced to the task force members to assist them in working through their particular issues.

One such tool introduced at the orientation session is a typology of structures of belief developed by social ethicist Dr. Robert Terry. Over several years, Terry has applied and refined this paradigm of social beliefs as a way to help managers in various kinds of organizations understand some of the basic orientations that inform social and ethical perspectives. One of the task forces later used this tool in a workbook in which they identified the basic orientation of the various speakers.

Terry's paradigm identifies six perspectives: Emergent Pluralist, Culturalist, Radical, Open Systems, Free Market, and Reactionary. For each perspective, Terry traces the basic model of reality, the key values, the prized mode of relationship, perceived threats to the key values, and additional factors such as how the people holding that basic perspective view the role of government, the role of the social scientist, potential internal conflicts, and alternative views that counter those contradictions.

During the session, we chose the issue of racism to illustrate the paradigm. Each perspective was examined to determine how its proponents would define the "problem," how they would characterize the problem in organizations, and the approach they advocate for working toward solutions to the "problem." Group members analyzed the logic of each perspective as applied to the issue of racism. In doing so, they began to see and understand the values and ethical assumptions underlying commonly encountered positions.

The discussion had additional impact because the participants were able to discover what their own basic orientations were. Before the discussion, a short written "test" based on Terry's paradigm was given to each task force member. The inventory consists of about twenty statements to which the individual is asked to indicate agreement or disagreement on a seven-point scale. Participants scored their own inventory. As we expected, this produced a good deal of interest and discussion about the implications of their own basic orientations to their task force topics.

It bears repeating that the context of this conceptual tool was a planned, task-oriented group—one that had time to wrestle with a management issue that was not a crisis. The group could think through the issues because the process was anticipatory in nature. The assumption, however, was that the tools used for the identifying and ordering moral issues, once employed in this context, could be used with increasing ease in other day-to-day management decisions.

The testimony process also encouraged the task force members to identify and order moral issues in that we self-consciously sought to bring to the group varying perspectives on each aspect of the task force subject. The Constituent Rights Task Force, for example, heard arguments from people ranging from an ACLU representative to corporate chief executives. Even focused specifically on employee rights, the members found many differing perspectives; between stakeholder perspectives—between customers and employees, for example—there were even more differences in how people view claims to rights with respect to the corporation.

We found that matrices are often very useful tools for helping people learn how to identify and order moral claims. Many people are visually oriented, and a matrix both helps to visualize the organization of certain perspectives and provides points of reference in group discussion. Members of the Community Development Task Force were asked at the close of the testimony phase to identify the strengths and weaknesses of neighborhoods. The results were assembled and ordered using a matrix. The process served to underscore again the variety of ways that people view the problems of community development and clarified and ordered the issues for subsequent evaluation.

Moral Evaluation: Powers and Vogel use "moral evaluation" to signify the process of weighing and reasoning about moral issues. They emphasize that, for business managers, it is imperative that the search for higher principles actually help inform decisions —that moral analysis be combined with consideration of institutional goals and purposes to yield an "answer" or course of action with measurable consequences.

It is this factor that makes the educational process in task-oriented groups so effective. At Northwestern Bank, the Management Policy Committee made clear to each of the task forces that they were expected to come up with specific recommendations for bank action. It was unacceptable for the task force members to spend six months in introspection and then present to management a lengthy discourse on the complexity and abstract nature of the problem (although in the case of the Individual Rights Task Force that would have been tempting). No matter how abstract or complex the issues, the task force members had to come up with an "answer," and it is precisely this imperative that forces the most rigorous evaluation— and the most learning—to take place.

The various instruments used for "moral ordering," such as matrices, provided the groundwork for the process of moral evaluation. For example, the Constituent Rights Task Force members were asked, first, to submit in writing their perceptions of the key issues grouped in categories as the person saw fit. These individual lists yielded a "master list" of rights issues. The task force then spent an intensive session sorting out the claims into three groups: legitimate claims, shoulds, and not legitimate.

The forcing of the answer enhances the learning process by providing the task force members with feedback about the adequacy of their decisions. Just as a student needs to see the results of a test in order to learn from the test, the business manager needs to see results in order to know whether the answer—and the moral analysis behind it—is "correct." An essential part of the learning process for members of the Constituent Rights Task Force is to see the effects of practices implemented, or not implemented, as a result of their analysis of the legitimacy of the rights claims.

Moral Disagreement and Ambiguity: The fourth capacity of judgment is the ability to tolerate moral disagreement and ambiguity. Powers and Vogel define this more fluidly than the other capacities:

> Both disagreement and ambiguity are real in ethics ... the challenge in pedagogical task [is] for "opening up" the space so that ethics has room and a place in business decisions, while honestly acknowledging that the justifications for moral matters are not ultimately as "coercive" as mathematics and may, in fact, finally rest on "decision."

The need to withstand pressure for closure when facing ambiguous moral dilemmas can be a problem in a management context. Managers often see differences in perspective as evidence of the "softness" of ethical analysis, and therefore ethical analysis is seen as less credible than straightforward business and financial analysis. The challenge is to help business people see that a variety of opinions on a particular question does not necessarily mean that the issue is hopelessly clouded in subjective feelings. If people can understand that, in many cases, what appears to be discrete opinions are actually pieces of a coherent perspective, they have taken an important step toward increasing their ability to tolerate competing moral claims.

We have used the stakeholder concept as one way of getting people accustomed to the idea of considering differing claims and self-interest motivations on particular issues, such as privacy rights. For example, the Privacy Task Force struggled with the dilemma of the customer's right to privacy and security of information conflicting with the possible violation of employee privacy. There were many illustrations of this conflict—one of them cropping up when the task force discussed the wisdom of every employee's fingerprints being forwarded to the FBI for a security check when, by law, only some employees in certain positions were required to have such a check. Obviously, here the interests of customers and employees were in conflict with each other. The task force deliberation was pitted with countless discussions of this kind. What was increasingly required of the members was tolerance for differences and ambiguity. What helped them achieve such tolerance was understanding the legitimacy of conflicting perspectives and some of the value assumptions on which these views are based.

In the end, however, each group had to arrive at a real conclusion and consensus that would make a difference in the way the bank deals with the issues. As mentioned earlier, the members did not have the luxury of an "academic" discussion because of the pressure to produce a definitive result. But the opportunity to deal proactively with an issue outside of a crisis environment gave the group a chance to consider the reasons for ambiguity and difference. The fact that the members had to take a position on issues did not dampen their enthusiasm for discussion; on the contrary, the opportunity to weigh differing perspectives made the issues more understandable and less emotionally laden, which helped free everyone to make informed choices.

Integrating Managerial Competence and Moral Competence: Powers and Vogel suggest that, even if managers have the four necessary capacities previously discussed, they need something more:

> For the manager the ability to make an ethical decision is of no value if it is not linked to managerial competence, the ability to create and coordinate the resources for which managerial decision must be made, rather than merely be shaped by them.

They contrast the two kinds of ethics—"head in hands" versus "ethics of anticipation," concluding that "the manager should be good at forecasting how such concerns should be dealt with, how they can all be maximized, or why they can only be partly met."

This point raises a significant question about *how* this can be done best, where the environment exists within businesses in which such "ethics of anticipation" can be encouraged and nurtured. One obvious answer is in the planning process. If an organization has a good planning process, examination of emerging ethical concerns among stakeholders, along with changing business conditions, is an excellent way to make room for developing "ethics of anticipation."

The task force program was purposely structured into the corporate planning process so that recommendations adopted by top management were, where appropriate, worked into departmental immediate and long-range plans. This procedure has several advantages, not the least of which is that the treatment of the issues is legitimated and structured into the objective-setting process as is any other business objective. This provides an opportunity for exploration of linkages between managerial and moral competence. Integrating consideration of ethical issues into the corporate planning process gives people an opportunity to learn moral judgment skills that can then be applied in other contexts and to more day-to-day decisions. It also makes it possible to pose the larger question of how the business itself takes into consideration potential ethical implications of particular business decisions.

In our experience, there appears to be a direct relationship between the development of this capacity and the capacity for moral identification and ordering. In order for managers to convert ethical decisions into institutional operations, they must have learned how to identify and order moral issues. Using these tools of moral judgment in real managerial context, such as planning, provides managers with the experience of doing two things at the same time: continuing to learn the process of moral judgment and working the process into an ongoing managerial decisionmaking procedure.

Sense of Moral Obligation: Powers and Vogel say that a sense of moral obligation is necessary to motivate and guide ethical analysis. They note that this element of moral judgment is least responsive to a teacher's influence, and the absence of the sense cannot be "corrected."

Our experience is that it is critical to have people with a sense of moral obligation in leadership positions and in sufficient quantity throughout the organization to affect its climate and reward system. Otherwise, the task of educating managers about ethical reflection becomes a futile exercise, and there will be little support or incentive for managers to consider the moral ramifications of economic decisions.

If this critical mass of people exists, however, it becomes less important for every member of the organization to feel morally obligated. That is, if the nonconverted can be convinced that it is in their best interest to engage in ethical analysis, and that such activity will pay off in a raise or fewer lawsuits or recognition, they will likely do so. And, ultimately, it matters less why people make the choices they do than that the choices are satisfactory according to the community's moral standards.

We have seen dramatic examples of marked behavior changes indicating a willingness to engage in ethical analysis, which have been unaccompanied by an apparent sense of moral obligation. One manager, who was very critical of the idea of even considering the ethical ramifications of certain investments (and very vocal about expressing his skepticism), became an equally vocal supporter less than a month later. The change had less to do with his conviction that the analysis was valuable than with his recognition that his manager thought it was valuable.

The intent of the task force is to nurture the sense of moral obligation among those who already have it, with the hope that they, in turn, will be motivated to nurture the same quality in their coworkers, thus allowing the task forces to develop recommendations that are structured upon these incentives for persons not motivated by moral obligation. There is evidence that the task force was, indeed, successful in nurturing the sense of moral obligation. Comments from participants' evaluations of the Community Development Task Force included:

> I have developed a stronger interest in community development, which will make me more aware of neighborhoods and more inclined to pursue other knowledge [about] communities. Will look for opportunities to put knowledge to work in community.

> Definitely intend to keep abreast of field of community development by reading and attending information sessions. Also, will be further involved with church and volunteer activities.

Over time, the task force process will develop the critical mass of people needed to alter the culture of the corporation.

Educational Tools

We have identified a number of methods that deserve future exploration with respect to their use in the task force process. *Simulations* are often excellent teaching tools because they provide an opportunity for concepts to be identified with experiences that, in turn, help people recall and make applications. Simulations can be integrated into various points in the task force process, such as the orientation of the group to the subject matter, during the input or testimony phase, or even at block points to help bring clarity to a prolonged disagreement over a particular conclusion.

One such simulation is *Star Power,* which is a very effective tool to help people order conceptual moral thinking about the issues of power and resource control in organizations and between groups. Of course, there are many other good simulations—some quite short and others more elaborate—that can be used to help in the development of moral imagination or in moral identification and ordering.

It would be very useful to develop a *stakeholder competing claim matrix* that could, in shorthand fashion, help individuals and groups identify constituent interests and claims and explore the compatibility or differences among the claims.

In studying and evaluating the task force process, we have become convinced of the value of *Dr. Robert Terry's paradigm* ordering and identifying differing moral perspectives on various issues. We intend to introduce and apply Terry's concepts more extensively with future task forces. For example, if a task force hears from a number of different people about a given issue, it would be instructive for the group to analyze the basic values and moral assumptions implicit in each viewpoint as well as the implications each perspective has for framing the problem and its solution.

Although it can be argued that task force membership in some degree represents more than one stakeholder perspective (e.g., in this case employees are all customers, community members who have a stake in credit-lending practices), it would be interesting to see what effect *bringing other stakeholders into task forces* would have on the stimulation of moral imagination and the identification of perspectives. People representing community interests could be included in a task force on community development; customers could continue to raise issues that employees might gloss over in a constituent rights task force; or spouses could provide different points of view in a task force looking at the relationship of work and family.

Although there are obvious problems that need to be addressed with respect to management control over such "outside" interests, the notion of including additional constituents in task forces can be valuable in increasing managers' learning.

Future Research

Thus far the effectiveness of the task forces as an educational process has been measured by personal observation combined with a subjective written evaluation by the task force members themselves. While both methods indicate that some often remarkable growth occurs among the participants, we can only speculate about the true magnitude and nature of the changes. We have identified a number of research tools that could be employed to gather such information: (1) Pre- and post-testing of task force members using the instrument (described earlier) based on Terry's paradigm and intended to assess the individual's basic orientation to social issues. We are interested in finding out whether participation in a task force has any effect on *basic ethical orientation*. (2) Pre- and post-testing, using a device intended to assess the individual's cognitive developmental stage of moral reasoning as described by Lawrence Kohlberg. We need to find out whether the task force experience has any effect on the *intellectual process* of evaluating ethical issues. We are also interested in finding out whether there is any relationship between *basic orientation* (as measured by the Terry instrument) and *moral reasoning* (described by Kohlberg). (3) Follow-up research to determine longer-term effects of task force participation. Possible techniques for obtaining such information include newspaper readership studies (often employed by public opinion researchers) to determine whether task force participants are more likely than nonparticipants to read news items about social or ethical issues. Another possibility is to interview task force participants (along with a control group) to ascertain whether task force participants can identify a greater number of current issues that have social or ethical implications. (4) Assessment of individuals' ability to identify value assumptions in ethical arguments. This involves asking the participant to analyze the underlying assumptions implicit in a statement provided by the interviewer.

Conclusion

The task force process helps to develop the six capacities of moral judgment described by Powers and Vogel by engaging individuals in analysis of real problems and their solutions. We believe that this aspect—learning by doing—immeasurably enhances the learning process and encourages continued application of the skills learned. Critical to the educational process is the fact that it is anticipatory: The task force participants are able to work through the issues and develop skills of moral judgment without the pressure of a crisis situation.

The effectiveness of this approach suggests that concepts of ethics education should not be limited to training sessions or workshops. Providing an environment in which people can learn for themselves how to make sound decisions on social and ethical issues may well work better than "teaching" ethics. We are looking forward to developing additional tools to use in the process and to documenting further the effects of task force participation with additional research.

NOTE

1. Charles W. Powers and David Vogel, *Ethics and the Education of Business Managers* (Hastings-on-Hudson, N.Y.: Institute of Society, Ethics, and the Life Sciences, the Hastings Center, 1980), pp. 40–45.

Chapter 5

Assessing the Sun Company's Ethical Condition: Voices from Within

Douglas Sturm

In 1980 the Corporate Ethics Committee of the Sun Company undertook a survey of the ethical sensibilities of several of its employees ranging from presidents of subsidiaries to workers on oil rigs. The immediate purpose of the survey was to discover what employees saw as points of ethical strain in the corporation's operation. The interviews were open-ended, and interviewees were encouraged to speak their minds freely. They did so with results extending far beyond what is customarily construed as "business ethics."

The concluding report of the survey constitutes the bulk of this chapter. Sun's Vice President for Corporate Affairs, Dale D. Stone, and Public Affairs Consultant, Eric A. Weiss, both of whom had key roles in the Corporate Ethics Committee, urged publishing the report because "it deals with an important subject in a novel and creative way and it reflects creditably on Sun." First, however, a few preliminary reflections about the place of ethics and ethical reflection in corporate life are in order.

Ethics and Ethos. Ethics, it has been said, is everybody's business. Curiously, however, not everybody thinks so. In particular, some members of the business community have insisted that business is strictly business. They believe ethics is a matter for home and church and that it has no place in the board room.

That view is shortsighted, for ethics, in one of its senses, is an unavoidable dimension of every human enterprise. A distinction has been made between popular and critical ethics. Ethos is another term for popular ethics. Every group, every practice, and every institution has an ethos, that is, a network of values and norms that govern the behavior of its members. Even a street corner gang has its code. And certainly a complex institution like the modern business corporation has its way of doing things, sometimes expressed in its policy statements, but more profoundly embedded in its culture. In that sense, ethics is indeed everybody's business.

But the ethos of an association may be questioned. Whenever anyone speaks approvingly or disapprovingly of the culture of a group, of its manner of acting, a shift has occurred from the popular level to the critical level. And everyone, it is presumed, has a criterion or standard from which to view the prevailing ethos. To scrutinize an institutional practice with an eye to its adequacy and possible improvement is to raise the mind from immediate operation to reflective analysis. In this sense, too, ethics is *potentially* everybody's business. And if the unexamined life is not worth living, ethics in this sense *ought* to be everybody's business.

The survey undertaken by the Sun Company was an effort to honor the reflective powers of employees and to assist the corporation in looking at its ethos from a critical standpoint.

Codes and Conversations. Over the past several years, a large number of corporations have formulated codes of ethics. In some cases, most likely, the codes are sheer window dressing. But, if taken seriously, they are an exercise in critical ethics. To confront a code is to be forced to think before acting. There are times and places where codes are helpful if not necessary for that purpose. It is difficult to imagine a modern civilization, for instance, without any code of law.

Yet sometimes codes are, at best, useless and, at worst, obstacles. They are useless if they are unknown, forgotten, or unenforced, and they are obstacles if they get in the way of honest and sharpsighted dissent.

An alternative means of doing critical ethics is conversation. Conversation is an interchange in views; it assumes that all parties have something valuable to tell each other even (maybe especially) when they disagree with each other. The simple fact of conversation forces reflection for one must think to speak and to hear. And, if one moves into conversation with all of one's being, the content of what is exchanged forces reflection even more, for one may find oneself persuaded to change one's views. Conversation may be a step toward conversion.

Conversation about ethical matters supposes several things. It supposes that one's own sights may be limited and might be corrected by hearing from another. It supposes that the other person is mature enough to have ethical insight and wise enough to see where things are going wrong. It supposes that the other person is vested with as much human dignity as oneself. It supposes the importance of creative listening.

Whereas codes are one directional, moving from authority to subject, conversations are two directional, moving reciprocally between person and person. An ethical conversation admits of a plurality of perspectives on ethical matters, but at the same time assumes there is something itself ethically sound and intrinsically good in the process of interchange. Each party is enriched in the process and the association as a whole is more humane as a result.

The Sun Company project was a modest attempt to stimulate conversation at least as a preliminary step to an eventual corporate code, if one were to be written, but more significantly as a satisfactory way in itself to engage in critical ethics generally.

Corporations and Constitutions. The modern business corporation, particularly if it is among the Fortune 500, is a complex organization. It cannot be characterized in a single word, and yet, most people would agree, it is a powerful organization both internally and externally. It has a broad and massive impact on its own members, often determining standard of living, place of residence, expenditure of energy, and character of relationship. But it also has an extensive and influential impact on the larger community given its location, what it produces, how it invests, and whom it employs.

Furthermore, even with patterns of decentralization and diversification, the modern corporation tends to be controlled hierarchically. Certainly the hourly employee has little say in the formation of the corporation's policies. The middle manager is often caught unawares upon the announcement of new procedures. Even someone in the executive suite may be shocked to learn of drastic changes in personnel.

It is not easy for those in positions of power and influence to engage in critical ethics about what they do and why they do it. That was a lesson learned some centuries ago in politics. That was one of the reasons for the rise of constitutionalism. A constitution provides a means for the voice of the people to be heard. It bestows rights and liberties, and it grants access to positions of influence. In short, it is a means of opening conversation—effective conversation—about policies that affect the community as a whole. Freedom of speech and freedom of association are among the fundamental rights protected by constitutions. In their positive sense, fundamental rights empower a people to speak their minds about current conditions and future possibilities.

Corporations have much to learn from constitutionalism. Maybe, as some have suggested, it is time to inaugurate certain constitutional forms in the design of corporate forms. The result would enhance a reflective approach to the ethos of the corporation.

Concession, Inherence, and Contexuality. Traditionally, there are two ways to think about the origin of corporations: concession theory and inherence theory.

According to concession theory, a corporation is a creation of the state. A corporation is not a natural entity, rather it is a fictional being brought into existence only by acknowledgement of law. Thus a corporation may be chartered, and in principle, its charter may be removed and the corporation dissolved. What the state giveth, the state may take away.

According to inherence theory, on the other hand, a corporation is an association of persons who have gathered together to do a job. It originates from the will of those who gave it substance out of their ideas and energies. It may be acknowledged by and thereby receive the protection of law, but its formation is in no way a concession of law.

In concession theory, a corporation is a dependent organization, subservient to the higher authority of law. In inherence theory, a corporation is an autonomous organization, controlled by and on behalf of its owners.

Today a third view of the corporation might be more sensible, a view that accounts for its social reality. A corporation is neither merely the creation of a state nor merely an instrument of its owners; it is part of the texture of the whole community of life, human as well as nonhuman. Given the web of interdependence that characterizes modern existence, a corporation is best understood in its contextuality. It takes from and gives to that context. Its strength and its weakness are contingent upon its surroundings even as its surroundings are strengthened and weakened by what it is.

In brief, although law and ownership are vital components in its origination, a corporation nonetheless belongs to its context. If that is so, critical ethical conversation about the ethos of a corporation must be extended beyond its normal boundaries.

The Sun Company survey did not go that far, although there were interviewees who thought it should. But the Sun Company survey is an affirmation of the need within the business corporation to move from ethos to critical reflection for the sake of the corporation itself and its meaning within the modern world. The survey is a declaration of the ethical necessity to form ways and means of bringing all constituencies of a corporation into reflective conversation about points of ethical stress in its operation. The maturity of a corporation is measured by the extent to which it provides regular opportunity to hear voices, including voices of suffering and opposition, from within and from without.

The report of the Sun Company survey is published here, except for minor stylistic changes, as it was presented to the Corporate Ethics Committee after its completion. Subsequent to the report, several recommendations for corporate action are outlined in keeping with the idea of critical ethics through open conversation.

Report Prepared for the Corporate Ethics Committee of the SUN Company

ASSESSING SUN'S ETHICAL CONDITION: VOICES FROM WITHIN

1. Introduction

Sun Company, like all business corporations, has many faces. To do full justice to the character of Sun, it is necessary to look at each face carefully. As a "creature of law," Sun is susceptible to legal analysis. As an organization, it may be examined according to managerial principles. As a means of amassing capital and creating wealth, the corporation is open to economic evaluation. As people interacting with each other, with segments of the rest of society, and with the world of nature, it is subject to ethical assessment.

Corporate life in America has been subjected to ethical assessment at least since the early years of the twentieth century (remember Teddy Roosevelt and the "trust busters"?), but much more intensively so in the last two decades. During those decades, people have become increasingly aware of the dominant role corporations occupy in modern society. They have become incensed with the scandalous behavior of some major corporation executives. And they have become deeply suspicious of large organization and bureaucratic structure whether public or private. In short, they have learned what Lord Acton taught over a hundred years ago, that is, power in whatever form tends to corrupt and they are too often the victims of that corruption.

In that context, several persons from corporate headquarters of Sun formed a committee to reflect on the ethical condition of the company and to consider ways to enhance its ethical character. These persons were moved in part by the trends of the times. During the past three to six years, many corporations have composed codes of ethics for their employees and have sponsored seminars and workshops on ethical issues. But these persons were moved as well by significant changes that have occurred at Sun over the past twelve years. These changes, it was thought, make it timely to undertake an assessment of Sun's ethical condition.

The ultimate objective of Sun's corporate ethics project is to assist all those who are part of the company to think about their work from an ethical perspective and to shape their conduct in that work accordingly.

There are two ways to proceed in this kind of project. One is to create a policy that gives all the answers before discovering what the questions might be. The other is to ask those concerned what the questions are and what sorts of answers might be helpful. Significantly, the committee chose the latter route, a route that is unique and risky. This chapter is an interpretation of the results.

Douglas Sturm of Bucknell University was hired to interview a variety of Sun's employees. Some interviewees were sought out, but in a way that would assure as much anonymity as possible. Other interviewees volunteered to participate in the project. In the *Managers' Memo* for June 27, 1980, the project was announced, and all employees who wished to contribute to the study were invited to do so. The announcement was repeated in other company publications. A brief interim report was included in the *Managers' Memo* for July 25, 1980, and again employees were urged to participate. In preparation for the interviews, the committee composed a roster of general questions, but interviewees were encouraged to speak freely on the subject. In general, interviewees were asked what kinds of ethical issues Sun employees face in their work, what obstacles stand in the way of dealing with them, what sorts of ethical issues confront Sun as a company, and what actions Sun can or should take to encourage ethical action.

Initially, twenty-five interviews were planned for the months of July and August, but before the conclusions of the interview period, fifty-two persons were interviewed. They included secretaries and district managers, legal staff and purchasing agents, presidents and foremen, auditors and system analysts, engineers and hourly workers. Of the fifty-two interviews, forty-two were solicited and ten were unsolicited. A further breakdown of the interviewees is given in the following tables.

Sex		*Locus in Sun*		*Years at Sun*	
Male	41	(according to groups)		0–9	10
Female	11	Oil and Gas	11	10–19	13
		Marketing	18	20–29	16
		Commercial	4	30–	13
		Canadian	0		
Race/Ethnicity		Energy Minerals	2	*Geographic Location*	
White	45	Logistics	4	Northeast	23
Black	6	Corporate	12	Midwest	6
Hispanic	1	Other	1	Southwest	23

Interviews lasted from one to three hours. Interviewees were frank and friendly, sometimes intense and passionate. A few interviewees did not think there were many places of ethical stress and strain in their positions if any at all. Others were pointed in their depictions of areas desperate for attention. Many initiated the interview with high praise for Sun and what the company had meant to and done for them. Many, as well, pointed to the corporate ethics project itself as an instance of a long-standing tradition of ethical concern in the Sun company.

Not surprisingly, what people saw as critical ethical issues and how they viewed them depended largely on their positions in Sun and in society generally. A male in materials management tended to see things differently from a female with environmental responsibilities. The views of a black in human resources would tend to diverge from those of a white in governmental relations. The genius of this portion of Sun's corporate ethics project is its acknowledgment of the diversity of voices within the corporation and of the right of each of those voices to an effective hearing especially in ethical matters. A vital stage in ethical judgment is to stand in the place of the other and to see the world as the other sees it. This is the stage of vicariousness or empathy, a virtue too often lacking in human relationships, personal and corporate.

In the subsequent interpretation of these interviews, something is lost and something is gained. What is lost is the texture of each particular interview, for each interviewee had a position to present, a story to tell, and all the issues presented were woven into that story. What is gained is a meaningful pattern of questions and categories that may press the project into its next stage. Furthermore, since confidentiality was assured, the interpretation of the interviews into a pattern of general categories will assist in hiding identities while nonetheless portraying the issues.

There are six parts to the interpretation, each gathering together a cluster of issues presented by several of the interviewees:

Standards of Business Conduct: A Question of Honesty
Personnel Practices: A Question of Justice
Market Behavior: A Question of Fair Bargain
Constituency Relations: A Question of Responsibility
The Corporation and the Public: A Question of Legitimacy
The Identity of Sun Company: A Question of Character

2. Standards of Business Conduct: A Question of Honesty

"Standards of business conduct" is used here to include the basic ethics of doing business as it has been understood in the Anglo-American tradition. On the negative side, it prohibits any conduct that would sully the commercial enterprise or pervert the market process. It forbids fraudulency and deceptive practices, conflicts of interest, the use of gifts or entertainment to influence buyer or vendor, exploitation of insider information, disclosure of proprietary information, violation of antitrust principles, and failure to use approved accounting procedures or to keep adequate records. On the positive side, the basic ethics of doing business means honesty in the full sense of the term.

In general, according to the interviewees, Sun Company has a reputation for honest dealing and has explicit policies bearing on all the areas mentioned above. But this does not mean that Sun is without any stresses or stains in basic business ethics.

Outright Thievery. Several interviewees, for instance, reported a dramatic increase over the past few years in the incidence of theft of company property and products by employees—a case of oil, a tank of gasoline, a piece of equipment, even, in some places, coffee money. The causes are uncertain. Persons who have been apprehended include some who have worked for Sun for years. One interviewee insisted that to deter theft, the company should move toward increased prosecution and publicity in cases that are certain and significant. Others, however, approved of current procedures. When a charge of stealing comes to light, it should be investigated quietly, thoroughly, and fairly. When the case is clear, the person involved should be fired, but then given some assistance in finding alternative employment, including, curiously, nondisclosure of the specific charge to a prospective employer. ("He was released," it is said, "because of violation of company procedures.") In cases of theft, there appear to be three points of ethical concern: the stealing itself (why does it occur?), the process of investigation (are procedures fair? do they protect the rights of the accused?), and recommendations to prospective employers (should a relevant fact about a former employee's record be withheld?)

Special Privileges and Favors. In some units of Sun Company, issues of noncompany (usually personal) use of company property and of accepting favors from vendors and contractors have been a source of contention. Until very recently, according to several interviewees, employees had become accustomed to certain privileges in these areas of conduct. The use of company equipment and scrap material to construct a trailer hitch, a television antenna, or a clothes line pole were common practice. There were abuses, but they were recognized as such. Furthermore, employees had come to expect and to enjoy a hunting or fishing trip, tickets to a sports event, a Christmas party, or bottle of whiskey given by a grateful supplier. In their minds, at least, they distinguished between gifts of appreciation for past business (ethically acceptable) and efforts to influence them for future contracts (ethically anathema).

The contention has broken out over where exactly to draw the line. To stop what appeared to be abuses, some operating units established strict standards prohibiting most such privileges and held seminars to communicate these standards and their implications to all employees. Some interviewees spoke of this move approvingly and expressed hope that the standards would be enforced rigorously and publicly. One interviewee thought the standards were appropriate in the abstract but were far more stringent than other companies and might be out of step with the times. Other interviewees reported a reaction of resentment to the standards: The privileges had been of long standing; abuses were few; and good feelings and cooperative working relationships had been established. The imposition of a new and strict policy seemed to treat employees as little children who had been doing wrong and to regard vendors as crooked culprits who should know better. One interviewee suggested that, in relations with vendors, Sun should merely require its employees to answer three questions: Will I be influenced by the proffered favor? Can I reciprocate? Am I willing to disclose the matter to my superiors? If, in all truthfulness, an employee can respond negatively to the first and affirmatively to the last two questions, then the favor is acceptable.

Two interviewees, both in high-level positions in materials management, expressed concern about the difficulty of securing effective control over all areas of business conduct in a large and complex organization. The "social distance" between headquarters and the field is remarkably great. A few managers may have responsibilities extending over thousands of locations where conflicts of interest, use of company property, relations with suppliers and buyers, and issues of restraint of trade assume their most concrete manifestation. Statements of guidelines, seminars, and case studies notwithstanding, there's many a slip 'twixt managerial intent and action on the line. While Sun should not cease in its efforts to police (a negative approach) or to educate (a positive approach), in the final analysis the honesty of the company depends on the integrity of the persons in its employ.

Hedging the Records. Sun's policy guidelines are clear about the need to keep appropriate and honest records. But in the practice of record keeping and reporting, some gray and not-so-gray problems have been noted. One interviewee, for instance, suggested that there are times when a shipload of oil might be booked on either the last day of one month or the first day of the next month. On a more important level, refineries, it was asserted, may hedge in the reporting of accidents so as not to spoil a long safety record and thus to avoid the reach of OSHA. Even more seriously, some interviewees alleged that there was evidence of executive manipulation of books to show profitability for purposes of promotion or special bonus, and so far as is known publicly, nothing was done when the manipulation was discovered. The interviewees were indignant at the manipulation but especially at the failure of the corporation to take corrective action publicly. Rank should have no privilege; dishonesty is dishonesty whether effected by truck driver or executive; to hide or to ignore improper conduct by executives is no way to encourage ethical behavior by persons in the field.

Greasing the Palm. Everyone knows that the ethics of doing business is not the same in all parts of the world. Differences result in painful decisions when an American company, such as Sun, engages in trading abroad, especially with the practice of "greasing the palm." One veteran employee of Sun insisted that Sun's position has always been clear: "Thou Shalt Not Grease." Despite protest about its lack of realism, the policy in the international field from the beginning was absolute and summary: All trading was to be above board, there was to be no graft, and violators would be fired. As a consequence, Sun has confronted difficulties and has suffered losses. Integrity has its price. But, claimed this interviewee, Sun has over the long range gained a reputation that has enhanced opportunities in some areas. Honesty, not won without struggle, may well be the best policy.

Yet things are not so simple as they seem. Another interviewee who has had responsibilities in international business argues that Sun's policy position is hypocritical if not unethical. It is hypocritical because there is no way to avoid some sorts of special arrangements and special payments in foreign countries, particularly in the Middle East. "Our objective is to make a profit decently"—but what is decent depends on the laws, customs, and reasonable expectations of the place of business. It is unethical to impose Western standards on the Eastern world. And it is unethical not to get equipment to customers in as expeditious a manner as possible even if that means providing customs' officials with a little "incentive." Is a contribution to the special cause of the ruler of a sheikdom any different from a contribution to the NAACP? Both are efforts to buy goodwill.

Even in the United States, resistance to "questionable payments" may be expensive. An interviewee reported that failure to give a sawbuck-hand-shake to the fire department of an eastern city resulted in an overzealous inspection (costing thousands of dollars to the company) and in an under-zealous response to a fire (costing even more). On the other hand, the same interviewee observed that Sun's new agency business on the waterfront has been deliberately and openly clean as a whistle (absolutely no kick-backs from vendors or to ship captains and absolutely no price fixing with other agents), and the results have been financially phenomenal. The up-shot: Sometimes honesty pays—but suppose it doesn't? What then?

3. Personnel Practices: A Question of Justice

Personnel practices include such matters as employment, transfer, promo-tion, compensation, and dismissal. How such matters are conducted is an issue of justice. Justice means (at least) distributing jobs and benefits ac-cording to principle. To do otherwise smacks of partiality, bias, or favor-itism.

According to many interviewees, personnel practices at Sun have changed radically over the past decade. In the "Old Sun," once a person was hired, employment was secured for life except in cases of egregious immorality. To be sure, advances depended on the determination (sometimes the whim) of superiors, transfers were unheard of, and compensation may have had little to do with performance. But, even during the Great Depression, Sun tended to keep its employees in position, which, in itself, is a kind of justice. In the "New Sun," however, systems have been adopted to enhance prac-tice according to principle. And yet no system is without its difficulties.

Intent and Limits of IPS. The presumed intent of the Internal Place-ment System (IPS) is to open up new opportunities for employees through-out the Sun Company. It is a "powerful tool of individual rights." It en-ables individuals to gain control over the development of their careers. It gives them chance to "compete" for new possibilities, thereby benefiting both them and the company.

But the intent is not matched by the fact. Interviewees called the system "hogwash," "window dressing," "hypocrisy." The system, despite its elab-orate mechanism of advertisement and application, is "wired." In part, "business need" dictates who shall succeed in opened positions. In part, "political connections" prevail. In part, new managers want to hire their own staff without regard to the system. Thus IPS creates false expectations and promotes cynicism. Furthermore, IPS does not operate consistently throughout Sun. For instance, one unit may require only one year in a position before an employee may take advantage of IPS, others, to reduce the costs of transiency, may require two years. In addition, some units of Sun are not part of the system at all.

No one suggested dispensing with IPS altogether, for it does offer opportunities for some persons. But several suggested (a) making it more consistent and effective in operation throughout Sun and (b) becoming more truthful about its limitations. If positions are not *really* open, they should not be presented as such. If it is true that the higher the position in the corporation, the less likely it is that the system pertains, this should be admitted.

Who's Worth What?   Both the Hay points system and the appraisal system purport to tie compensation in a principled way to position and performance. But interviewees expressed severe doubts about the result. The systems were described as "farcical," "inequitable," "deceptive," "dishonest," and even "immoral." Despite their apparent objectivity, the systems allow too much room for discretionary judgment. They intend to make more explicit what had been a mystery in the "Old Sun," namely, the presumed basis on which benefits were distributed. But the human element has not been removed. There is far too much room for maneuverability in assigning the scales, and more than one interviewee charged that the system is used for punitive purposes against employees who offer constructive criticisms of the company's operation. Disparities among the operating units of Sun in the assignment of Hay points were noted. One interviewee complained that to fix the average appraisal of the employees in a subunit in advance is to make a mockery of the evaluation. The limit of, say, a "5.5 average" is artificial and does not permit an honest and just appraisal of the employees.

Separation Anxiety.   The severance of someone from employment is never pleasant, for one's work is closely linked with one's self-esteem. The loss is more than economic; it is social and psychological; it touches on the meaning of one's personal life. The agony of separation is felt most keenly by the person fired; but even those who fire confront difficult ethical questions.

What, mused one interviewee, is the equity of discharging a female employee who has been blatantly slothful on the job when so many "Good Old Boys" have basked for years in a sinecure at Sun? Several interviewees expressed deep concern over the impact of reorganization on employment. Reorganization may be justified on grounds of productivity or efficiency, but it is the individual employee who suffers the result. Many are released through no fault of their own, and yet the very fact of dismissal makes them feel less worthy than those retained. Even those retained suffer pangs of anxiety and insecurity for they know they may be subjects of the next reorganization. All efforts to be fair in layoffs cannot fully compensate for the injuries, loss of morale, and lessened loyalty to the company that results.

Two interviewees insisted that there was something "plainly wrong" when, with the accession of a new top executive, a number of subordinate managers are removed either by the appearance of promotion (being "kicked upstairs") or by being forced into early retirement. The "golden handshake" does not undo the injustice. One interviewee noted the irony of Sun making large grants through its contributions program while releasing employees because of reorganization (to "cut costs"). Finally, several interviewees puzzled over the propriety of giving a strong recommendation to a prospective new employer on behalf of an employee whose performance has been less than satisfactory.

Equal Employment Opportunity.   Despite rhetoric to the contrary ("All men are created equal..."), discrimination has been a dominant characteristic of American life. The slavery system was its most heinous, but not its only manifestation. The Emancipation Proclamation and Women's Suffrage were mere beginnings of its obliteration. The drive for Equal Employment Opportunity (EEO) that emerged in the 1960s is a recent stage toward overcoming this deeply ingrained injustice in the social order. Its implementation, however, has been a source of controversy, and it is no wonder that that controversy is present in American corporate life.

EEO practices were of express concern to more than half the interviewees. Yet perspectives differed sharply over the character of the ethical problem and what Sun should do about it.

A few complained about the EEO principle as such. The argument was simple: Sun is a business and should be run strictly as a business. The *only* principle that should prevail in employment is competence, qualifications, and ability to do the job and to do it well. All other considerations are utterly irrelevant and, if introduced, will confuse proper procedures. Most strongly put, hiring incompetents is unethical.

Several, however, thought the problem was not so much EEO as the manner of its implementation. Supervisors and managers, it was said, are less concerned about the intent of EEO than about their records in meeting "quotas." They are, in effect, pressured by the system to hire and to retain minorities and women regardless of how qualified they might or might not be. As a result, other employees are resentful; supervisors themselves complain; those hired feel unwelcome and are frustrated; and business itself suffers. "Reverse discrimination" was the charge leveled against this process.

Yet one interviewee, a white male from the field, insisted that reverse discrimination, even granting its negative side, is an ethical obligation during this long period of agonizing historical transition to a time when race, ethnicity, and sexual identity are irrelevant to one's political and economic status.

Several interviewees would concur in the judgment articulated by one of them: Sun is not a bigoted company, but it is racist. A bigot is deliberately and flagrantly discriminatory. Racism, particularly in its systemic forms, may not be intentional but its manifestations are palpable to those affected. To be sure, Sun hires minorities, but without understanding the need for preparation. The young black entering Sun as a first job experiences cultural shock. There are differences between the white and black culture. The young black is often without any understanding of the corporate environment, which has been historically white, or what sort of behavior and attitudes are expected. Particularly in earlier years, blacks were placed in contexts or given assignments where they were destined to fail. It is difficult to know where or how assistance can be provided. The human resources function, it is alleged, is more geared to assist middle management than the beginning employee. While there are very informal networks of support and assistance among blacks, there is fear that the creation of a formal organization would provoke backlash. A number of interviewees suspected that, however unintentional it might be, there are limits to the career development of minorities in Sun. There are no models or mentors for blacks in the higher echelons of management. Promotion among blacks (and women) seems not to be as rapid as among white males. One interviewee cited several examples of highly qualified blacks who were given no encouragement to stay at Sun and who, after a short time, left for other companies at a considerable advance in career.

Sundry suggestions were made for modifying Sun's position. (a) A management development program explicitly geared for minorities should be designed. (b) A strong public affirmation of Sun's commitment to EEO should be made by the top executive office. (c) A significant portion of Sun's contributions program should be channeled toward training promising minorities (and women) in technical areas, such as engineering and accounting, with the commitment to hire those who complete their degrees successfully. (d) Whenever a position becomes available in top management at corporate headquarters, it should be filled with a qualified minority. (At present, one interviewee noted, Radnor shows "very little color"!) (e) The reward system should reinforce the managers and supervisors who take calculated but honest risks in the placement and promotion of minorities and women even if they fail.

Why should such suggestions be accepted? Because justice demands it is one argument. Because it's just plain good business is another. In effect it is in the self-interest of Sun to take an aggressive stance on equal employment. The world at large is dominantly nonwhite; pressures in American society are moving slowly but strongly toward equal opportunity; the reputation of respect for Sun will be enhanced as it adopts more forcefully than it has the EEO principle.

Some interviewees cited cases of blatant racism in Sun. There is simply no excuse, for instance, when a young woman of Southeast Asian ancestry is called "our little gook" by her superiors. If the reports are correct, there are places in Sun where there is open hostility between white and black workers and where middle managers are without the ability, either by training or by disposition, to conciliate.

A Woman's Place.   A number of interviewees suspected that, on balance, a white women at Sun is more likely to be favored than a black—male or female. But, even if this is so, it does not mean that women have attained their just and proper place everywhere in the company.

Sun apparently has its share, although perhaps no more than its share, of outright sexism and sexual harassment. Instances cited by interviewees were vivid and depressing such as the case of the disgruntled supervisor who suggested a secretary go into prostitution if she wanted to make more money. The ethical problems stressed in the interviews, however, tended to be of a more institutional and cultural character.

Two interviewees indicated evidence of salary discrimination between males and females. One suggested that the Hay point system had been used in some instances to keep females in a lower position. Several were not at all certain that prospects for promotion and career advancement were as good for women as for men. One was informed that, once she was married, her job must have become less important to her. There is a strong feeling that a woman with children, particularly young children, would simply not be considered for an advanced executive position in Sun—not because there is a policy against the possibility, but because that appears to be the character of the company.

The cultural or attitudinal aspects of the problem of discrimination against women are often subtle, but nonetheless real. Men in the company, particularly men in higher management, seem more at ease with women who are younger and women who are in lower positions than they (the men) are. They seem unable to deal with women who are either on a par or in superior positions to them. Men appear threatened by women with high skills or women who have strong character: Such women are called "too aggressive" when they are simply doing their jobs and doing them very well. There is a general feeling that whatever position—managerial or geological, staff or line—is undertaken by a woman, it must not be very hard or highly technical. As sociologists have argued, to be a token person (e.g., the one and only female) in a social setting creates extraordinary tensions and difficulties. There is a kind of "male culture" even as there is a kind of "white culture" that tends to prevade Sun.

One interviewee mentioned an even more subtle ethical problem she discerns at Sun, that of the self-image of many of the women, especially the younger women in the offices. They are flattered rather than offended by comments of a sexually suggestive character, with flirtation, even with sexual advances by male supervisors. They fail to see that they are being used, and that, curiously, what seems so flattering is not only degrading but also may very well be dysfunctional to their careers.

There is a women's organization in some Sun units through which these issues can be and are addressed. One interviewee suggested that Sun could (and should) become a leader of women's concerns in the corporate world by creating the kinds of institutional arrangements that would enable a capable woman to pursue a career and have a family at the same time: establish an in-corporation day care center; form shared-time positions that two or more persons might occupy; provide for more flexible time possibilities; arrange for jobs where some of the work could be done at home; locate computer terminals, where they are essential, in the home of the employee. The implicit judgment is that if having a family jeopardizes a career, injustice is the result.

The Old, the Young, and the Disadvantaged. Many employees have worked in Sun Company for years and years, even decades and decades. It would appear that Sun "takes care of its own." Yet several interviewees alleged that Sun suffers from a pattern of age discrimination. One asserted that it is difficult for anyone over fifty years of age to get a promotion. Another surmised that given the competition for highly qualified and recently educated persons in technical fields, the company tends to favor the young for promotions in order to keep their talents at Sun, but the consequence is that those over fifty-five are captives to their positions, without challenge and without possibility of advancement. Thus the plaintive question: "Is fifty-five too late?"

But there is another side to the matter. A number of interviewees mentioned the problem of the "incompetent senior employee." Some persons have worked at Sun for twenty years or more, remaining at entry level jobs, and yet they have begun to slow down, perform their work below standard and now constituting a drag on the work in a unit. Others may have performed admirably during their early years at Sun and advanced appropriately, but now they have become burned out and are no longer able to contribute to the company in a creative way. What is the company's obligation in such cases? On the one hand, it seems unjust to keep them in the employ of the company because they are a drain on its resources and energies. One interviewee, referring to them as the "Good Old Boys," suggested they are, indirectly, "superthieves" since they take from the company much more than they contribute in return. On the other hand, it would appear unjust to separate them for, over the years, they have given the enterprise much of their lives and they are close to retirement. No one cannot blame them for the absence of corrective measures that should have been taken much sooner. To fire them would be to crush part of the meaning of their lives.

While the ethical quandary of the incompetent senior employee may be in some instances nearly insoluble, one interviewee has suggested that it might be avoided by assuring periodic change and challenge to employees throughout their careers lest they stagnate and become complacent as the years progress.

In contrast, another interviewee (himself at retirement age) thought Sun had a problem in providing jobs with sufficient challenge and responsibility for the young. Sun has a disproportionately large number of young people with creative ability, good training, and excellent qualifications but not enough positions to match their outstanding capacities. Not enough has been done to enhance their role within the corporation. New opportunities must be provided to do justice to their potentialities and to enable Sun to reap the benefits of their training. (On the other hand, several interviewees reflected openly about the extent and implications of the attributes of contemporary youth culture that a significant number of newer employees were bringing into the company: casual, permissive, low-keyed, laid-back, "expecting the world to be brought to their doorstep." Maybe, the interviewees mused, the old work ethic is becoming anachronistic and even the technically qualified young person is devoid of the drive that characterized the ambitious entrepreneur or hard-driving manager. What this new culture does for the future of the corporate enterprise remains unclear.)

Two interviewees made an explicit point about the need (the ethical obligation?) for Sun to adopt a proactive role in hiring the handicapped. To be sure, many feel uncomfortable around people with defects and deformities, but that is no reason to ignore their presence in society or to shut them out from meaningful employment or promotion. To equip places of work for the handicapped, to create roles they can perform, to train them where necessary, to seek them out is first of all a matter of doing them justice. But it is also sensible business practice, for they constitute a vast but yet untapped reservoir of talent. And, besides, if they are working, they do not need to be on welfare.

4. Market Behavior: A Question of Fair Bargain

Throughout the history of Western ethical and legal thought, there has been a good bit of discussion about fairness in business relationships. Hence the concepts of fair wage, fair price, and fair bargain. Although no one has come up with a definition of these concepts that is wholly acceptable to everyone, it seems easier to discern what is manifestly unfair in particular cases than to determine beforehand what will be certainly fair to all conceivable circumstances. Yet the issue of fairness haunts those who approach business relationships with ethical sensitivity.

A significant number of interviewees pointed to areas of Sun's commercial dealings where the issue of fairness is at stake.

Sun, according to one interviewee, is among the world's leading dealers in lube oils. The lube oil business has not been very profitable in the past. But under current market conditions in the petroleum industry, it is entirely possible to push prices up to show a healthy if not a handsome return. The blunt fact is that Sun has sufficient market power and therefore sufficient flexibility in pricing to do so. But should it? The higher someone is in the structure of management, the easier it is to accept the words of the economists who declare what the market will bear and what is therefore justifiable and fair. The salesman, however, who must deal directly with the customer sees the other side of the equation and knows the anguish of the buyer who is pressed by the inflationary spiral. Higher profit (a sign of economic health) may correlate too neatly with higher inflation (a sign of economic disease). What is a fair allocation of the gains and the losses in the current pricing of lubes?

A more intricate issue about the pricing of lubes was raised by two interviewees. Sun deals with both unbranded and branded lube oils. The former is sold to independent wholesalers or other companies (e.g., John Deere), who blend, label, and sell the oils under their own trademark. But, at least in some areas, representatives of Sun's branded lubes have been known to undersell—intentionally to undersell—the lubes of those to whom Sun has supplied its unbranded product. Indeed, one might conjecture a strong temptation to adopt a marketing strategy to manipulate the prices of unbranded and branded oils to the long-term advantage of Sun Company and to the detriment of the independents. Yet, the wholesalers, remarked one interviewee, are the "best friends we have in Sun": "Should we undercut our own best customers?"

In keeping with ordinary business practice, Sun contracts to develop its products according to a customer's specifications. The final product, for a variety of reasons, does not always match the specifications perfectly. Yet, given the usage the customer intends, the product, somewhat imperfect given original specifications, may still work satisfactorily. An "offspec" product in such cases could be shipped, used, and the imperfection never discovered. To dispose of the "offspec" product or to re-refine is costly. Apart from the legalities of the case, what is the fair thing to do?

The code of ethics of the American Association of Petroleum Landmen calls for fair dealing in the effort to secure land rights for exploration and drilling. But, according to some interviewees, it is sometimes difficult to know what is fair. In the process of negotiation the landman is "obliged to get as good a deal as possible." One should not lie, but then, to what extent is it permissible to withhold information? Furthermore, should the character of one's negotiating technique depend on whether one is dealing with a seasoned professional or, say, an eighty-year old widow who has lived on the land in question all her life? Again, suppose Sun is bargaining for rights on several parcels of land in the same area, has arrived at a satisfactory "going price" after consultations with two or three of the owners, has settled on a contract with most of the landowners in the area given the price, but one owner, particularly one holding a critical parcel, holds out for a higher price? Is it fair to grant the higher price only to the one who holds out?

In international trading, Sun is engaged in complex dealing with suppliers, shippers, and buyers. The process leaves open the possibility for many slips and, consequently, many claims. It is not always clear who is at fault for the slips, for instance, in the timing of shipments. Who or what was the cause of delay and therefore who should be liable for the costs of delay are uncertain. Thus, declared one interviewee, in claims settlement, there is no absolutely "right answer." But are some answers more right than others? Suppose one party happens to make a windfall as a result? Is the principle of fairness satisfied simply by the agreement of all parties?

Two interviewees noted that, given the current accelerated drilling schedule of American oil companies, there is a shortage of available oil rigs.
Consequently, those in the field scurry around to make arrangements with
drilling contractors in anticipation of future needs. A problem arises, however, when during the time gap between arrangements and anticipated
drilling, corporate management alters its plans. This has occurred increasingly, resulting in some loss of credibility and goodwill with the contractors.

One interviewee observed that, in marketing, there was a high degree of
managerial discretion in making economic arrangements with potential
dealers. Having arrived at a figure for "economic rent," taking account of
factors of land, facility, and operating costs, it is possible for managers to
discourage potential dealers by hitting them immediately with full costs, or
to encourage them by working out a long-range plan. In effecting such a distinction, what considerations should weigh in the balance? How can one be
sure one is treating all potential dealers fairly?

Finally, Sun engages in many joint ventures with other large corporations, with partnerships, and with individual entrepreneurs. One interviewee in particular described a number of cases of joint venture where driv-
ing a "hard bargain" was, in his judgment, nonetheless a matter of fair
dealing. His point: Tough business is not (necessarily) unethical business.

In one instance, Sun's partner had estimated the profit of their venture
at an amount significantly higher than Sun's more realistic (but undis-
closed) calculations. Since, for purposes of the contract, Sun accepted the
partner's estimate but arranged that Sun's percentage would come out of
the venture first, and since Sun's calculations proved in the end to be more
accurate, Sun completed the venture with the lion's share of the profits.

In an instance of hotel development and management, Sun had engaged
a partner in a five-year trial period after which, if stipulated conditions
were met, the arrangement was fixed "in perpetuity." After three years
had passed it was clear that Sun would derive its anticipated profits, but
the partner would not. The partner requested a modification of the contract. Sun refused, saying "a bargain is a bargain."

In these and other instances, the interviewee insisted that Sun had been
fair. That may be. The only question is, on what grounds? Are there gen-
eralizable principles of fairness on the basis of which one may guide one's
dealing in the marketplace to assure that they are indeed fair?

5. Constituency Relations: A Question of Responsibility

Over the course of the past several decades, corporations in America have
become increasingly aware of the need to develop new forms of relationship with the public. Especially during recent years it has been acknowledged that there are several quite different publics concerned with corporate enterprise. Furthermore, it has been acknowledged that these publics
(often called constituencies or stakeholders) are both external and internal
to the corporation as an entity. Precisely how the corporation ought to
shape its relationship with these constituencies is a question of respon-

sibility. In virtually all of the interviews, something of relevance to this question was presented. In the next section of the chapter, the focus will be on the generic relation of the corporation to the public at large. In this section, the focus will be on the relation of Sun to particular groups outside and inside the corporation. In both sections, a question of the status of the corporation is at stake. Is the corporation a *property* owned by stockholders to be possessed, utilized, and manipulated as they see fit subject only to minimal legal limits and accountable finally to no one but themselves? Or is the corporation a *social process* linked inextricably with a complicated set of other social processes in which each is dependent on and accountable to all others for the sake of the common good? Perhaps the property model and the social model are extremes, but if so, what is the most appropriate balance between the two? That is the question of responsibility.

Governments and Communities.   Interviewees differed widely in their attitude toward governmental agencies—federal, state, and local. One simply observed that the role of governments is to represent the wishes of the people and Sun should accept whatever guidelines and regulations governments set down. With that limitation, Sun should not worry itself further about "social responsibility," but do its business in a hardheaded and straightforward way. Another interviewee, however, saw government agencies as in fact (if not in intent) an enemy of business. The relationship between corporation and government is adversarial, and the corporation should become aggressive in countering all efforts at corporate regulation. In the long haul, the corporation represents the interests of the people better than government. The market system is a more accurate gauge of what will benefit society than the presumed democratic processes of an administrative state.

Other interviewees asserted that, in their spheres of work, the policy and practice of Sun are to cooperate with government agencies in an open and helpful way. Sometimes, however, difficulties are encountered as in joint ventures when partners of Sun fail to fulfill all governmental requirements or falsify affidavits and reports.

In a striking statement, one interviewee, who had spent time working in public affairs and in community organization as well as in Sun, asserted that each of these sectors has its own orientation, its own criteria of success, even its own language. Governments intend effective public programs; community organizations seek to improve the life circumstance of their members; corporations are motivated by profit. Each aim is honorable. The problem is, the sectors are without an appreciative understanding of each other. One solution is for Sun, together with other corporations, to effect new forms of partnership with municipalities. Citing a particular case, the interviewee argued that, for instance, the mere construction of an office building in the inner city is an inadequate expression of social responsibility. In addition, the company should ascertain who will bear the costs of the special tax benefits it seeks for the building; whom the contracted work on the actual construction will benefit; what impact the building will have on transportation, residential, and employment patterns in the city; and in general how the building fits into a general program of urban development. Responsible partnership with a municipality means Sun must establish close working relationships with urban planners and politicians and with community organizations. To do this effectively, the managers and executives of Sun must become more intimately acquainted than they are at the present time with the concrete community context of Sun's work.

In the phrasing of another interviewee, what Sun as a company does is only to a limited extent "its own business"; it is, after all, a corporation with a public impact and it must be receptive to what the impacted public has to say about its policies and plans. This interviewee cited the case of an energetic but abrasive citizens' group that was probing into negotiations between Sun and a state environmental agency about the disposal of toxic wastes. The question before Sun was whether to ignore the group altogether or to initiate a forum for an open and frank interchange with the group. The more responsible route, according to this interviewee, was the latter, but the issue was a point of serious contention within Sun's offices.

Media and the Right to Know.   Several interviewees remarked that Sun seems to have a good working relationship with the media, particularly the press. During the recent "energy shortage" period, Sun initiated a series of periodic briefings and energy seminars for representatives of the media. In availability and candidness, Sun went far beyond other oil companies.

But Sun, like other corporations, faces an issue that has not yet been satisfactorily resolved: Where should the line be drawn between a public's right to know (and thus the media's right to probe) and a corporation's right to silence? Sometimes business considerations dictate secrecy. But sometimes that principle can be used as an illicit excuse to keep a public in the dark. One interviewee cited cases of an acquisition by Sun, the resignation of an executive, and an accident in one of Sun's units as times when this issue was encountered in recent years and when the resolution was not every time as responsible as it could and should have been.

Sun, according to this interviewee, should adopt as a written guideline the principle that it is more honorable to be truthful even if the result is an "unfavorable" story than to equivocate or to hide the inner workings of the corporation from the press. Paradoxically, cooperation with the media in an "unfavorable" story may redound to the benefit of the company and show it in a favorable light!

Another interviewee, however, warned that relations between corporations and media can become *too* cozy. The role of the media in a free society requires that they maintain a critical distance from their subjects. Neither the intent nor the result of cooperation with the media should be the suppression of what is genuinely newsworthy.

Mother Nature: Does She Have Rights?   According to one interviewee, Sun, in some areas of its operation, has long had a policy of environmental concern on the principle, "don't mine what you won't reclaim." In the West, Sun has been engaged in cooperation with environmental groups and governmental agencies in reclamation research. The effort has been to demonstrate how it is possible to disturb the land for purposes of mining, but then to reclaim the land and to do so without need for irrigation.

Another interviewee observed that, in retrospect, Sun's past operations may seem environmentally shoddy, but they were in keeping with if not in advance of the industry's practices at the time. In light of current concerns, he thought the passage of environmental protection and occupational safety and health laws was a good move: "I breathe that air and drink that water, too." But there are limits to what a corporation should be required to do. Some pipelines were laid decades ago. The materials used are susceptible to rust and decay. Some have sprung leaks and caused environmental damage. Sun has a regular program to repair and to prevent leaks. But it would be irresponsible for Sun to replace all rusty pipelines. The costs would be too great. Besides, if forced to do so, Sun would most likely abandon its pipelines and turn to trucks, which alternative has its own environmental disadvantages.

A second interviewee making the same kind of point noted the need for a "tradeoff" between concern to protect the environment and desire to maintain a style of life heavily dependent on high energy usage.

In such cost–benefit calculations (i.e., the tradeoff), the question of responsibility is: What should be weighed in the balance, who should determine what lines are to be drawn, who will gain the benefits and who suffer the losses, and what role should an energy company play in considering these issues?

One interviewee, generally pleased with Sun's environmental record, nonetheless lamented the impossibility of getting higher management to perceive Mother Nature in a new light, one superseding cost-benefit analysis. In pleading for capital expenditures for environmental projects, for instance, one may argue successfully for what the law requires or for what public agencies expect. But to argue that trees, water, air, and wildlife have rights, *prima facie* or inalienable, will not get a single copper penny out of the company.

Corporate Contributions: To Whom, for What?   Significantly, none of the interviewees took the tack of some classical economists that corporate managers have absolutely no business contributing any monies from Sun's coffers to any cause, however worthy. On the contrary, several thought Sun was too modest about its grants and should be more bold in telling the world of the causes it has succored.

One interviewee, however, thought the contributions program was too diffuse. Since there are many more needy causes than funds available, a more responsible approach might be to establish clear priorities and to concentrate Sun's grants—whether in the arts, in medical research, or in social service. Other interviewees had definite suggestions. As already noted, one thought the contributions program might be used to enhance Sun's EEO commitment in a focused way by providing monies for the technical education of minorities and females. Another argued that Sun's contribution funds should be channeled toward specific urban development projects in which, through sustained involvement, Sun might improve the lot of the disadvantaged and enhance the quality of city life.

Incidentally, despite stated policy to the contrary, one interviewee suspected that the contributions committee is more heavily subjected to the special pleading of executives than is proper in making some of its selections. Rank, it seems, has its privileges even where, in principle, it has none. But that is a mark of irresponsibility.

Employee as Constituent. One interviewee complained about the "diminished role of the employee" at Sun. The corporation as such seems more concerned about governmental agencies, public media, and shareholders than about employees. But employees are more deeply involved in and dependent on the corporation than these others; in that sense employees are the most important of all constituents. A significantly large number of interviewees disclosed areas where responsibility to (and responsibilities of) employees posed critical ethical questions.

Labor unions seem to be a point of contention at Sun. One interviewee remarked that Sun was without unions until about a decade ago and since that time there seems to be an increase in labor unrest. He confessed he could not understand what would motivate persons to join unions, for the costs (e.g., of dues and of loss of wages during strikes) seem to outweigh the benefits. On the other hand, two other interviewees complained about how bitter Sun's management has been about unions. One of them described the attitude of management as condescending toward the worker. Whenever union members or officials offer suggestions about how to improve job performance through altered arrangements, management suspects their motives and discards the suggestions. On the management side, one interviewee noted that when once assigned the task of improving relations with labor, he still confronted the difficult ethical question of how far to go in divulging the truth in negotiations. One should not lie, but then one cannot be totally open and frank, or negotiations cannot proceed as they normally do.

Many of the hourly employees are persons of long experience, they are highly skilled, in some cases they are well educated, yet, according to several interviewees, they tend to be treated as youngsters. They know their jobs and are mature, talented persons, and yet managers and supervisors seem not to trust them to do their jobs without constant instruction and surveillance. As a result there are a lot of frustrated people in the shops, in the offices, and in the field. There is a tendency in Sun for policies, programs, and plans to come from the top of the organization down. Little if any effort is made to take advantage of the wisdom and experience of those affected before policies are announced. Concepts that look good in design may not work out in practice and those engaged in the practice might have something to tell the designers were they asked. Plans for the use of fire retardant clothing, for a new refinery mechanic concept, and for the re-arrangement of secretarial space and secretarial accountability were cited as examples. It might prove more efficient and satisfactory to plan patterns of work in the field itself than in the "glass cage" of a planner's office. An alternative version of the same point was made by a field supervisor who, when asked what major change he would propose at Sun, responded: "provide explanatory reasons whenever a directive is handed down or a policy changed; in short, treat us in the field as persons who want to understand and can understand what is going on; and give us opportunity to respond."

On the latter point, several interviewees expressed concern about the fate of the whistleblower and the inner critic at Sun. One interviewee reported a speech made by an executive to employees in which he decreed, "We in Sun are a family and do not discuss our problems freely with others." The tone was condescending, and the implication was that employees should not voice any criticisms about working conditions. Another interviewee, recording the same sentiment, noted that outspoken people are turned off in the area of Sun where he works. The result is unfortunate, for it eliminates those checks and balances in the organization through which corrective action is made possible. "If you can't tell people, especially your superiors, where things are wrong, or where they are wrong, then how can we improve conditions?"

Two other interviewees, each from a different unit of Sun, told convincing stories of how they had been penalized because of efforts at corrective action. In one case, the employee had pointed out the inadequacy of prevailing procedures for controlling, recording, and measuring one of Sun's products and had designed more effective alternatives. In his judgment, the loss of assets by means of inadequate procedures was itself unethical, but even more unethical was the manner in which his criticism was received. He became known as a "complainer," and treated punitively at appraisal time. In the other case, the employee had conducted an assigned study on reorganization of a department that, though praised by his immediate supervisor, was rejected as "contrary to Sun's philosophy" by the next higher supervisor, and this employee also felt the impact at the time of the annual performance evaluation.

Throughout the interviews, a significant number of instances of maltreatment of employees by supervisors, managers, and even by top executives were recounted. In one case, a supervisor became belligerent when asked by an employee why, in a report prepared by the supervisor, he (the employee) had not been given credit for his contribution to a particular project: "Watch out! I can be brutal." In another instance, the managers in an office discussed openly the (presumably confidential) work records of their subordinates, thereby embarrassing them and violating principles of privacy. In other examples, secretaries have been called on the carpet for leaving their offices even when the cause was family emergency. In several instances, interviewees complained that principles of confidentiality had been breached in other studies conducted by Sun and they suffered the consequences. In one dramatic case, a top executive of the company gave a dressing down to a person in high managerial position, perhaps for good business cause, but in a personally abusive manner and in the presence of other members of the staff.

All of the above seem to be instances of degrading, dehumanizing behavior. They demonstrate a lack of civility, an unnecessary deficiency in the good graces of responsible human behavior, perhaps even a failure to understand what forms of relationship enable an association to get on with its work in the most effective manner. There is as little justification for a managerial tyrant as there is for a political one.

Modern managers may be in an impossible bind. As an executive remarked, on the one hand, they must be experts in all things—finance, administration, production, public relations. On the other hand, they confront the pressure of the "bottom line"—performance measured by profit. Unless a corporation by its policies and principles helps them see an essential connection between humane behavior and profitable performance, they see the "bottom line" as the only thing that counts and act accordingly.

But the "bottom line," some interviewees argued, is an insufficient criterion of corporate responsibility. Where the corporation has an impact on the lives of persons, it has a correlative obligation to make sure that impact is not detrimental. One sphere mentioned by four interviewees where this principle is particularly important is the family. Sun's practices are not without their repercussions on family life. On the managerial level, Sun takes its toll in the general stress of doing business and in the particular demands on at least some of its executives and managers to move from place to place. In the field, Sun keeps some of its employees, especially in drilling, from their families for days at a time. While there may be no direct correlation between these features of Sun's life and the incidence of broken families, there is most likely some degree of correlation, and in so far as that is so, Sun has a responsibility to promote corrective if not preventative action.

Responsibility in human relationships is two-sided: As in a dialogue, each party is responsive to the other. Several interviewees took note of a change in the ethos of employees at Sun, a change that is disturbing to them. Where once employees had a career at Sun and felt a sense of loyalty to the company, now they have a job and the company is simply a place of work. Where once the "work ethic" motivated employees to devote themselves to the tasks at hand, now they may perform their assignments well enough, but they do so for the income and the prestige they personally derive from it. The result is that they are more concerned about their rights than about their duties—this is the "Age of Entitlement." The new ethos, thought these interviewees, might not serve the corporation very well as it becomes increasingly dominant.

Political Activism: Temptation and Reactions. Sun has two programs that promote political activism among its immediate constituents: SUNPAC and the Responsible Citizens' Program. A number of interviewees made comments about both of these programs.

SUNPAC contributes monies (all of which are donated voluntarily by persons allied with Sun) to political candidates whose records and platforms conform to the program's criteria. According to one interviewee, the program is susceptible to many temptations of wrongdoing, but, at least on the corporate level, those temptations have been resisted. In a sense, resistance is easy, for everyone involved knows that such political action committees are scrutinized carefully and sanctions for wrongdoing are heavy. The major difficulty the program has encountered in this interviewee's judgment is the loose-jointed connection between corporate SUNPAC and the political action committees of the subsidiaries. In a number of instances, the staff of a subsidiary committee has acted in an irresponsible manner: A contribution was made to a political campaign where it was perfectly legal but against company policy; a corporate aircraft was offered to a group of state officials for personal use; a letter soliciting funds for a politician's pet project suggested contributions from the right parties might have an influence on him; a letter delivering a contribution to a congressman included a "thank you for past considerations." There is need, suggested this interviewee, for more meticulous control of all the PACs in SUN to assure that everything is done scrupulously.

Other interviewees were not quite so sanguine about the actions of corporate SUNPAC. One charged SUNPAC with irresponsible inconsistency: SUNPAC's stated intent is to support candidates who share the program's principles; SUNPAC's practice, however, is (sometimes) to support candidates because of the power they wield in the Houses of Congress even when their voting records do not conform with SUNPAC's orientation.

A second interviewee insisted that SUNPAC's solicitations constitute a personal affront; they are semicoercive; they overreach into the lives of the employees. A communication informing employees about the records and principles of political candidates would be acceptable, but a petition for funds to support (or to oppose) particular candidates detracts from an employee's maturity of judgment. A third interviewee opposed the program as a "threat to the political freedom of the employee." A fourth found receipt of the letters from SUNPAC "embarrassing." A fifth declared that, among some of his acquaintances in Sun, the letters had a reverse effect—they would support candidates opposed by the program!

Several interviewees expressed appreciation for the Responsible Citizens' Program as it had been conducted in their areas. One was particularly lavish in his praise, for the RCP had provoked him into active politicking. Another, however, allowing that RCP was beneficial in intent (and might be so in fact where it is conducted in a wholly nonpartisan and voluntary manner), was incensed when an RCP event in his area was made mandatory. In his judgment, it is irresponsible so much as to hint that employees should be expected to attend RCP events or that those employees who do so are "better" than those who do not.

The Legal Professional: To Whom Responsible? Corporations are composed of management and labor, and yet increasingly they are composed of professionals (knowledge-workers) as well—engineers, account-ants, geologists, lawyers. The professional is a unique kind of constituent, for in many cases, the professional has a dual loyalty, to the corporation and to the professional guild. Sometimes these two loyalties come into conflict. In the interviews this possibility emerged particularly in the com-pany's relation to law and to the legal professional.

Through several interviews, a negative attitude toward law was reported. One interviewee, a person with both legal and managerial training, noted that Sun has never directly and openly urged anyone to flout the law, but there is strong pressure exerted through the operation to stretch the law. One is not led to ask about the purpose of laws and regulations, but rather to ask what the corporation can "get away with." The effort is to gain the greatest advantage for the corporation through its interpretation of the law, to "go up to the limit," and where there is disagreement with an agency, to fight the case. Another interviewee, giving voice to his own managerial orientation, thought the corporation should comply with laws once they are secured, but not without strong resistance and reaction. The corporation should fight against all efforts to regulate it. OSHA and EEO are but two examples of laws that obstruct the efficient doing of business. A third interviewee cited a particular activity where Sun winks at the law: the overloading of trucks. Enforcement of highway laws on overloading is lax; trucking firms generally ignore the rules; the economies that result from overloading are appreciable; in such circumstances it is easy to ra-tionalize some hedging on the law.

One place where this attitude to law is felt sharply is in Sun's treatment of the legal professional. The legal professional is in the sensitive position of being an officer of the court and a representative of the legal order as well as an employee of the company. The tendency at Sun, as at other cor-porations, is for the latter capacity to overreach the former. In the inter-views, the suggestion was forwarded that Sun should correct the imbal-ance in three ways: First, the function of legal advice and counsel should be incorporated at all stages of corporate planning at the executive level. Lawyers should not merely be asked to check out a *fait accompli*. Second, to preserve independence of professional judgment, lawyers should report directly to others on the legal staff, not to someone whose managerial ex-pertise is strictly business. Third, the performance of lawyers should be assessed according to their legal qualities and not according to economic return.

Yet to be understood is that the corporation is a "creature of law," it ex-ists at the pleasure of law, and the legal perspective on corporate activity should not be subordinated to the managerial or the economic perspective.

6. The Corporation and the Public: A Question of Legitimacy

Legitimacy is an ethical category that goes beyond sheer lawfulness. There are instances when one is led to say: "Well, that may be legal, but it's not right!" (Take, for example, a home mortgage foreclosure when the family involved suffered an unexpected and severe economic loss because of illness or accident.) There are other instances when unlawful behavior is seen as honorable and legitimate. (An historical example is the activity of the French resistance movement during World War II.) Legitimacy, in the words of legal historian James Willard Hurst, "means that no arrangement of relations or of power recognized in law should be treated as an end in itself or as autonomous." Sociologists speak of legitimacy as meaning public acceptability.

Corporations have always been subject to judgments of legitimacy, but the terms of judgment have not always been the same. In an earlier period, the *utility* of the corporation in promoting economic growth was deemed sufficient to assure its legitimacy, that is, its acceptability to the public. But in more recent decades, a judgment of legitimacy has depended on the corporation's *accountability* to assessments of various parts of its operation by agencies and persons outside the corporation itself: hence the movement toward antitrust laws, securities and exchange laws, safety regulations, rules governing advertising and product purity, and so on.

Within the past two decades, corporations have experienced what some have called a "legitimation crisis." In various ways, the public has expressed its wariness of corporate enterprise. The gas and oil industry has experienced this crisis in a particularly acute manner in the past few years.

In one way or another, almost all of the interviewees spoke about this crisis, for they had experienced it in personal and disturbing ways. Petroleum shortages (real or imagined), steeply increasing prices for gasoline and fuel oil (all too real), and reports of comparative profits in the oil industry (however interpreted) have created in the public a rather dour, if not downright angry, attitude toward the oil industry. As a result, many of the interviewees reported tense moments when meeting new acquaintances. A new acquaintance upon learning of the interviewee's association with an oil and gas company would react with acrimonious deprecation. Many of the interviewees, recoiling against such reactions, made efforts not to reveal their place of work. A few reported that even their children suffered from negative reactions in their schools. As one interviewee put it, "Those who work in Sun now carry a cross because of the dim view the public takes of oil companies." Another asserted, "I feel my work is legitimate, but the public feels it is not." One interviewee spoke of this tension as a "moral crisis," for it provokes among employees a deep sense of uncertainty about the worth of what they are doing for a living. When the oil industry is criticized, they feel *they* are criticized. Their work is a major part of their lives; when that work comes under question, directly or indirectly, they are naturally disturbed.

Interviewees characterized the attitude of the public in various ways. The public, said one interviewee, is "skeptical about big industry and about big oil." Many of them know very little about what goes on in industry, how it works. Thus ignorance plays a large part in their reaction. Another noted a "high degree of cynicism" about corporations and their executives.

In part the cynicism seems justified given scandals in the private sector as well as in government. Watergate was a dramatic moment in recent American history; in a way Watergate was seen as a "microcosm of what has happened throughout the country." The moral conflict over the Vietnam war has been another influence in the public's thinking about large organizations, public and private. Still others referred a "loss of confidence and trust" in the oil companies by the public and a "tremendous credibility gap" between the public and the petroleum industry.

Several interviewees suggested the need to educate the public about the meaning and justifiability of profits. Sun, declared one interviewee, fulfills a valuable function in society by producing energy supplies. If they think about it, people do not want to return to more primitive forms of life; but if not, they need energy, and in present circumstances this means they need oil and oil products. It is the fulfillment of this function that justifies profit. Another interviewee charged that the general public has lost sight of the positive accomplishments of an oil company: gasoline, lubes, plastics, jobs and wages, and contributions to social causes, education, and research. In other words, the company is devoted to meeting the wants and needs of the public and there is no good reason for the public's negative attitude.

Other interviewees noted that the public may misunderstand the meaning of profits. Profits are merely return on investment derived when the investment has been successful and justified by taking the risk. Furthermore, it is unfair to charge that oil company profits are "too high" merely on grounds of a comparison with a previous year. The more revealing figure is rate of return on investment. But the public has been misled by screaming headlines and by ignorance about the basics of economic procedures.

Thus, according to this set of interviewees, Sun should show the public that the company is fulfilling a social need and that its return on investment is justifiable. That, they thought, might help close the credibility gap.

Others were not so sure. Two interviewees raised question about the simplicity of the "profit ethic" according to which profit is justifiable as a clear sign of fulfilling a social need. That direct correlation fails to take account of two factors: First, in some circumstances, companies have sufficient market power to make unreasonably high profits quite independently of meeting actual need, and, second, the fulfillment of some social needs (e.g., public transportation) requires a long-term vision and an expenditure that tends not to be rewarded, at least immediately, in the marketplace.

Several other interviewees, while arguing that Sun together with other oil companies should "tell its story," were open to the possibility that the story has more than a single side. The public's cynicism may have a point, and if so, that point should be heard, too. Maybe, one remarked, even the ordinary employee of the oil company has been "snookered" (outmaneuvered) into thinking the industry is not involved in some kinds of shenanigans. Another observed that one cannot experience, say, a massive oil spill as he had done, without beginning to have doubts about the consequences of the enterprise even where it is, largely, honest and aboveboard. Still another pondered that the public anxiety may stem from conflicting signals about energy resources: On the one hand, there is a strong argument to the effect that oil is "running out," and that other energy resources are also in short supply or will be extraordinarily expensive to produce and risky to human safety and health. On the other hand, no officials in government or top executives in industry are truly acting as if there is any sort of emergency at hand; fuel, while increasingly expensive, seems in ample supply; there is no obvious and evident emergency at hand. Given these conflicting signals, it is no wonder the public is frustrated and turns that frustration against those structures that seem to be the only beneficiaries of the crazy, mixed-up circumstance.

Most interviewees who addressed themselves to this problem agreed that Sun, which normally assumes a low profile in public, has an obligation to do something. According to one, "what Sun most lacks is a top notch public relations program to dispel the confusions of the public and, for that matter, of the ordinary employee." The oil companies should "fight back" when criticized unjustly. They should demonstrate through carefully designed campaigns what they are doing in all areas in which they are brought to task, for example, in reclamation of land used for exploratory and mining or drilling purposes. They should "tell the truth" as it is. One interviewee felt that much of the criticism of the corporations was based on past practices and the public was just plain ignorant about current practices. The criticism is based on "out-of-date perceptions." But effective instruction of the public (and, as many insisted, of the employees as well) will depend on the use of spokespersons who are themselves credible and who are sophisticated in what they know and how they communicate.

Those interviewees, however, who felt there might well be more than a single side to the current energy story advised against Sun taking simply a defensive posture. Slick press releases are an insufficient way to address the question of legitimacy. Some of them invoked Sun's philosophy of two-way communications, and urged that Sun adopt some type of forum in which persons and groups with appreciably different perspectives might discuss corporate public relations in general and the issues of profits and energy resources in particular. To have such a forum in a setting in which employees of the company and members of the public could hear the many sides of the story debated reasonably and in a sustained manner might go a long, long way toward addressing the profounder aspects of the legitimation crisis.

7. The Identity of Sun Company: A Question of Character

Persons and organizations are not the same kind of entity. A person is an organic whole. An organization, however, though it may pretend or make an effort to be an organic whole, is always to some degree an aggregation of independent minds. Yet there is a sense in which persons and organizations are alike. Both possess a cluster of attributes that constitutes their character and both undergo historical change in interaction with their environment.

As not all persons are the same, so are all organizations not the same. Business corporations, even those engaged in similar endeavors, differ from each other. They gain a reputation for tending to act and react in typical, if not stereotypical, ways. Those inside a corporation are as aware of this as those outside it.

Corporations, however, are not static. In part, modes of organizational behavior alter in response to conditions—economic, political, cultural— that impinge on the corporation from without. In part, the style and form of a corporation are contingent on internal determinations—changes in personnel, dissension from the ranks, even the emergence of new ideas.

Indeed, there are moments of dramatic transition in the lives of persons and organizations. Such moments are often traumatic, for they constitute a time of fundamental decision. At stake is a question of ethos or character. The question—"Who am I"?—is linked to the question—"Who should I become?" An identity crisis is a crisis in one's basic ethic. Such a crisis is difficult enough in personal life, but perhaps even more difficult in organizational life, for organizations are composed of multiple and different personalities and quite divergent sensibilities.

Virtually every one of the interviewees in this study had something to say about transitions in the identity of Sun Company. The topic was of obvious importance and, to the interviewees, of ethical significance. They were aware that identity is more than a matter of projected image. It is a matter of organizational form and practice. In the deepest sense of the term, the identity of a corporation is the character of its impact on those inside and outside its boundaries.

Interviewees spoke of an Old Sun and a New Sun, although their characterizations and especially their evaluations of the two were not always the same. To some interviewees, both Old and New are still current in the actual operation of the company, for the transition is still underway, and the fundamental decision of character has yet to be clearly made. They are concerned with how it is to be made, procedurally (who will make the decision?) and substantively (what will the decision be?), for they know that the character of the company constitutes the context and meaning of their work life.

Key events in the recent history of Sun's transition from Old to New were cited by interviewees as the Sunray-DX merger, the accession of Robert Sharbaugh to the chief executive office, and the ill-fated Becton Dickinson acquisition. Each event signaled a change, evident or potential. The merger, it was said, brought together two companies with different orientations to and styles of doing business. The accession of Robert Sharbaugh brought an entirely new philosophy of management to bear on the company and resulted in vast organizational innovations. The acquisition of Becton Dickinson sent shock waves of anxiety throughout the company about how the New Sun was going to conduct its business, and, in its aftermath, additional changes have been made.

Interviewees used a variety of terms to symbolize the overall transition. In capsule form, it was characterized as "from paternalism to managerialism," "from a family company to a professional organization," "from a dictatorial to a behavioral approach to conducting business." One interviewee described the shift more complexly as from a traditional integrated oil company to a modestly diversified (but dominantly energy) corporation, from a centralized to a relatively decentralized organization, from a medium-sized to a large-sized company, from a style of leadership that is visible and personal to one that is remote and anonymous, from centrally directed to self-initiated employee development, from a family controlled board of directors to one increasingly composed of outsiders, and from a people-oriented to a capital-intensive enterprise.

Some interviewees were nostalgic about the Old Sun and were not wholly reconciled to the changes. One, for instance, became part of Sun following the completion of his education. He decided to work with Sun because of the kind of company it was. He devoted his talents and energies to his job, moved up through the ranks, and was proud of the company and of his contribution to it. The corporate reorganization effected under Robert Sharbaugh came as a surprise and a shock to him. With decentralization, he found himself assigned to a unit that was "not doing well," but was of such a character and in such a role that it could not do nearly as well as other units, however much effort was put to the task. With the new system of assigning Hay points to positions, he found himself fixed so that he could not receive the advances he believed were deserved. Even with the system for new placements, he felt stymied because of his age. "My major complaint," he said, "is, I did not choose this." The change, he asserted, was arbitrary.

Other interviewees expressed approval of the changes, at least in principle. According to some, the business environment demanded that such changes be made. The company *had* to become more attentive to profits and losses; it *had* to diversify at least to some extent to maintain itself; newer employees, especially those highly educated, *expected* a more professional approach to management and career development.

A few, however, thought the changes were not profound enough to bring Sun into its proper place in the modern business world. A more radical reorientation of character was required. Two interviewees in particular asserted that productivity is the central principle of a genuinely modern business ethic. It is the criterion that should govern all else in the enterprise—organizational structure, personnel practices, mergers and acquisitions, sales and marketing. On this basis, one interviewee pronounced the paternalistic tradition at Sun as "abhorrent." The favoritism and bias manifest in the hiring, promotion, and retention practices of a paternalistic company are "absolutely pathetic." It is ethically repugnant for a company not to get optimal results from its enterprise and not to adopt measurable criteria for success. He predicted that if Sun does not move quickly out of its current middle-of-the-road approach, it will not be able to generate sufficient return on investment to remain a viable corporation in the modern context.

Still other interviewees were neither nostalgic about the paternalism of the Old Sun nor unqualifiedly pleased with the professionalism (or intended professionalism) of the New Sun. Both the Old Sun and the New Sun suffer from ambiguity of character.

Of the Old Sun, one interviewee asserted that its paternalism was arrogant, dictatorial, secretive, nepotistic, overprotective, lacking in creative daring. On the other hand, it was honest, trustworthy, upright, and caring. The executives who ruled with an iron hand nonetheless were persons of moral integrity. And the employees who were cast into positions of dependency nonetheless were secure in their positions. More than a single interviewee remarked about Sun's policy during the Great Depression: a cut in the work week, but no one turned out.

Of the New Sun, favorable comments were made about the opportunities it provides for employees to take initiative for career development and about efforts undertaken to make the company more profitable. But a number of features of the New Sun were the focus of special criticism.

A persistent focus of criticism in the interviews was the principle of decentralization of the corporation into "modules"—operating units and subsidiaries. While decentralization has its benefits, as it has worked out in Sun it is cumbersome in administration and confusing to the public and the employees. The drive toward profitability has led some of the units into unhealthy competition with each other. It puts so much pressure on each unit to perform, other values and considerations beyond the "bottom line" tend to get lost. In some cases, it has increased the temptation to hide losses where possible and to be less than fully honest about the condition of an operating unit. It split into different units persons who had been accustomed to cooperating with each other. There are instances of employees of one operating unit "bad-mouthing" another. Some employees have expressed uncertainty about their identity: Are they working for Sun or for the operating unit? Furthermore, decentralization places units that have been traditionally service-oriented into an awkward and almost demeaning position given the difficulty they find in competing with other units in profitability. One interviewee contended, "The profit ethic by itself is irresponsible!" Presumably this principle applies both to the character of the company as a whole and to relations among operating units. Several expressed hope that the new system of clustering units into groups might alleviate the ills of decentralization and lead toward a common sense of identity and more active cooperation among the modules.

The issue of divestiture was another point of concern connected with decentralization. One interviewee (who proposed that Sun adopt a strict business ethic of profit and productivity) argued there is no justifiable alternative but to divest every operating unit showing a loss. The alternative (the "grandfatherly" approach), which had been characteristic of the Old Sun and continues to plague its operation, is out of keeping with modern managerial methods. Other interviewees were not nearly so certain. For one thing, the losses and benefits of divestiture are not merely monetary. To divest or to close an operation is to put large numbers of people out of work, to disrupt lives of families and communities, to dampen the morale of persons throughout the rest of the corporation, and to suffer loss of the physical and human resources of the severed unit. On the other hand, to maintain a unit that is consistently losing money is to have a drain on the rest of the company; and that, too, has an effect on morale and on conditions of work of employees throughout the entire corporation. For a second thing, a company faces the issues of *how* to divest, what procedures to employ, whom to consult in making the decision, and whether to be selective about the kind of corporation that will assume ownership and control of the divested unit.

According to several interviewees, the Becton Dickinson acquisition also provoked serious question about the character of the New Sun. The Becton Dickinson acquisition "could not have happened under the Old Sun." Or, at least, the manner of acquisition would have been wholly different and would not have resulted in SEC action against Sun. Various interviewees opined that the acquisition may have not been illegal (the matter, they noted, was settled before it got to the courts), but the methods used in its consummation were ethically questionable: It was a "boiler room operation." One employee remarked that she was personally embarrassed by the event. The issue raised was whether the Becton Dickinson affair was typical of the character of the New Sun; if so, she (and others) wanted none of it. One interviewee stated, "Our confidence in the heads of the corporation was shattered; we were uncertain whether we could trust the integrity of those involved in the deal."

Another criticism of the New Sun may be a function either of its size or its organizational form or its basic orientation. One interviewee framed the criticism this way: The most critical issue now facing the company is loss of individuality. Others echoed the same sentiment. In "this crazy organizational structure," people feel cut off, separated from what is going on, isolated from the company as a whole. Top officials have no time for the rank and file. Leadership tends to be remote, too concerned with "doing business." In the Old Sun an individual's judgments mattered, but in the New Sun one's voice gets lost. In another version of the same critique, one interviewee noted there is much talk about "open and honest communication" at Sun, but the talk is empty rhetoric. Another interviewee, however, of a somewhat different school of thought, labeled the "open and honest communication philosophy" as "hypocritical bullshit": Those who espouse it do not mean it, and they should not mean it, for no decent business can operate that way; productivity requires strong directive leadership from the top down.

Interviewees are thus aware that Sun has experienced and is still undergoing a period of painful change. They have an intense interest in that change, for the identity of Sun is tied to their identity as participants in the process and to the conditions of their working life. On the question of whether the character of the Old Sun or the New Sun or some entirely new amalgamated Sun should prevail, they are divided as one might expect from an aggregation of talented and sensitive people. But they are clearly asking for leadership in dealing with the matter. Indeed one spoke of a "crisis of leadership" in Sun; another of the need for vivid and persuasive leadership and direction; a third for some clarity of the goals of Sun. But the leadership must not be a sham, nor should it be merely verbal. It must be visible and personable; it must be sincere and responsive to reaction; it must be shaped into policies and programs that are consistent with statement and goals.

8. Epilogue: Creeds, Codes, and Conscience—the Ethical Process

A few final words are germane to this report on Sun's ethical condition. For many years, Sun Company was directed by a man known for his moral integrity. In about midcentury, a Creed was formulated for Sun giving written voice to the principles he represented. This Creed has been revised, most recently in 1977 under the instruction, significantly, of Robert Sharbaugh (see Appendix). Several interviewees mentioned the Creed, but in various and different ways. One called it "unique," signifying the basic orientation of the company. Another called it "pollyanna," signifying not much of anything. A third was impressed by it but wondered if it really represented current thinking of the executives of Sun. A fourth averred that the Creed had *never* meant much of anything, for people are what they are, and a Creed is not going to affect their morality one way or the other. A fifth thought the Creed's orientation and the profit motive represented two divergent moralities inconsistent with each other. A sixth interviewee admitted he scurried about to find a copy in preparation for the interview; it took him four days to do so. After all, he said, it has been sent through the mail some years ago, and that is not a very effective way to communicate its message. Another observed that the Creed by itself is just too abstract. What might be interesting is to have a sequence of meetings among people throughout Sun—board members, top executives, middle and low-level managers, hourly employees—to discuss the Creed, what it means to each, and how it should be interpreted.

Taking this project itself as a lesson, it may be that while creeds and codes have a place, the process of intercommunication is a more significant and effective way to encourage ethical reflection. With very few exceptions, the interviewees were eager and ready to talk. They had issues on their minds. They wished not only to speak but to listen. They saw the value in the give and take of conversation, for it is through that process that consciousness is awakened and new insights arise. Conscience is an inner dialogue; its counterpart in organization is intercommunication, especially intercommunication among persons with differing perspectives and philosophies. As this project of listening to voices from within is unique (how many other corporations have dared to take the risk?), maybe Sun should take one more unusual step: establish means, through the Sun Institute and elsewhere, to have continuing conversation about hardheaded ethical issues across all lines inside and outside the corporation.

One last note—several interviewees suggested the need for Sun, as another expression of inner conscience, to institute a means to hear out the critical, the dissident, and the injured. The means for this might be a special office in Human Resources, one with a hot-line telephone and with authority to act. Or the means might be the creation of the ombudsman's office.

But then one might, just as well, do what Andrew Hacker once proposed for all corporations: appoint a vice president in charge of heresy—not to snoop it out, but to keep it alive. What ever happened, by the way, to the court jester? 'Twas he, it is said, who kept the conscience of the king!

THE CREED WE WORK BY

A STATEMENT OF PRINCIPLES

Recognizing that business is among the institutions affecting the well-being of mankind, and that the philosophy as well as the performance of particular corporations is of proper public interest, we the Directors of Sun Company, Inc., set forth these beliefs:

e believe human development to be the worthiest of the goals of civilization and independence to be the superior condition for nurturing growth in the capabilities of people. ∎

We believe freedom of choice is the critical requisite of any form of social organization that effectively provides for self-determination. Competition both encourages and makes practical the exercise of that freedom. And competition is in turn encouraged when meritorious achievement is recognized by commensurate reward. ∎

We believe economic competition spurred by the profit motive gives unparalleled thrust to production, provides the material base for superior living standards, and preserves the widest latitude for the exercise of individual preferences. ∎

We believe that while business cannot survive if incapable of performing profitably, its sole obligation does not consist literally of producing profits. Instead, it must also nourish values cherished by the society of which it is a part. ∎

We believe we are obligated to be responsible in conducting the affairs of Sun Company to the interests of its customers, employees and stockholders. Also, we must be responsive to the broader concerns of the public, including especially the general desire for improvement in the quality of life, equal opportunity for all, and the constructive use of natural resources. ∎

We believe we must be sensitive to the needs and aspirations of others, and that it is important we seek understanding in turn of the goals of Sun Company, its policies and the manner in which it attempts to discharge its responsibilities. Consequently, we will strive to maintain open communications with all affected by or concerned with our Company. ∎

We believe that managers of organizations hold a trust, and that their stewardship demands scrupulous treatment of the loyalties and resources committed to their direction. We acknowledge this principle as it applies specifically to us. ∎

Finally, we know that the conduct and character of our Company will depend ultimately upon the many thousands of persons who contribute to its functions. Each plays a part; each possesses a unique degree of skill and dedication; each holds and is entitled to a personal creed. It will be our conscious purpose to encourage, by precept and especially by example, competency and a common practice of fairness, honesty and integrity as the hallmark of Sun Company. ∎

SUN COMPANY

Recommendations

The Sun Company survey was a one-time event, although the Corporate Ethics Committee has followed through on several areas addressed in the report and has contemplated ways of keeping the process alive. That, of course, is what is most important—to keep the process alive.

The shortcoming of a Code of Ethics is that it fails in this respect. On the surface, a code seems a simple way to bring critical ethics into the corporation for once and for all. But it is simple to the point of neglect. It neglects the dynamic character of a corporation. It neglects the plurality of perspectives found among persons working for a corporation. It neglects the particularities of circumstances in which decisions are made. It neglects the need for continuous reflection about the impact of a corporation's policies and procedures on the actual lives of people.

Ethical responsibility is not just a matter of knowing and applying rules. It is as much a matter of listening, reflecting, and response. Unless a corporation is to rest satisfied with its given ethos and ideology, it must establish regular means of listening to all parties who have something to say, reflecting about the sensibility and implication of what has been said, and responding in a respectful and respectable way. Regular means must be instituted to keep the process going. What are the possibilities?

1. An Ethical Concerns Audit.   There is good reason to make the kind of survey undertaken at Sun a periodic event. Once or twice a year employees can be given opportunity to speak directly with someone about their perceptions of ethical stresses and strains in the corporation. The interviewer should be someone from outside of the corporate world to insure the integrity of the audit and to remove any suspicion of an executive spy. Interviews should be open-ended. Confidentiality should be scrupulously maintained. The audit should be authorized by the executive office and the report should be presented directly to those in that office. But the report should also be available to all persons working for the corporation to inform them of the results and to stimulate them to keep ethical concerns in mind.

2. An Ombudsman's Office.   Taking their cue from the Swedish invention of the ombudsman, many administrative organizations, public and private, have created a similar institution. The ombudsman's purpose is to hear complaints from individuals, to investigate them, and to resolve them as satisfactorily as possible. Governments, hospitals, and educational institutions have tried various versions of the office. In an age of large complex organizations, the individual needs some way of cutting through the proverbial bureaucratic red tape and avoiding the awkwardness of complaints to an immediate superior (who may be, of course, the object of complaint!). In some cases, an ombudsman's office works well; in others, not so well. The difference rests in part on vested interests and in part on the personality and power of the person in the office. Granting possible limitations, a corporate responsibility ombudsman might prove a valuable means to keep the process of critical ethics alive. The office should have a "hot line" that anyone at anytime could call to air a grievance, to blow a whistle, to pose a question, or to discuss a difficulty. The ombudsman should have ample discretion and sufficient clout to pursue issues that are raised, especially without anyone worrying about job security.

3. A Policy Formation Hearing.   Corporations might learn a lesson or two from the congressional and administrative branches of government. Congressional committees hold hearings prior to the final writing of their bills. Similarly, administrative agencies have hearings on proposals for new regulations or for changes in old regulations. Through hearings interested parties can register their judgments, point out difficulties, inform panels about conditions of life from their perspective, and offer alternatives. To be sure, hearings can be and have been rigged. But, in principle, they are a means of empowering those who are affected by policies to influence those who make them. Why should corporations not adopt a similar procedure? In their own sphere of influence, corporations are governments of an unofficial character. There is no reason why they should not be open to hearing from interested individuals and groups before policies are fixed that will affect their lives. Plant relocations, mergers and divestitures, organizational reforms, overseas expansion, and new personnel practices and marketing techniques are all matters that affect the texture of life. A corporation, if it is to incorporate procedures for critical ethics, needs a way of listening to those whose lives are involved.

4. A Critical Issues Forum.   A corporation, it is said, is an organized way of "doing business" and should be left alone to do what it can best do. External matters are just that—external—and should be of no direct concern to the corporation.

That view is not only too narrow; but it also shows a misunderstanding of the full meaning of the modern business corporation in the context of modern life. Corporation and society are inextricably intertwined. Critical social issues invariably influence corporate activity and, in turn, corporate practices have an indirect if not direct impact on critical social issues.

Sexism and racism, urban decay and air pollution, soil erosion and energy shortage, war and revolution, poverty and crime may not appear to be relevant to "doing business," but they are. A corporation thus needs a means of exploring the interconnection between critical issues and its way of doing things. It needs a forum whereby it can hear from those who insist that corporate ethos and practice are part of the problem and through which it can demonstrate where and how it has made responsible efforts to be part of the solution.

5. A Corporate Ethics Seminar. Conversations are more or less sophisticated as they are more or less informed. A sophisticated conversation about ethical matters requires a special kind of information. There are traditions, philosophical and religious, dealing explicitly with fundamental ways of thinking about ethical questions. There are varying perspectives and divergent schools of thought. There are basic categories and inherited principles. The Sun Company report employed, for instance, the ethical categories of honesty, justice, fair bargain, responsibility, legitimacy, and character. The interviewees did not use these concepts, but one who knows the traditions of ethical discourse is able to classify, distinguish, and thus make more intelligible what it is that is being said. Yet, if a corporation is to encourage reflective ethical thought, these traditions should become part of its working vocabulary. Words are powerful instruments. They enable one to see things not otherwise seen and to do things not otherwise thought possible. For purposes of basic instruction in ethical thinking, a corporate ethics seminar is a possibility. The seminar should be led by those who know the traditions, persons versed in the disciplines of history, philosophy, and religious thought. Furthermore, to gain the wisdom of mental distance about corporate life, it would be valuable to bring in those who can instruct about the history and sociology of the corporation even as, at the present, corporations use psychologists to assist in understanding the character of personal relations.

These five ways of regularizing the process of critical ethics in a corporation rest on a set of premises—that ethics is everybody's business, that corporate life is nowadays part and parcel of our everyday life, and that any corporation establishing means for open and serious conversation about ethical concerns is a more humane enterprise than it could otherwise be. That is the most basic lesson to be learned from the Sun Company survey.

PART II

What Is Business Ethics?

Chapter 6

Ethics Without the Sermon

Laura L. Nash

As if via a network TV program on the telecommunications satellite, declarations such as these are being broadcast throughout the land:

Scene 1. Annual meeting, Anyproducts Inc.; John Q. Moneypockets, chairman and CEO speaking: "Our responsibility to the public has always come first at our company, and we continue to strive toward serving our public in the best way possible in the belief that good ethics is good business.... Despite our forecast of a continued recession in the industry through 1982, we are pleased to announce that 1981's earnings per share were up for the twenty-sixth year in a row."

Scene 2. Corporate headquarters, Anyproducts, Inc.; Linda Diesinker, group vice president, speaking: "Of course we're concerned about minority development and the plight of the inner cities. But the best place for our new plant would be Horsepasture, Minnesota. We need a lot of space for our operations and a skilled labor force, and the demographics and tax incentives in Horsepasture are perfect."

Scene 3. Interview with a financial writer; Rafe Shortstop, president, Anyproducts, Inc., speaking: "We're very concerned about the state of American business and our ability to compete with foreign companies. . . . No, I don't think we have any real ethical problems. We don't bribe people or anything like that."

Scene 4. Jud McFisticuff, taxi driver, speaking: "Anyproducts? You've got to be kidding! I wouldn't buy their stuff for anything. The last thing of theirs I bought fell apart in six months. And did you see how they were dumping wastes in the Roxburg water system?"

Scene 5. Leslie Matriculant, MBA '82, speaking: "Join Anyproducts? I don't want to risk my reputation working for a company like that. They recently acquired a business that turned out to have ten class-action discrimination suits against it. And when Anyproducts tried to settle the whole thing out of court, the president had his picture in *Business Week* with the caption, 'His secretary still serves him coffee'."

Whether you regard it as an unchecked epidemic or as the first blast of Gabriel's horn, the trend toward focusing on the social impact of the corporation is an inescapable reality that must be factored into today's managerial decision making. But for the executive who asks, "How do we as a corporation examine our ethical concerns?" the theoretical insights currently available may be more frustrating than helpful.

As the first scene in this article implies, many executives firmly believe that corporate operations and corporate values are dynamically intertwined. For the purposes of analysis, however, the executive needs to uncoil the business–ethics helix and examine both strands closely.

Unfortunately, the ethics strand has remained largely inaccessible, for business has not yet developed a workable process by which corporate values can be articulated. If ethics and business are part of the same double helix, perhaps we can develop a microscope capable of enlarging our perception of both aspects of business administration—what we do and who we are.

SIDESTEPPING TRIASSIC REPTILES

Philosophy has been sorting out issues of fairness, injury, empathy, self-sacrifice, and so on, for more than 2000 years. In seeking to examine the ethics of business, therefore, business logically assumes it will be best served by a "consultant" in philosophy who is already familiar with the formal discipline of ethics.

As the philosopher begins to speak, however, a difficulty immediately arises; corporate executives and philosophers approach problems in radically different ways. The academician ponders the intangible, savors the paradoxical, and embraces the peculiar; he or she speaks in a special language of categorical imperatives and deontological viewpoints that must be taken into consideration before a statement about honesty is agreed to have any meaning.

Like some Triassic reptile, the theoretical view of ethics lumbers along in the far past of Sunday School and Philosophy I, while the reality of practical business concerns is constantly measuring a wide range of competing claims on time and resources against the unrelenting and objective marketplace.

Not surprisingly, the two groups are somewhat hostile. The jokes of the liberal intelligentsia are rampant and weary: *"Ethics and Business*—the shortest book in the world." "Business and ethics—a subject confined to the preface of business books." Accusations from the corporate cadre are delivered with an assurance that rests more on an intuition of social climate than on a certainty of fact: "You do-gooders are ruining America's ability to compete in the world." "Of course, the cancer reports on _____ (choose from a long list) were terribly exaggerated."

What is needed is a process of ethical inquiry that is immediately comprehensible to a group of executives and not predisposed to the utopian, and sometimes anticapitalistic, bias marking much of the work in applied business philosophy today. So I suggest, as a preliminary solution, a set of 12 questions that draw on traditional philosophical frameworks but that avoid the level of abstraction normally associated with formal moral reasoning.

I offer the questions as a first step in a very new discipline. As such, they form a tentative model that will certainly undergo modifications after its parts are given some exercise. Exhibit A poses the 12 questions.

To illustrate the application of the questions, I will draw especially on a program at Lex Service Group, Ltd., whose top management prepared a statement of financial objectives and moral values as a part of its strategic planning process. Lex is a British company with operations in the United Kingdom and the United States. Its sales total about $1.2 billion. In 1978 its structure was partially decentralized, and in 1979 the chairman's policy group began a strategic planning process. The intent, according to its statement of values and objectives, was "to make explicit the sort of company Lex was, or wished to be."

Exhibit A.   Twelve Questions for Examining the Ethics of a Business Decision

1	Have you defined the problem accurately?
2	How would you define the problem if you stood on the other side of the fence?
3	How did this situation occur in the first place?
4	To whom and to what do you give your loyalty as a person and as a member of the corporation?
5	What is your intention in making this decision?
6	How does this intention compare with the probable results?
7	Whom could your decision or action injure?
8	Can you discuss the problem with the affected parties before you make your decision?
9	Are you confident that your position will be as valid over a long period of time as it seems now?
10	Could you disclose without qualm your decision or action to your boss, your CEO, the board of directors, your family, society as a whole?
11	What is the symbolic potential of your action if understood? if misunderstood?
12	Under what conditions would you allow exceptions to your stand?

Neither a paralegal code nor a generalized philosophy, the statement consisted of a series of general policies regarding financial strategy as well as such aspects of the company's character as customer service, employee–shareholder responsibility, and quality of management. Its content largely reflected the personal values of Lex's chairman and CEO, Trevor Chinn, whose private philanthropy is well known and whose concern for social welfare has long been echoed in the company's personnel policies.

In the past, pressure on senior managers for high profit performance had obscured some of these ideals in practice, and the statement of strategy was a way of radically realigning various competing moral claims with the financial objectives of the company. As one senior manager remarked to me, "The values seem obvious, and if we hadn't been so gross in the past we wouldn't have needed the statement." Despite a predictable variance among Lex's top executives as to the desirability of the values outlined in the statement, it was adopted with general agreement to comply and was scheduled for reassessment at a senior managers' meeting one year after implementation.

1. Have you defined the problem accurately?

How one assembles the facts weights an issue before the moral examination ever begins, and a definition is rarely accurate if it articulates one's loyalties rather than the facts. The importance of factual neutrality is readily seen, for example, in assessing the moral implications of producing a chemical agent for use in warfare. Depending on one's loyalties, the decision to make the substance can be described as serving one's country, developing products, or killing babies. All of the above may be factual statements, but none is neutral or accurate if viewed in isolation.

Similarly, the recent controversy over marketing U.S.-made cigarettes in Third World countries rarely noted that the incidence of lung cancer in underdeveloped nations is quite low (from one-tenth to one-twentieth the rate for U.S. males) due primarily to the lower life expectancies and earlier predominance of other diseases in these nations. Such a fact does not decide the ethical complexities of this marketing problem, but it does add a crucial perspective in the assignment of moral priorities by defining precisely the injury that tobacco exports may cause.

Extensive fact gathering may also help defuse the emotionalism of an issue. For instance, local statistics on lung cancer incidence reveal that the U.S. tobacco industry is not now "exporting death," as has been charged. Moreover, the substantial and immediate economic benefits attached to tobacco may be providing food and health care in these countries. Nevertheless, as life expectancy and the standards of living rise, a higher incidence of cigarette-related diseases appears likely to develop in these nations. Therefore, cultivation of the nicotine habit may be deemed detrimental to the long-term welfare of these nations.

According to one supposedly infallible truth of modernism, technology is so complex that its results will never be fully comprehensible or predictable. Part of the executive's frustration in responding to question 1 is the real possibility that the "experts" will find no grounds for agreement about the facts.

As a first step, however, defining fully the factual implications of a decision determines to a large degree the quality of one's subsequent moral position. Pericles' definition of true courage rejected the Spartans' blind obedience in war in preference to the courage of the Athenian citizen who, he said, was able to make a decision to proceed in full knowledge of the probable danger. A truly moral decision is an informed decision. A decision that is based on blind or convenient ignorance is hardly defensible. One simple test of the initial definition is the question:

2. How would you define the problem if you stood on the other side of the fence?

The contemplated construction of a plant for Division X is touted at the finance committee meeting as an absolute necessity for expansion at a cost saving of at least 25 percent. With plans drawn up for an energy-efficient building and an option already secured on a 99-year lease in a new industrial park in Chippewa County, the committee is likely to feel comfortable in approving the request for funds in a matter of minutes.

The facts of the matter are that the company will expand in an appropriate market, allocate its resources sensibly, create new jobs, increase Chippewa County's tax base, and most likely increase its returns to the shareholders. To the residents of Chippewa County, however, the plant may mean the destruction of a customary recreation spot, the onset of severe traffic jams, and the erection of an architectural eyesore. These are also facts of the situation, and certainly more immediate to the county than utilitarian justifications of profit performance and rights of ownership from an impersonal corporation whose headquarters are 1000 miles from Chippewa County and whose executives have plenty of acreage for their own recreation.

The purpose of articulating the other side, whose needs are understandably less proximate than operational considerations, is to allow some mechanism whereby calculations of self-interest (or even of a project's ultimate general beneficence) can be interrupted by a compelling empathy for those who might suffer immediate injury or mere annoyance as a result of a corporation's decisions. Such empathy is a necessary prerequisite for shouldering voluntarily some responsibility for the social consequences of corporate operations, and it may be the only solution to today's overly litigious and anarchic world.

There is a power in self-examination: with an exploration of the likely consequences of a proposal, taken from the viewpoint of those who do not immediately benefit, comes a discomfort or an embarrassment that rises in proportion to the degree of the likely injury and its articulation. Like Socrates as gadfly, who stung his fellow citizens into a critical examination of their conduct when they became complacent, the discomfort of the alternative definition is meant to prompt a disinclination to choose the expedient over the most responsible course of action.

Abstract generalities about the benefits of the profit motive and the free market system are, for some, legitimate and ultimate justifications, but when unadorned with alternative viewpoints, such arguments also tend to promote the complacency, carelessness, and impersonality that have characterized some of the more injurious actions of corporations. The advocates of these arguments are like the reformers in Nathaniel Hawthorne's short story "Hall of Fantasy" who "had got possession of some crystal fragment of truth, the brightness of which so dazzled them that they could see nothing else in the whole universe."

In the example of Division X's new plant, it was a simple matter of defining the alternate facts; the process rested largely on an assumption that certain values were commonly shared (no one likes a traffic jam, landscaping pleases more than an unadorned building, and so forth). But the alternative definition often underscores an inherent disparity in values or language. To some, the employment of illegal aliens is a criminal act (fact 1); to others, it is a solution to the 60 percent unemployment rate of a neighboring country (fact 2). One country's bribe is another country's redistribution of sales commissions.

When there are cultural or linguistic disparities, it is easy to get the facts wrong or to invoke a pluralistic tolerance as an excuse to act in one's own self-interest: "That's the way they do things over there. Who are we to question their beliefs?" This kind of reasoning can be both factually inaccurate (many generalizations about bribery rest on hearsay and do not represent the complexities of a culture) and philosophically inconsistent (there are plenty of beliefs, such as those of the environmentalist, which the same generalizers do not hesitate to question).

3. How did this situation occur in the first place?

Lex Motor Company, a subsidiary of Lex Service Group, Ltd., had been losing share at a 20 percent rate in a declining market; and Depot B's performance was the worst of all. Two nearby Lex depots could easily absorb B's business, and closing it down seemed the only sound financial decision. Lex's chairman, Trevor Chinn, hesitated to approve the closure, however, on the grounds that putting 100 people out of work was not right when the corporation itself was not really jeopardized by B's existence. Moreover, seven department managers, who were all within 5 years of retirement and had had 25 or more years of service at Lex, were scheduled to be made redundant.

The values statement provided no automatic solution for it placed value on both employees' security and shareholders' interest. Should they close Depot B? At first Chinn thought not: Why should the little guys suffer disproportionately when the company was not performing well? Why not close a more recently acquired business where employee service was not so large a factor? Or why not wait out the short term and reduce head count through natural attrition?

As important as deciding the ethics of the situation was the inquiry into its history. Indeed, the history gave a clue to solving the dilemma: Lex's traditional emphasis on employee security and high financial performance had led to a precipitate series of acquisitions and subsequent divestitures when the company had failed to meet its overall objectives. After each rationalization, the people serving the longest had been retained and placed at Depot B, so that by 1980 the facility had more managers than it needed and a very high proportion of long-service employees.

So the very factors that had created the performance problems were making the closure decision difficult, and the very solution that Lex was inclined to favor again would exacerbate the situation further!

In deciding the ethics of a situation it is important to distinguish the symptoms from the disease. Great profit pressures with no sensitivity to the cycles in a particular industry, for example, may force division managers to be ruthless with employees, to short-weight customers, or even to fiddle with cash flow reports in order to meet headquarters' performance criteria.

Dealing with the immediate case of lying, quality discrepancy, or strained labor relations—when the problem is finally discovered—is only a temporary solution. A full examination of how the situation occurred and what the traditional solutions have been may reveal a more serious discrepancy of values and pressures, and this will illuminate the real significance and ethics of the problem. It will also reveal recurring patterns of events that in isolation appear trivial but that as a whole point up a serious situation.

Such a mechanism is particularly important because very few executives are outright scoundrels. Rather, violations of corporate and social values usually occur inadvertently because no one recognizes that a problem exists until it becomes a crisis. This tendency toward initial trivialization seems to be the biggest ethical problem in business today. Articulating answers to my first three questions is a way of reversing that process.

4. To whom and what do you give your loyalties as a person and as a member of the corporation?

Every executive faces conflicts of loyalty. The most familiar occasions pit private conscience and sense of duty against corporate policy, but equally frequent are the situations in which one's close colleagues demand participation (tacit or explicit) in an operation or a decision that runs counter to company policy. To whom or what is the greater loyalty—to one's corporation? superior? family? society? self? race? sex?

The good news about conflicts of loyalty is that their identification is a workable way of smoking out the ethics of a situation and of discovering the absolute values inherent in it. As one executive in a discussion of a Harvard case study put it, "My corporate brain says this action is O.K., but my noncorporate brain keeps flashing these warning lights."

The bad news about conflicts of loyalty is that there are few automatic answers for placing priorities on them. "To thine own self be true" is a murky quagmire when the self takes on a variety of roles, as it does so often in this complex modern world.

Supposedly, today's young managers are giving more weight to individual than to corporate identity, and some older executives see this tendency as being ultimately subversive. At the same time, most of them believe individual integrity is essential to a company's reputation.

The U.S. securities industry, for example, is one of the most rigorous industries in America in its requirements of honesty and disclosure. Yet in the end, all its systematic precautions prove inadequate unless the people involved also have a strong sense of integrity that puts loyalty to these principles above personal gain.

A system, however, must permit the time and foster the motivation to allow personal integrity to surface in a particular situation. An examination of loyalties is one way to bring this about. Such an examination may strengthen reputations but also may result in blowing the whistle (freedom of thought carries with it the risk of revolution). But a sorting out of loyalties can also bridge the gulf between policy and implementation or among various interest groups whose affiliations may mask a common devotion to an aspect of a problem—a devotion on which consensus can be built.

How does one probe into one's own loyalties and their implications? A useful method is simply to play various roles out loud, to call on one's loyalty to family and community (for example) by asking, "What will I say when my child asks me why I did that?" If the answer is "That's the way the world works," then your loyalties are clear and moral passivity inevitable. But if the question presents real problems, you have begun a demodulation of signals from your conscience that can only enhance corporate responsibility.

5. What is your intention in making this decision?

6. How does this intention compare with the likely results?

These two questions are asked together because their content often bears close resemblance and, by most calculations, both color the ethics of a situation.

Corporation Buglebloom decides to build a new plant in an underdeveloped minority-populated district where the city has been trying with little success to encourage industrial development. The media approve and Buglebloom adds another star to its good reputation. Is Buglebloom a civic leader and supporter of minorities or a canny investor about to take advantage of the disadvantaged? The possibilities of Buglebloom's intentions are endless and probably unfathomable to the public; Buglebloom may be both canny investor and friend of minority groups.

I argue that despite their complexity and elusiveness, a company's intentions do matter. The "purity" of Buglebloom's motives (purely profit-seeking or purely altruistic) will have wide-reaching effects inside and outside the corporation—on attitudes toward minority employees in other parts of the company, on the wages paid at the new plant, and on the number of other investors in the same area—that will legitimize a certain ethos in the corporation and the community.

Sociologist Max Weber called this an "ethics of attitude" and contrasted it with an "ethics of absolute ends." An ethics of attitude sets a standard to ensure a certain action. A firm policy at headquarters of not cheating customers, for example, may also deter salespeople from succumbing to a tendency to lie by omission or purchasers from continuing to patronize a high-priced supplier when the costs are automatically passed on in the selling price.

What about the ethics of result? Two years later, Buglebloom wishes it had never begun Project Minority Plant. Every good intention has been lost in the realities of doing business in an unfamiliar area, and Buglebloom now has dirty hands: some of those payoffs were absolutely unavoidable if the plant was to open, operations have been plagued with vandalism and language problems, and local resentment at the industrialization of the neighborhood has risen as charges of discrimination have surfaced. No one seems to be benefiting from the project.

The goodness of intent pales somewhat before results that perpetrate great injury or simply do little good. Common sense demands that the "responsible" corporation try to align the two more closely, to identify the probable consequences and also the limitations of knowledge that might lead to more harm than good. Two things to remember in comparing intention and results are that knowledge of the future is always inadequate and that overconfidence often precedes a disastrous mistake.

These two precepts, cribbed from ancient Greece, may help the corporation keep the disparities between intent and result a fearsome reality to consider continuously. The next two questions explore two ways of reducing the moral risks of being wrong.

7. Whom could your decision or action injure?

The question presses whether injury is intentional or not. Given the limits of knowledge about a new product or policy, who and how many come into contact with it? Could its inadequate disposal affect an entire community? two employees? yourself? How might your product be used if it happened to be acquired by a terrorist radical group or a terrorist military police force? Has your distribution system or disposal plan ensured against such injury? Could it ever?

If not, there may be a compelling moral justification for stopping production. In an integrated society where business and government share certain values, possible injury is an even more important consideration than potential benefit. In policymaking, a much likelier ground for agreement than benefit is avoidance of injury through those "universal nos"—such as no mass death, no totalitarianism, no hunger or malnutrition, no harm to children.

To exclude *at the outset* any policy or decision that might have such results is to reshape the way modern business examines its own morality. So often business formulates questions of injury only after the fact in the form of liability suits.

8. Can you engage the affected parties in a discussion of the problem before you make your decision?

If the calculus of injury is one way of responding to limitations of knowledge about the probable results of a particular business decision, the participation of affected parties is one of the best ways of informing that consideration. Civil rights groups often complain that corporations fail to invite participation from local leaders during the planning stages of community development projects and charitable programs. The corporate foundation that builds a tennis complex for disadvantaged youth is throwing away precious resources if most children in the neighborhood suffer from chronic malnutrition.

In the Lex depot closure case I have mentioned, senior executives agonized over whether the employees would choose redundancy over job transfer and which course would ultimately be more beneficial to them. The managers, however, did not consult the employees. There were more than 200 projected job transfers to another town. But all the affected employees, held by local ties and uneasy about possibly lower housing subsidies, refused relocation offers. Had the employees been allowed to participate in the redundancy discussions, the company might have wasted less time on relocation plans or might have uncovered and resolved the fears about relocating.

The issue of participation affects everyone. (How many executives feel that someone else should decide what is in *their* best interest?) And yet it is a principle often forgotten because of the pressure of time or the inconvenience of calling people together and facing predictably hostile questions.

9. Are you confident that your position will be as valid over a long period of time as it seems now?

As anyone knows who has had to consider long-range plans and short-term budgets simultaneously, a difference in time frame can change the meaning of a problem as much as spring and autumn change the colors of a tree. The ethical coloring of a business decision is no exception to this generational aspect of decision making. Time alters circumstances, and few corporate value systems are immune to shifts in financial status, external political pressure, and personnel. (One survey now places the average U.S. CEO's tenure in office at five years.)

At Lex, for example, the humanitarianism of the statement of objectives and values depended on financial prosperity. The values did not fully anticipate the extent to which the U.K. economy would undergo a recession, and the resulting changes had to be examined, reconciled, and fought if the company's values were to have any meaning. At the Lex annual review, the managers asked themselves repeatedly whether hard times were the ultimate test of the statement or a clear indication that a corporation had to be able to "afford" ethical position.

Ideally, a company's articulation of its values should anticipate changes of fortune. As the hearings for the passage of the Foreign Corrupt Practices Act of 1977 demonstrated, doing what you can get away with today may not be a secure moral standard, but short-term discomfort for long-term sainthood may require irrational courage or a rational reasoning system or, more likely, both. These 12 questions attempt to elicit a rational system. Courage, of course, depends on personal integrity.

Another aspect of the ethical time frame stretches beyond the boundaries of question 9 but deserves special attention, and that is the timing of the ethical inquiry. When and where will it be made?

We do not normally invoke moral principles in our everyday conduct. Some time ago the participants in a national business ethics conference had worked late into the night preparing the final case for the meeting, and they were very anxious the next morning to get the class underway. Just before the session began, however, someone suggested that they all donate a dollar apiece as a gratuity for the dining hall help at the institute.

Then just as everyone automatically reached into his or her pocket, another person questioned the direction of the gift. Why tip the person behind the counter but not the cook in the kitchen? Should the money be given to each person in proportion to salary or divided equally among all? The participants laughed uneasily—or groaned —as they thought of the diversion of precious time from the case. A decision had to be made.

With the sure instincts of efficient managers, the group chose to forgo further discussion of distributive justice and, yes, appoint a committee. The committee doled out the money without further group consideration, and no formal feedback on the donation was asked for or given.

The questions offered here do not solve the problem of making time for the inquiry. For suggestions about creating favorable conditions for examining corporate values, drawn from my field research, see Exhibit B.

10. Could you disclose without qualm your decision or action to your boss, your CEO, the board of directors, your family, or society as a whole?

The old question, "Would you want your decision to appear on the front page of the *New York Times?*" still holds. A corporation may maintain that there's really no problem, but a survey of how many "trivial" actions it is reluctant to disclose might be interesting. Disclosure is a way of sounding those submarine depths of conscience and of searching out loyalties. It is also a way of keeping a corporate character cohesive. The Lex group, for example, was once faced with a very sticky problem concerning a small but profitable site with unpleasant (although in no way illegal) working conditions, where two men with 30 years' service worked. I wrote up the case for a Lex senior managers' meeting on the promise to disguise it heavily because the executive who supervised the plant was convinced that, if the chairman and the personnel director knew the plant's true location, they would close it down immediately.

At the meeting, however, as everyone became involved in the discussion and the chairman himself showed sensitivity to the dilemma, the executive disclosed the location and spoke of his own feelings about the situation. The level of mutual confidence was apparent to all, and by other reports it was the most open discussion the group had ever had.

The meeting also fostered understanding of the company's values and their implementation. When the discussion finally flagged, the chairman spoke up. Basing his views on a full knowledge of the group's understanding of the problem, he set the company's priorities. "Jobs over fancy conditions, health over jobs," Chinn said, "but we always *must disclose.*" The group decided to keep the plant open, at least for the time being.

Disclosure does not, however, automatically bring universal sympathy. In the early 1970s, a large food store chain that repeatedly found itself embroiled in the United Farm Workers (UFW) disputes with the Teamsters over California grape and lettuce contracts took very seriously the moral implications of a decision whether to stop selling these products. The company endlessly researched the issues, talked to all sides, and made itself available to public representatives of various interest groups to explain its position and to hear out everyone else.

When the controversy started, the company decided to support the UFW boycott, but three years later top management reversed its position. Most of the people who wrote to the company or asked it to send representatives to their local UFW support meetings, however, continued to condemn the chain even after hearing its views, and the general public apparently never became aware of the company's side of the story.

11. What is the symbolic potential of your action if understood? if misunderstood?

Jones Inc., a diversified multinational corporation with assets of $5 billion, has a paper manufacturing operation that happens to be the only major industry in Stirville, and the factory has been polluting the river on which it is located. Local and national conservation groups have filed suit against Jones Inc. for past damages, and the company is defending itself. Meanwhile, the corporation has adopted plans for a new waste-efficient plant. The legal battle is extended and local resentment against Jones Inc. gets bitter.

As a settlement is being reached, Jones Inc. announces that, as a civic-minded gesture, it will make 400 acres of Stirville woodland it owns available to the residents for conservation and recreation purposes. Jones' intention is to offer a peace pipe to the people of Stirville, and the company sees the gift as a symbol of its own belief in conservation and a way of signaling that value to Stirville residents and national conservation groups. Should Jones Inc. give the land away? Is the symbolism significant?

If the symbolic value of the land is understood as Jones Inc. intends, the gift may patch up the company's relations with Stirville and stave off further disaffection with potential employees as the new plant is being built. It may also signal to employees throughout the corporation that Jones Inc. places a premium on conservation efforts and community relations.

If the symbolic value is misunderstood, however, or if completion of the plant is delayed and the old one has to be put back in use—or if another Jones operation is discovered to be polluting another community and becomes a target of the press—the gift could be interpreted as nothing more than a cheap effort to pay off the people of Stirville and hasten settlement of the lawsuit.

The Greek root of our word *symbol* means both signal and contract. A business decision—whether it is the use of an expense account or a corporate donation—has a symbolic value in signaling what is acceptable behavior within the corporate culture and in making a tacit contract with employees and the community about the rules of the game. How the symbol is actually perceived (or misperceived) is as important as how you intend it to be perceived.

12. Under what conditions would you allow exceptions to your stand?

If we accept the idea that every business decision has an important symbolic value and a contractual nature, then the need for consistency is obvious. At the same time, it is also important to ask under what conditions the rule of the game may be changed. What conflicting principles, circumstances, or time constraints would provide a morally acceptable basis for making an exception to one's normal institutional ethos? For instance, how does the cost of the strategy to develop managers from minority groups over the long term fit in with short-term hurdle rates? Also to be considered is what would mitigate a clear case of employee dishonesty.

Questions of consistency—if you would do X, would you also do Y?—are yet another way of eliciting the ethics of the company and of oneself, and can be a final test of the strength, idealism, or practicality of those values. A last example from the experience of Lex illustrates this point and gives temporary credence to the platitude that good ethics is good business. An article in the Sunday paper about a company that had run a series of racy ads, with pictures of half-dressed women and promises of free merchandise to promote the sale of a very mundane product, sparked an extended examination at Lex of its policies on corporate inducements.

One area of concern was holiday giving. What was the acceptable limit for a gift—a bottle of whiskey? a case? Did it matter only that the company did not *intend* the gift to be an inducement, or did the mere possibility of inducement taint the gift? Was the cut-off point absolute? The group could agree on no halfway point for allowing some gifts and not others, so a new value was added to the formal statement that prohibited the offering or receiving of inducements.

The next holiday season Chinn sent a letter to friends and colleagues who had received gifts of appreciation in the past. In it he explained that, as a result of Lex's concern with "the very complex area of business ethics," management had decided that the company would no longer send any gifts, nor would it be appropriate for its employees to receive any. Although the letter did not explain Lex's reasoning behind the decision, apparently there was a large untapped consensus about such gift giving: by return mail Chinn received at least twenty letters from directors, general managers, and chairmen of companies with which Lex had done business congratulating him for his decision, agreeing with the new policy, and thanking him for his holiday wishes.

THE "GOOD PUPPY" THEORY

The 12 questions are a way to articulate an idea of the responsibilities involved and to lay them open for examination. Whether a decisive policy is also generated or not, there are compelling reasons for holding such discussions:

The process facilitates talk as a group about a subject that has traditionally been reserved for the privacy of one's conscience. Moreover, for those whose consciences twitch but don't speak in full sentences, the questions help sort out their own perceptions of the problem and various ways of thinking about it.

The process builds a cohesiveness of managerial character as points of consensus emerge and people from vastly different operations discover that they share common problems. It is one way of determining the values and goals of the company, and that is a key element in determining corporate strategy.

It acts as an information resource. Senior managers learn about other parts of the company with which they may have little contact.

It helps uncover ethical inconsistencies in the articulated values of the corporation or between these values and the financial strategy.

It helps uncover sometimes dramatic differences between the values and the practicality of their implementation.

It helps the CEO understand how the senior managers think, how they handle a problem, and how willing and able they are to deal with complexity. It reveals how they may be drawing on the private self to the enhancement of corporate activity.

In drawing out the private self in connection with business and in exploring the significance of the corporation's activities, the process derives meaning from an environment that is often characterized as meaningless.

It helps improve the nature and range of alternatives.

It is cathartic.

The process is also reductive in that it limits the level of inquiry. For example, the 12 questions ask what injury might result from a decision and what good is intended, but they do not ask the meaning of good or whether the result is "just."

Socrates asked how a person could talk of pursuing the good before knowing what the good is; and the analysis he visualized entailed a lifelong process of learning and examination. Do the 12 short questions, with their explicit goal of simplifying the ethical examination, bastardize the Socratic ideal? To answer this, we must distinguish between personal philosophy and participation as a corporate member in the examination of a *corporate* ethos, for the 12 questions assume some difference between private and corporate "goodness."

This distinction is crucial to any evaluation of my suggested process for conducting an ethical inquiry and needs to be explained. What exactly do we expect of the "ethical," or "good," corporation? Three examples of goodness represent prevailing social opinions, from that of the moral philosopher to the strict Friedmaniac.

1. The most rigorous moral analogy to the good corporation would be the "good man." An abstract, philosophical ideal having highly moral connotations, the good man encompasses an intricate relation of abstractions such as Plato's four virtues (courage, godliness or philosophical wisdom, righteousness, and prudence). The activities of this kind of good corporation imply a heavy responsibility to collectively know the good and to resolve to achieve it.

2. Next, there is the purely amoral definition of good, as in a "good martini"—and a moral fulfillment of a largely inanimate and functional purpose. Under this definition, corporate goodness would be best achieved by the unadorned accrual of profits with no regard for the social implications of the means whereby profits are made.

3. Halfway between these two views lies the good as in "good puppy"—here goodness consists primarily of the fulfillment of a social contract that centers on avoiding social injury. Moral capacity is perceived as present, but its potential is limited. A moral evaluation of the good puppy is possible but exists largely in concrete terms; we do not need to identify the puppy's intentions as utilitarian to understand and agree that its "ethical" fulfillment of the social contract consists of not soiling the carpet or biting the baby.

It seems to me that business ethics operates most appropriately for corporate man when it seeks to define and explore corporate morality at the level of the good puppy. The good corporation is expected to avoid perpetrating irretrievable social injury (and to assume the costs when it unintentionally does injury) while focusing on its purpose as a profit-making organization. Its moral capacity does not extend, however, to determining by itself what will improve the general social welfare.

Exhibit B. Shared Conditions of Some Successful Ethical Inquiries

Freed time frame	Understanding and identifying moral issues takes time and causes ferment, and the executive needs an uninterrupted block of time to ponder the problems.
Unconventional location	Religious groups, boards of directors, and professional association have long recognized the value of the retreat as a way of stimulating fresh approaches to regular activities. If the group is going to transcend normal corporate hierarchies, it should hold the discussion on neutral territory so that all may participate with the same degree of freedom.
Resource person	The advantage of bringing in an outsider is not that he or she will impose some preconceived notion of right and wrong on management but that he will serve as a midwife for bringing the values already present in the institution out into the open. He can generate closer examination of the discrepancies between values and practice and draw on a wider knowledge of instances and intellectual frameworks than the group can. The resource person may also take the important role of arbitrator—to ensure that one person does not dominate the session with his or her own values and that the dialogue does not become impossibly emotional.
Participation of CEO	In most corporations the chief executive still commands an extra degree of authority for the intangible we call corporate culture, and the discussion needs the perspective of the legitimization by that authority if it is to have any seriousness of purpose and consequence. One of the most interesting experiments in examining corporate policy I have observed lacked the CEO's support, and within a year it died on the vine.
Credo	Articulating the corporation's values and objectives provides a reference point for group inquiry and implementation. Ethical codes, however, when drawn up by the legal department do not always offer a realistic and full representation of management's beliefs. The most important ethical inquiry for management may be the very formulation of such a statement, for the *process* of articulation is as useful as the values agreed on.
Homegrown topics	In isolating an ethical issue, drawing on your own experience is important. Philosophical business ethics has tended to reflect national social controversies, which though relevant to the corporation may not always be as relevant—not to mention as easily resolved—as some internal issues that are shaping the character of the company to a much greater degree. Executives are also more likely to be informed on these issues.
Resolution	In all the programs I observed except one, there was a point at which the inquiry was slated to have some resolution: either a vote on the issue, the adoption of a new policy, a timetable for implementation, or the formulation of a specific statement of values. The one program observed that had no such decision-making structure was organized simply to gather information about the company's activities through extrahierarchical channels. Because the program had no tangible goals or clearly articulated results, its benefits were impossible to measure.

The good puppy inquiry operates largely in concrete experience; just as the 12 questions impose a limit on our moral expectations, so too they impose a limit (welcome, to some) on our use of abstraction to get at the problem.

The situations for testing business morality remain complex. But by avoiding theoretical inquiry and limiting the expectations of corporate goodness to a few rules for social behavior that are based on common sense, we can develop an ethic that is appropriate to the language, ideology, and institutional dynamics of business decision making and consensus. This ethic can also offer managers a practical way of exploring those occasions when their corporate brains are getting warning flashes from their noncorporate brains.

Chapter 7

Teaching Business Ethics: Aims and Methods

Manuel Velasquez

Just as there is more than one way to skin the proverbial cat, so also there is more than one way to provide managers with training in business ethics. One way is to bring the classroom to the manager by setting up ethics training programs within a company's walls. These kinds of in-house programs are discussed at some length in other chapters of this book. A second way of providing ethics training is to bring the manager to the classroom by bringing the manager to a university campus that offers seminars, workshops, or courses in business ethics.[1]

This second approach has a number of advantages. For example, on-campus programs can be cheaper since the firm does not have to hire and train its own teaching staff, and on-campus programs can broaden the manager's ethical perspectives since the manager will be exposed to views different from those prevalent within his or her own company. University programs, however, can also have certain disadvantages. On-campus programs, for example, generally take up more of a manager's time and they can easily focus on issues that are not relevant to the manager's own company or industry. If properly conducted, however, on-campus programs in business ethics can provide managers with effective tools for dealing with the ethical problems they will encounter in their working lives.

The aim of this chapter is to describe the contributions that business schools can make to providing ethics training for managers. We begin by looking briefly at the kinds of ethics training programs that business schools have been developing and then turn to discussing some concrete methods by which ethics training might be enhanced.

MANAGEMENT EDUCATION IN ETHICS: CURRENT APPROACHES

During the last several years an increasing number of business schools around the country have recognized a growing need to develop more adequate approaches to business ethics and a need to incorporate business ethics into their management training programs. Three main factors forced business schools to face up to these needs.

The first factor was the breakdown of traditional approaches to business ethics.[2] If one were to read through the contents of texts and articles on business ethics written during the first half of this century, one would find that they usually focused on such issues as respect for private property and the immorality of theft, on personal honesty and company loyalty, on the necessity of competition and the immorality of anticompetitive practices, on the honoring of contracts, and on just wages. The controlling assumptions behind this traditional approach to business ethics were (1) that most businesses are small, and are constrained by the pressures of the competitive domestic economy in which they operate and (2) that society's best interests will be achieved by encouraging respect for the elements necessary for the existence of such an economy: competition, private property, freedom of contract, employee loyalty, and so on. Since the 1920s, however, it has become increasingly clear that these assumptions no longer adequately characterize our economy. The major economic institution is no longer the small business but the large multinational corporation with thousands of employees in dozens of plants; most of the basic industrial markets are no longer competitive in the classical sense but are now highly concentrated and dominated by a relatively few large oligopolies; and the large-scale operations and technologies that modern corporations employ have social and environmental impacts that escape traditional market control mechanisms. In this changed business environment the traditional ethic with its outdated assumptions was no longer able to identify and answer the major new ethical questions that the modern manager faced: questions of market power, oligopoly competition, pollution, the quality of working life, occupational health, race relations, affirmative action, foreign bribery, consumer safety and welfare, privacy, weapons production, corporate governance, disclosure, organizational politics, conflicts of interest. If business schools were to adequately prepare managers for the real world they would have to develop new methods of ethical analysis that could deal with these issues, and they would have to arm their students with these ethical tools.

The second factor that forced business schools to pay more attention to ethics was the creation of the professional manager. As firms began to combine into large integrated corporations at the end of the nineteenth century, they created a pressing need for people skilled in administering the complexities of large-scale organizations.[3] The administrative skills needed to coordinate the activities of hundreds of employees working in a dozen different locations became a prized commodity, first for the railroad industry, then for manufacturing, and last, in our own day, for retailors and financial institutions. To meet this need colleges eventually developed specialized business (or "commercial") curricula designed to impart the generalized administrative and financial skills for which large-scale organizations were calling. The professional manager was born: a person whose basic role was to manage the resources of large-scale organizations and who entered this role after a period of specialized training in a professional school. Because of their training and because of the position they occupied, professional managers were able to exert considerable power over several constituencies who now depended on their expertise: stockholders, workers, consumers, and creditors. The question that the possession of these advantages began to raise in business schools was: What professional norms should govern managers in exercising these specialized skills on behalf of their less knowledgeable and less powerful constituencies?[4] As management has become professionalized, therefore, it has begun to seek what every profession eventually seeks: a set of ethical standards that can guide professionals in using these specialized skills and power on behalf of their more vulnerable clients. Inevitably, business schools have become the focus of this search for a set of ethical norms that can govern managers in their professional activities.

The third factor that has led business schools to develop new ethics programs has been the rise in public pressures on business that have developed over the last two decades. First there have been the pressures from external public interest groups—including consumer advocacy groups, environmental groups, and various ethnic and women's groups—who perceive businesses as unresponsive to their morally legitimate concerns. A second set of pressures came from the corporation's own internal constituencies, including employees and unions, which have demanded safer and more satisfying working conditions, and stockholder groups who have proposed shareholder resolutions on socioethical issues as diverse as investments in South Africa, the sale of infant formula in Third World countries, redlining, military sales, and so on. And, third, there have been the public pressures that have taken the form of laws and regulations including the Equal Employment Opportunity Act, the Air Pollution Control Act, the Truth in Lending Act, and the Foreign Corrupt Practices Act, all of which were prompted by what the public perceived as improper corporate practices. These three kinds of pressures have made it imperative for businesses to find ways of bringing ethical considerations into their decision-making process. Again, business schools have been forced to respond to this need by taking ethics training more seriously.

For a variety of reasons, then, professional schools of business have now begun to offer managers enrolled in their on-campus programs (in MBA programs as well as in shorter "leadership training" programs) an opportunity to study business ethics. Periodic surveys conducted during the 1970s, in fact, have revealed an astonishing increase in the number of professional schools offering special courses in socioethical issues.[5] This trend accelerated in 1976 when the main accrediting agency for business schools (the American Assembly of Collegiate Schools of Business) required all accredited business schools to include in their programs the study of "ethical considerations." Innumerable courses on socioethical issues in business have been developed since then. These courses have tended to focus on four main kinds of issues:

Business Law Courses   These courses are aimed at giving the manager an understanding of current law as it affects the manager and the business firm. They are generally taught by faculty with a legal background and tend to incorporate a study of case law and descriptions of legal statutes. Typical topics would include the law of agency, the law of corporations, product liability, contracts, and so on.

Regulatory Environment Courses   These courses aimed at giving the manager an understanding of how regulatory policy is formed, how it may be influenced, and how corporations can respond to it. They are sometimes indistinguishable from courses on public policy formation and on the structure of government agencies. Typical topics include the history and activities of the federal regulatory agencies, antitrust regulation, consumer regulation, environmental law, and so on.

Social Issues Courses   These courses are aimed at giving the manager a broad understanding of social institutions and of current social concerns, an understanding of how these concerns impact on and affect the firm, and an understanding of the processes by which firms can and do respond to these concerns. They tend to rely heavily on the social sciences to provide a basic framework for analysis. The faculty comes from a diversity of backgrounds, including economists, political scientists, and professors of management and even marketing. Topics typically include business–government relations, business ideologies, social responsibility, consumerism, corporate governance and disclosure, ecology, and worker health and safety.

Philosophical Courses   These courses aim at giving the manager an understanding of various ethical concepts and of various issues concerning the nature and proper social role of business. Some take an explicitly religious approach, whereas others draw from secular moral philosophy; some focus on the personal moral conduct of the individual manager, and others focus more on broader socioethical issues raised by corporate conduct; still others focus on a philosophical analysis of the corporation, profits, advertising, the economy, and so on.

These courses are generally quite successful at what they do. But they do not always provide the ethical and social understanding that, I think, is essential to meet the growing needs for moral education in management that I sketched above. Courses that focus on law and government regulatory processes may give the impression that the only responsibility of the manager is to obey the law or perhaps to influence the lawmaker. Courses that focus on social issues sometimes smuggle in unexamined normative assumptions and may fail to address the basic moral issues that face managers today. And courses that focus on philosophy are usually too abstract and neither oriented enough toward managerial concerns nor well integrated with basic social science research.

Ideally, I believe, if on-campus training in business ethics is to meet the needs of the managers I described earlier, it should incorporate components found in all four kinds of courses, as well as others that are sometimes overlooked. I shall try to describe the sorts of things that training in business ethics should include by describing the sorts of competencies that training in business ethics should develop. As the reader will see, some of these competencies demand a background that no single academic discipline can provide.

THE DEVELOPMENT OF MORAL SENSIBILITY

Lawrence Kohlberg, a leading psychologist, has developed a typology of moral development that conceives of moral development as the expansion of one's concerns so as to include an ever-widening range of persons and interests.[6] The individual matures morally as he or she learns first to satisfy his or her own interests and to deal with others in doing so. At a second or "conventional" level of development, the individual expands his or her concerns to include not only self-interest, but also the interests and norms of the groups to which he or she personally belongs: the family, peer groups, the nation, the firm. At this more developed stage the interests of the individual are seen as subordinate to the beliefs and needs of the group and one's own society. At the third or "post-conventional" level of development, the individual expands his or her concerns to encompass the welfare of humanity as a whole and expresses this concern by appealing to the universal concepts of justice, human rights, and social welfare.

One way of looking at the task of the teacher of ethics is to see the teacher as someone who facilitates this development. That is, the task of the teacher of ethics is to provide for his or her client a set of experiences and concepts that will enable the client to understand, appreciate, and employ the universal point of view that Kohlberg calls the "post-conventional" level of moral development. The task of the teacher of ethics, in short, is to help the manager become adept at habitually incorporating the interests of others into his or her decisionmaking processes.

Ethics is definitely not to be equated with feeling. Nonetheless, the study of ethics becomes a sterile and irrelevant intellectual exercise if it does not engage the learner's feelings in the developmental process described above. A prerequisite to being able to incorporate the interests of others into one's decisionmaking processes is that one be able to feel, to empathize, with those who are affected by one's decisions. The manager studying ethics, then, must learn how to regularly put himself or herself in the position of other persons; learn how others perceive a situation; learn to sense what others feel and suffer. Without this ability to identify with and care for others on a sensible level, it is simply impossible to examine the moral dimensions of life in any meaningful way.

The device that many teachers of business ethics, including myself, have found most useful for developing this sensitizing process is the case discussion. The members of a class are presented with a description of a situation in which a manager or a firm has to make some hard moral choices, or they are asked to write up situations that they have personally encountered in their own work experiences. The members of the class are then encouraged to look at the situation from various points of view; they are encouraged to vicariously put themselves in the positions of the various actors; they are encouraged to challenge and question each other's responses to the case; they are asked to select the morally relevant features of the case; and they are asked to find a rationally defensible resolution for the case that adequately takes into account the interests of everyone involved. In my view, case discussions are an essential component of teaching business ethics. Case discussions provide an understanding of the practical difficulties and pressures that managers must face when trying to bring ethics into their everyday decisions, and, if carefully selected, they ensure that the topics and issues discussed are relevant to the daily concerns of the members of the class.

THE DEVELOPMENT OF MORAL REASONING

It is not enough to respond emotionally to a moral problem. Any course in business ethics should develop the cognitive and reasoning skills of the manager. First, the manager must learn to recognize a moral issue and then be able to identify the moral issues embedded in a managerial situation even when that situation is described in nonmoral economic language.

Second, the manager must be able to identify the factors and alternatives relevant to resolving a given moral issue and to separate them from the irrelevant factors. Three kinds of skills are needed: First, the manager must learn to look for the ways in which decisions impact on the well-being of persons: Who benefits and who is harmed? Second, the manager must become sensitive to the moral rights of the individuals affected by the decision. Third, the manager must learn to notice the distributional effects of a decision: How are benefits and burdens distributed among the members of the group affected by his or her decision?

Third, and most importantly, the manager must learn to order these factors in a coherent framework that will allow him or her to adopt a rationally defensible position on the moral issues confronted and to communicate this position to others in an intelligible language. This means that the manager should have an ability to use the basic moral ideas: justice, human rights, social welfare, liberty, moral obligation, moral paternalism, human dignity, and autonomy. But more critically, it means that the manager should have a working familiarity with some of the fundamental criteria or principles that have been developed to deal with moral issues. Since this is the most critical aspect, I shall describe the sort of principles that I have in mind and the way in which they might be approached in courses on business ethics.

Three kinds of principles come immediately to mind. First, and perhaps most familiar, are the principles that concentrate on the consequences that decisions or policies have on the well-being of all the persons directly or indirectly affected by the decision or policy. These are called "utilitarian" principles and they hold that:

> Of any two decisions or policies, the morally better decision or policy is the one that will produce the greatest net social benefits or the least net social harm.

Different kinds of utilitarian principles can be developed by varying what counts as a social benefit and what counts as social harm.[7] The basic strategy behind all utilitarian principles, however, can be summarized in three steps: First, the decisionmaker must identify each of the practical alternatives open to him or her. Second, the decisionmaker must, as carefully as possible (within whatever time and financial constraints are present), determine the social benefits and the social costs each alternative will produce (if possible in quantifiable terms). Third, the decisionmaker should select the alternative that promises to produce the greatest net social benefit.

A second family of principles focuses on the right that each individual has to be treated in certain ways, regardless of the benefits or costs that such treatment might involve. The classical examples of these kinds of principles are those developed by Immanuel Kant. One principle he developed is as follows:

> A person's decision (or policy) is morally right only if it treats others in ways in which the decisionmaker would be willing to have everyone (including himself) be treated whenever they were in similar circumstances.[8]

To employ Kant's principle, the decisionmaker must move through a two-step process. First, the decisionmaker must identify the circumstances that in his or her mind call for that decision. Second, the decisionmaker must ask whether he or she would want to live in a society in which everyone, when they were confronted with similar circumstances, made decisions with similar sorts of effects. If the decisionmaker would not want to live in such a society, then the decision is wrong.

Another principle that Kant developed is:

> A person's decision (or policy) is morally right only if the decision does not use others merely as a means for advancing the decisionmaker's own interests, but also both respects and develops their capacity to choose freely for themselves.[9]

This version of Kant's principle implies that human beings each have an equal dignity that sets them apart from things like tools or machines and which is incompatible with being manipulated, deceived, or otherwise unwillingly exploited to satisfy self-interest. The principle in effect says that a person should not be treated as an object incapable of free choice, that is, not treated in ways to which he or she did not give his or her free informed consent nor in ways that diminish his or her capacity to choose freely. By this principle, for example, an employee may legitimately be asked to perform the unpleasant (or even dangerous) tasks involved in a job, if she freely (knowingly and voluntarily) consented to take the job understanding that it would involve these tasks. But it would be wrong to subject an employee to health risks without her knowledge. The principle would exclude the use of deception, force, manipulation, or other coercive kinds of treatment. In general it would require that consumers, workers, and investors be provided with whatever information they need to make choices that are rational and in accord with their personal preferences and well-being.

Finally, a third family of principles focuses on the distributional effects of decisions: What effect will a decision have on the fairness with which benefits and burdens are distributed in a group. These kinds of principles are usually called principles of justice.[10] The most fundamental principle of justice is that equals should be treated equally and unequals unequally. Or, in more detail:

> Individuals who are similar in all relevant respects should be given similar benefits and burdens, and individuals who are dissimilar in the relevant respects ought to be treated dissimilarly in proportion to their dissimilarity.[11]

Suppose, for example, that Tom and Bill are both doing the same work for me and that there are no relevant differences between them or the work they are doing. Then, in justice, I should pay them equal wages. But if Tom has been working twice as long as Bill and if length of working time is the relevant basis for determining wages for the kind of work they are doing, then to be just I should pay Tom twice as much as Bill. There are a number of hard questions connected with this basic principle of justice, of course, particularly with what counts as a "relevant" difference between individuals. A manager, for example, may be forced to make hard choices between using seniority or using merit as the basis for deciding who is to be given preference in a job training program.

Each of these three kinds of principles focuses on an aspect of moral issues that is not emphasized by the others. Because no single kind of principle fully analyzes all the factors relevant to making a moral decision, the decisionmaker should be familiar with the three kinds of principles and with the three kinds of morally relevant facts that each principle forces him to consider. Occasionally, of course, the principles may conflict with each other: A decision that respects the moral rights of certain individuals may not be the one that produces the greatest net social benefits. In such cases the decisionmaker has no recourse but to conscientiously weigh the conflicting moral factors presented by each principle, and opt for the one that he or she conscientiously judges to be the most important in the circumstances at hand. It is not always an easy matter.

THE DEVELOPMENT OF PERSONAL RESPONSIBILITY

It is not enough for the manager to be provided with an array of criteria for determining what is right and what is wrong. The manager must also have an understanding of when he or she is responsible for doing right and when he or she is excused from doing wrong. Here, too, there is a long moral tradition that can offer some help and guidance to the manager if it is adequately adapted.

Responsibility has traditionally been analyzed in terms of three factors: freedom, knowledge, and causality.[12] To the extent that a decisionmaker is not free to act otherwise, he is not responsible for the harmful consequences of his decision; to the extent that those consequences are unknown to him, he is also not responsible; and to the extent that the consequences do not result from his action or inaction, he is again not responsible.

Training in business ethics should provide familiarity with the concepts of freedom, knowledge, and causality, not in the abstract, but as they relate directly to a managerial context. What kinds of corporate pressures, rewards, sanctions, and performance standards are operative on the manager at different levels of the corporation? What effects do the culture of the corporation and pressures to conform to this culture have on the individual? To what extent do these various pressures narrow the manager's freedom? What kinds of information systems exist in the corporation? What kinds of information do these systems carry and what do they systematically filter out? How do these information systems affect the knowledge of the various managers within the firm? What kinds of control systems does the corporation have? How are decisions made and how are they monitored? What implications do the absence of effective controls have on the manager's responsibility? These are the sorts of questions that training in business ethics should examine if it is to develop an informed sense of moral responsibility.

DEVELOPING AN UNDERSTANDING OF THE MANAGERIAL AND SOCIAL CONTEXTS

In order to apply moral principles to the real world, the decisionmaker must have some information and theory about what the world is really like. The instructor who hopes to teach business ethics, therefore, must approach the subject armed with a knowledge of the political, economic, legal, and social characteristics of the world within which business organizations operate. This is no easy task: There are a number of complex topics that courses in business ethics should address and which require the teacher of business ethics to have some familiarity with the findings and theories of the social sciences. Let me suggest some of the more important subjects and indicate the background data these topics call for.

Employee Rights

Several factors have led to an increased interest in the question of employee rights: (a) the perception that managers exercise substantial discretionary power over their subordinates and that modern technology has effectively expanded this power, and (b) the human relations movement, which has brought the concept of human dignity into the workplace. Several distinct rights have been discussed during the last few years, including: the right to privacy, that is, the right of the employee to do whatever he or she chooses to do outside working hours and the right to control information about his or her own private life; the right to freedom of conscience, that is, the right to refrain from carrying out any order that violates the commonly accepted moral, legal, or religious norms to which the employee adheres; the right to due process, that is, the right to a fair and impartial hearing when the employee believes that his or her rights are being violated; the right to participate, that is, the right to be informed about and to take part in the decisions that affect the employee.[13] Recent discussions of these rights raise several questions. Do employees have these moral rights? How far do these rights extend? What are their limits? To answer these questions one must know something about the ways in which managers exercise authority and the kinds of information and control that effective management requires. Not only must one have a grasp of moral principles, then, but also these principles must be integrated with a detailed knowledge of how large-scale organizations function.

Organizational Politics

Every large-scale organization provides ample opportunity for employees to exercise their political and manipulative skills. Employees within organizations may find themselves embroiled in intrigues, in ongoing battles for organizational resources, in feuding between coalitions, in scrambles for career advancement, and in maneuvering to influence organizational goals. Employees use a variety of political tactics in these maneuverings, including image-building, associating with the influential, blaming or attacking others at critical moments, withholding information, using innuendo to create a desired impression, developing allies, making others feel obligated to oneself, and so on. Obviously, such political behaviors can become manipulative and deceptive; they can injure those who themselves have few political skills; and they can be used to advance narrow interests at the expense of wider organizational or social goals. The teaching of business ethics should address the moral issues raised by these behaviors.[14] What separates morally legitimate and necessary organizational politics from those that are unethical? To answer this question requires some understanding of organizational behavior and some familiarity with how people function in different organizational contexts. Moral principles cannot by themselves provide such understanding; here the teacher of business ethics has to rely heavily on the experience of the business manager and the findings of the organizational theorist.

Affirmative Action

Although affirmative action programs have been undertaken by virtually every large corporation, there are still many misunderstandings, doubts, and questions about their moral legitimacy. My own view is that affirmative action programs are morally legitimate instruments for achieving morally legitimate ends. But this is a view that one can adopt only after struggling with several messy kinds of questions: What kind of moral justification, if any, do these programs have? Does preferential treatment for women or minorities constitute a form of reverse discrimination? Do such programs provide any social benefits? Do they respect the rights of individuals? Will they result in a more just distribution of society's benefits and burdens? These are questions that should be raised when this important issue is examined in courses on business ethics. Answering these questions, however, requires not only an understanding of the moral principles involved, but also a grasp of the sociological context and managerial practicalities that are needed to understand how problems of discrimination can be dealt with most effectively. Here again the teacher of business ethics has to understand how management functions as well as what the social sciences say about discrimination in American society.

Risk and Personal Injury

The terms "risk" and "personal injury" are most often linked in discusssions concerned with two issues: product safety and worker safety. But whether one is concerned with the level of risk appropriate for a consumer product or the level of risk that a worker can reasonably be allowed to carry, the basic ethical questions are largely the same and just as troubling.[15] How much risk of injury should the manager allow customers or workers? What obligations does the manager have to inform workers or consumers of the risk associated with a product or a job? What price should be put on the willingness to carry risk? Do consumer markets and labor markets accurately measure and compensate for risk? Again, these are not questions that can be answered by a simpleminded appeal to moral principles. To answer them one must know something about the costs of information, the costs of insurance, the patterns of consumer and employee preferences, and the structure of consumer and labor markets. Consequently, although questions of risk and personal injury are particularly acute and urgent, especially for managers involved in manufacturing, they cannot be very deeply and adequately discussed by the teacher unless he or she joins hands with economists, knowledgeable engineers, and experienced managers.

Political Activities

Several well-known events have made political issues an important topic for business ethics: the discovery of the illegal domestic campaign contributions and foreign payoffs that companies were making during the Watergate era; the rising level of government regulatory activity that has taken place over the last two decades; the organization of the Business Roundtable and other corporate lobbies; the legalization of political action committees within corporations; court decisions approving the use of advocacy advertising to influence the electorate. All of these events raise questions about the moral propriety of influencing local, state, and federal political processes. What methods of influence are appropriate and what methods are inappropriate? What political activities can legitimately be expected of the employee and which cannot? What kinds of lobbying and advertising are appropriate and which are not? Not only do these moral issues have no easy solutions, but it is clear that they also require the expertise of the political scientist since they require an understanding of the functions of government, a knowledge of the effects of political lobbying and political advertising, and a familiarity with the law on political action committees, lobbying, and so on.

Market Ethics

To a large extent, we are still a market-oriented society. And markets, if they are to function effectively, must impose on their participants a special set of norms. In particular, normative prohibitions on theft, price collusion, the evasion of contractual obligations, employee disloyalty, and on trespass are necessary components of a market ethic. A course on business ethics should, I think, examine these aspects of a market ethic. To what extent are they still justified? How have changes in our society made them irrelevant? What do they mean within the context of large bureaucratic organizations? Providing adequate analyses of these questions also, I believe, requires more than an acquaintance with ethical theory. Adequate analysis calls for some knowledge of the structure and functions of modern economies and contemporary businesses. Here the teacher of business ethics must again join hands with the social scientist and the manager.

External Effects

Environmental pollution is the economist's favorite illustration of an external effect: the effects of producing or using a commodity that are both costly to society and that are not incorporated into the market price of the commodity. They are costs that escape the discipline of the market. There are other kinds of external effects besides pollution, of course, including the effects of closing down or relocating a plant, the effects that corporate activities have on a manager's family life, the effect that the operations of a firm have on urban decay, and so on. The problems all external effects raise, however, are similar: What responsibilities does the firm have toward external constituencies who must bear some of the costs of the firm's activities, when there are no economic reasons for the firm to do anything for these constituencies? Again, this crucial issue should be addressed in courses on business ethics, since it lies at the heart of some of the most pressing moral issues that confront businesses today. But to answer the question requires, again, a knowledge of the effects of business operations: Moral principles are not enough.

CONCLUDING REMARKS

I close with some brief conclusions based on these suggestions concerning the capacities that training in business ethics should develop. First, the moral philosopher cannot teach business ethics all alone. It is necessary to join hands with the social scientist and the practicing manager. Second, business ethics is still in a very crude stage of development. The topics that I sketched above are developed in only very rudimentary ways. Third, business ethics must, above all, be practical. The topics it addresses and the methods it employs must be inserted into a managerial context, and they should be aimed at making ethical considerations a regular part of decisionmaking in the corporation.

NOTES

1. For a compact description of these kinds of programs see Charles W. Powers and David Vogel, *Ethics in the Education of Business Managers* (Hastings-on-Hudson, New York: The Institute of Society, Ethics, and the Life Sciences, The Hastings Center, 1980).
2. See T. A. Petit, *The Moral Crisis in Management* (New York: McGraw-Hill, 1967).

3. Alfred D. Chandler, Jr., *The Visible Hand* (Cambridge, Mass.: Harvard University Press, Belknap Press, 1977).
4. See Edgar H. Schein, "The Problem of Moral Education for the Business Manager," *Industrial Management Review,* 8 (1966): 3–11.
5. Thomas F. McMahon, *Report on the Teaching of Socio-Ethical Issues in Collegiate Schools of Business/Public Administration,* Center for the Study of Applied Ethics, University of Virginia, 1975; Rogene Buchholz, *Business Environment/Public Policy; A Study of Teaching and Research in Schools of Business and Management,* Center for the Study of American Business, Working Paper No. 41, 1979.
6. Lawrence Kohlberg, "Moral Stages and Moralization: The Cognitive–Developmental Approach," in Thomas Lickona, ed., *Moral Development and Behavior: Theory, Research and Social Issues* (New York: Holt, Rinehart and Winston, 1976), pp. 31–53.
7. Thomas A. Klein, *Social Costs and Benefits of Business* (Englewood Cliffs, N.J.: Prentice-Hall, 1977), applies utilitarian principles to contemporary business decisions; Henry Sidgwick, *Outlines of the History of Ethics,* 5th ed. (London: 1902) traces the history of utilitarian thought.
8. Immanuel Kant, *Groundwork of the Metaphysics of Morals,* translated by H. J. Paton (New York: Harper & Row, 1964), p. 70; I have paraphrased Kant's principle in order to avoid a lengthy explanation of his technical vocabulary.
9. Ibid., p. 105; again, I have paraphrased Kant to avoid his technical vocabulary.
10. For a discussion of various principles of justice, see Norman E. Bowie, *Towards a New Theory of Distributive Justice* (Amherst: The University of Massachusetts Press, 1971).
11. C. Perelman, *The Idea of Justice and the Problem of Argument* (New York: Humanities Press, 1963), p. 16.
12. For a traditional analysis of moral responsibility see Henry J. Wirtenberger, *Morality and Business* (Chicago: Loyola University Press, 1962), pp. 14–30.
13. All are discussed in Alan F. Westin and Stephen Salisbury, eds., *Individual Rights in the Corporation* (New York: Pantheon, 1980).
14. Gerald Cavanagh; Dennis Moberg; and Manuel Velasquez, "The Ethics of Organizational Politics," *Academy of Management Review,* 6; 3 (July 1981): 363–374.
15. William W. Lowrance, *Of Acceptable Risk* (Los Altos, Calif.: William Kaufmann, 1976).

PART III

The Practical Application of Ethics in Business

Chapter 8

Essentials of an Ethical Corporate Climate

Gerald E. Ottoson

*Neglecting to take steps to insure an ethical corporate cli-
mate has proved to be an ill-considered risk for many organizations. Tarnished reputations, costly reparations, and ruined careers
are just some of the results that have accompanied revelations of
unethical business practice. It is easier—and cheaper—to take preventive measures than to live with the consequences.*

The world has been waiting for the day when a disclosure of mal-
feasance in the ranks would be followed by an admission from the
top that at least *some* of the fault lay there. It has been a long wait.
"Mea culpa" is not a popular phrase with executives, be they from
business, government, a university, or any other institution. The
eagerness with which leaders claim credit for excellent results
achieved by their organizations is rarely matched by their prompt-
ness in accepting blame when unethical conduct is uncovered. On
such occasions, they may opt to don the cloak of the betrayed, the
innocent, the deceived, or the overburdened. Rarely will the gar-
ment selected be a hair shirt.

The disclaimers are many and, it should quickly be pointed out,
sincere. No one here is saying that the dismay of the executive who
is confronted with shady dealings within the organization is anything but genuine. Statements like "I trusted them and they betrayed
me," "I had no way of knowing," "They kept me in the dark," and
"I was too busy with high level concerns to get involved in the details" are the shocked reactions of the leader who has just been surprised by an embarrassing disclosure within the ranks and is using
the "I didn't know it was loaded" defense.

The point is that the gun of temptation is always loaded. All of us
are heirs to human frailty. When the opportunity to cut corners is
coupled with the anonymity provided by a large and complex organization, there exists a potentially explosive situation.

Over the past decade or so two new elements have been added to the scene. For one, in times of shortages and economic stress the pressure to yield to temptation is always intensified. One needs only to recollect the gasoline lines of the late 1970s to recall how limited access to scarce resources affected many of us.

The second factor is that the public has become far less forgiving of transgressions in the business community. There is no need to review all the reasons for the new social awareness, but it does exist and it demands a higher standard of ethical conduct than ever before. These two new elements dictate that more attention be paid to the prevention of questionable dealings. It is no longer appropriate to ask, "How can we minimize our losses if an unethical business act becomes the headline of tomorrow's newspaper?" More and more thoughtful leaders are now beginning to seek answers to the question, "What can we do to prevent such occurrences in the future?" As an answer, I suggest we can *dis*courage unethical conduct in organizations by employing the same kinds of strategies we use now to *en*courage constructive and beneficial actions. We claim to know how to motivate subordinates to do good work. We should be able to use that knowledge with equal skill to help our employees avoid ethical pitfalls. I was recently asked how to create an institutional climate that would discourage unethical conduct. I listed five key conditions, all of which are already commonly accepted as positive motivators of performance. They are, in broad terms, Communication, Example, Objective Setting, Monitoring, and Reinforcement.

As we examine each of them, it will become apparent that we already have the ability to create organizational environments that will promote ethical awareness. The principles are known; however, we need to develop applications.

COMMUNICATION

The first condition that must exist is a written code of ethics —a series of clear, specific, and direct statements from the very top that define in unmistakable terms the ethical standards that the organization demands. It is not essential, but certainly highly desirable, for these statements to be collected in one place. Whether they are bound in a separate document or issued as a part of a larger manual is not important. What is critical is that there be no doubt in anyone's mind exactly where the company, the university, or the government agency stands in how it wants its people to conduct their business affairs.

In industry, clear definition of performance standards is typical in establishing production quotas, accounting procedures, and quality control limits, to name but a few. Such standards are always in writing—and never left to the uncertainties of oral communication. They are always all in one place. There is no reason why behavior standards cannot be communicated with equal care. The codifier of ethical directives should be aware, however, that writing down the organization's guides of conduct is not as easy as it might first appear. There are two traps and they are almost completely opposite each other.

The first impulse is to write the code of ethical conduct in broad and ringing declarations. The trouble with these sweeping generalities is that they quickly take on the air of motherhood statements. They are so broad and so general that they give people little or no guidance in their day-to-day behavior. Going to the other extreme may be even more dangerous, however. Setting out detailed rules in an attempt to cover all conceivable situations creates such a huge volume of specifics that people tend to use the rulebook as a complete guide to action. There is a tendency to substitute rules for judgment. The hidden danger is the temptation to use the absence of a direct rule as a reason for plunging ahead even when one's conscience says "no."

Rules that are set down initially with the expectation that they will be floors for ethical behavior soon become interpreted as ceilings for it. People rationalize their actions by saying, "It's not covered in the Rule Book so it must be OK."

For the written statements in the code of ethical conduct to be useful to the employees of the corporation, to the faculties and administrations of the universities, or to the servants in the public agencies, they have to be somewhere between these two extremes. They have to be guides for behavior and standards for conduct but not fixed rules by which all decisions are controlled. An excellent example of a well-constructed document is "A Code of Worldwide Business Conduct" of the Caterpillar Tractor Company.

Example

Having made clear statements of what is expected in the way of ethical conduct within the organization, we come to the second condition that is essential. It grows from the first. It is simply that examples must be set from the top of, and throughout, the organization that will demonstrate the substance and the vitality of those statements. The examples may be of many kinds. The one that comes most readily to mind is that the professional conduct of the most visible people in the organization—the top echelon—must be beyond reproach. The rest of the organization will follow the example of those to whom it looks for leadership. If the leadership indicates anything less than a total commitment to the codes of conduct that have already been expressed, the rest of the unit will surely follow the unspoken word rather than pattern itself after what it sees as empty phrases.

Another way that examples can be set is through programs of action sponsored by the institution. Such programs invariably require the investment of time, money, or both, making them visible proof of the organization's sincerity in matching deeds to words. The opportunities are endless. A few examples follow.

One "Fortune 500" company conducts a three-day executive seminar entirely devoted to discussions and analyses of corporate business ethics. Maintaining this program costs the company a considerable sum, but, because there is a real concern for making certain that all of the executives are constantly aware of and sensitive to their obligations regarding business ethics, the company continues to underwrite the program. Attendance at the seminar is looked on as a badge of distinction. The participants are proud to be involved and proud of their company's sponsorship of the program.

Another example is a very large effort, called Product Responsibility, in one of the leading chemical companies. The program, in essence, says that the company feels a responsibility for all of the products it makes and sells. It feels this responsibility from the time raw materials come into one of its manufacturing plants until the product is sold to a customer, used by the customer, and ultimately disposed of, either by the customer or the consumer. The company insists, for instance, that all of its customers handle the products in a way that is safe and that will endanger neither individuals nor the environment. It has canceled sales contracts with customers who are either unable or unwilling to follow the prescribed standards. Any business person who has ever turned down a sale knows how painful that can be. This company, however, feels that the discomfort of turning down a sale is considerably less than the uneasiness it would feel if it sold to a customer whose integrity could not be trusted.

Perhaps one of the most constructive ways in which a commitment to an ethical business posture can be demonstrated is to become involved in the community and its concerns. Opportunities are many, including supporting charitable causes; participating in community fund-raising campaigns; and giving grants to colleges and universities, special incentives to encourage greater participation by minorities, or grants to public television—the list can go on and on. Many companies not only sponsor such activities but also make it attractive for their employees to become involved. Matching gift programs, giving time off for community service, and granting leaves of absence for *pro bono publico* work are all ways of encouraging individuals to recognize their roles in the wider community.

OBJECTIVE SETTING

I am convinced that most of the unethical acts I have seen committed in business were performed by essentially honest people. But they were people who felt under great pressure to achieve. In their desire to make good—to "win"—they compromised themselves. Here we see decent, law-abiding human beings, the kind of neighbors we all cherish, suddenly engaging in behavior totally contrary to our expectations and their own values. What goes wrong? In the majority of cases the breakdown can be traced to a feeling that results are all that matter and superiors are not concerned with the means employed.

Of course we all must strive for excellence, but we also must attempt to stimulate subordinates to greater productivity. In our enthusiasm to get things done, in our natural desire to compete, and in the internal urge we all feel to achieve, it is very easy to convey the impression to one's subordinates that the results—the end—are all that matter; we imply that they should keep their eyes on the goal and not worry too much about the means employed in getting there.

The message, "we only pay off on results," is rarely conveyed directly. It is usually transmitted unconsciously when high expectations and great challenges are being voiced with more enthusiasm than thought. We must always school ourselves and the people around us to remember that we do ourselves, our employees, and our companies a great disservice by exerting unconscionable pressure on our subordinates.

If the word is simply passed to "cut costs," no one should be surprised later to find that indiscriminate personnel cuts have been made toward that end. When the human resources of an organization are looked upon only as means of achieving budget cuts, the dignity of individuals will run a poor second. If, in the face of rising stores of unsold inventory, a forceful executive demands that his sales force "Move that product!" he is inviting any number of unethical practices designed to empty the warehouse.

What do events like these tell us about objective setting? Three things. First, the establishing of goals must be a joint process, shared by subordinate and superior alike. When targets are imposed on people, it violates their fundamental concept of self-determination. All of us are entitled to the right to know and to either consent or dissent in matters affecting us. To deny a subordinate a role in the process of objective setting invites the following mode of thinking: "I had no say in the whole thing so I take no responsibility in how it is to be done either."

Second, the objectives need to be reasonable. One of the real strengths of the joint process of goal setting is the balancing effect of two intellects mulling over the same challenge. No benefit will result to the company, or the individual involved, if the objective is set so low that no incremental effort is required. A major purpose of goal setting is to develop intellectual strength through the "stretching exercises" required to reach new plateaus of achievement. To deny an employee this opportunity for growth is neither good business nor good ethics.

There is the potential for a far more serious error, however, if the objective is set unrealistically high, for one of two things is bound to occur. The employee may, after striving unsuccessfully to reach an unattainable goal, give way to discouragement, give up the struggle, and then certainly suffer a loss of self-esteem. Creating situations in which the image of self is diminished is bad ethics. The other course of action that may occur when objectives are seen as unreachable by conventional means is to resort to ethically unacceptable methods. There is no need to chronicle here the painful incidents of bribery, undue influence, price-fixing, reciprocal deals, misleading advertising, and other shameful actions that have attracted so much negative publicity.

It is at this point that the third requirement appears. Most of these incidents could have been prevented if, at the time of objective setting, a sensitive boss would have avoided establishing impossible goals and would have made it clear that *how* the goals are to be reached is as important as what the goal is. If the boss fails in either regard, the boss is being callous to the ethical demands of his or her responsibility. It was mentioned earlier that much of the pressure that results in regrettable methods is unconscious on the part of the boss. The prudent manager will not simply leave "means" to the employee. Conscious, planned discussion is mandated so that there is complete understanding of the ethical standards expected.

MONITORING

There must be some planned process for constantly reviewing the actions of the people within the organization. Clear statements of ethical conviction and the setting of good examples will not automatically ensure that everyone will follow the lead. It would be naive not to have some provision for "minding the store." This simply requires setting up a system of checks and balances. There is no implication of distrust in such a system. The review feature provides a safeguard, and again, a variety of techniques are available.

The most obvious review that all employees receive is from their immediate supervisors. Discussions at this level are generally adequate to resolve any ethical questions. If differences of opinion still exist, appeals up the line for a resolution of the conflict are in order.

The possibility will always exist that a supervisor and employee will agree and will both be wrong in their judgment, or the two of them may act in concert to conceal an action they know to be questionable. In cases like these, simple reviews "up the line" are insufficient; monitoring by other parties is called for.

One of the most useful tools for this purpose is a strong staff organization. The function of a good staff group is exactly that of assisting in determining *how* a task will be done. The line organization decides what it wishes to achieve—the staff should have influence on the means of attaining the desired end. Two sets of individuals—line and staff—who are reporting to different heads can maintain equilibrium.

Another way that this balance can be achieved is by having people report administratively through one line and functionally through another. This dual relationship precludes any kind of action that will not be scrutinized by two quite different parties. The system is demonstrated in companies that use the general manager form of organization structure. The general manager of a product line bears the line responsibility for the performance of the group. Concurrently, there are functional executives who coordinate and control the specific functions (marketing, research, manufacturing, etc.) assigned to them. A simple way of describing the dual roles is to think of the general manager as being concerned with *what* the employees do and the functional officer as controlling *how* they do it.

In recent years there has been an increase in the number of organizations that have established committees, internal and external, with a charter to monitor the activities of the entire unit. The committees may confine their investigations to matters entirely internal or they may look at the impact that certain actions have on external society. When committees of this kind are made up of outside members of the board of directors (or a similar body), they are especially useful since they have no vested interest in protecting either a particular person or a particular unit in the organization. They can do their work with total objectivity.

It is also worth noting the valuable contribution to the maintenance of high standards made by professional groups themselves. Especially in industry, there is significant policing done within professions such as engineering, purchasing, and law, to name but a few.

REINFORCEMENT

The fifth, and final, condition that must be present for the encouragement of an ethical corporate climate is the agreement that virtue will be rewarded while violations of ethical principles will be dealt with promptly. As painful as it may be, when someone is found to have broken any of the codes of ethical conduct in the company, penalties must be imposed. People who have worked in large organizations for any period of time have learned that there is no such thing as a well-kept secret. Any occurrence outside the norm soon becomes known widely. The informal communication network is a highly effective medium for spreading news. We delude ourselves if we think we can conceal or gloss over malpractices of any kind. Not only does the whole workforce soon know of the incident, but they also wait and watch to see the outcome. They do not ask for "frontier justice" but neither will they accept retributive penalties that are scaled inversely with the level of the culprit in the organization. Punishments must be prompt, certain, and appropriate to the gravity of the case. If clearly stated codes of conduct have been forcefully communicated to the organization, then surely anyone who knowingly violates the code must suffer the consequences. Anything less will make a mockery of these statements and will provoke cynical reactions. Cynicism is the mortal enemy of ethics.

On the other hand, there should be procedures built into the organization to reward employees whose actions dignify and strengthen the stated ethical aims of the company. For years, it has been common for companies to recognize individual employees who have done outstanding work in the community by featuring them in company publications. This is an admirable practice and should be continued. There is a need, however, to go beyond just noting such performance in the house organ. More and more, leading corporations are giving great weight to their employees' performances in other than short-term profitability. In a number of cases, as much as 50 percent of an employee's rating for compensation purposes is based on nonfinancial elements—how well the employee has, for instance, participated as a responsible member of the community; how good a job he or she has done in developing staff members under them so that these workers can become more productive, not only for themselves, but for the company; how good a job has been done in ensuring the hiring of the disadvantaged and the handicapped, and how well the promotions of such people have been handled; and any number of things that are not measurable on the bottom line.

To summarize, these five key conditions can be expressed as follows. Clear statements of ethical conduct made from the top, preferably in writing and preferably all in one place; examples set that bear out the notion that we not only preach, but we also practice; objective setting that recognizes the worth and dignity of the individual; monitoring of the activities of everyone within the organization so that we can be constantly aware of what's going on and a system of rewards and punishments set up so that people recognize the fact that we, in the language of the street, "put our money where our mouth is."

We have all the tools and all the knowledge we need to create these conditions. All that is needed is the will.

Chapter 9

Government Regulation
vs.
Self-Regulation
of Marketing Ethics:
A Cost-Benefit Approach

Priscilla A. LaBarbara

During the past decade much attention has been focused on the subject of business ethics in general, and marketing ethics in particular. Marketing comprises those activities that concern the identification of unmet consumer wants, the design of goods and services to satisfy those wants, and the development of distribution systems to bring the goods and services to the customer. In fulfilling its basic objective of satisfying consumer wants and needs, marketing is the most visible function of a business enterprise. Major marketing components such as the product offering and advertising can be directly scrutinized and evaluated by the public. As a result, marketing is the business area that has received the greatest criticism for its unethical practices.

This chapter is concerned with government regulation and industrywide self-regulation as two major approaches to raising the ethical level of marketing practice. Prior to discussing these alternatives, an overview of the ethical dimensions of marketing is presented. Next, the costs and benefits of government regulation and self-regulation of marketing are investigated. Following this discussion, some approaches to raising the ethical consciousness of marketers are outlined. Finally, two examples of successful marketing self-regulation programs are discussed.

THE ETHICAL DIMENSIONS OF MARKETING

A difficult problem with defining ethical marketing practices stems from the fact that everyday marketing activities raise questions of ethics. In a classic book about the responsibilities of the business person, Bowen (1953) raised some basic ethical issues. It is striking that each of Bowen's questions centers on the marketing area in contrast to any of the other business functions:

> Should he conduct selling in ways that intrude on the privacy of people, for example, by door-to-door selling ... ? Should he use methods involving ballyhoo, chances, prizes, hawking, and other tactics which are at least of doubtful good taste? Should he employ "high pressure" tactics in persuading people to buy? Should he try to hasten the absolescence of goods by bringing out an endless succession of new models and new styles? Should he appeal to and attempt to strengthen the motives of materialism, invidious consumption, and "keeping up with the Joneses?"

Bowen's last question underscores that the very role of marketing in our economy and the values in our society that marketing helps to shape raise ethical concerns. For example, it can be questioned whether demand-creation leads to the distortion of priorities. Such distortion can result in the production and acquisition of more material things, which take precedence over the production and consumption of community goods. Furthermore, it is unknown whether people's desire for more goods, which advertising has stimulated, really contributes to consumer satisfaction and happiness.

In addition to ethical concerns about the general role of marketing, Bowen suggests that there are ethical issues involved in each of the basic components of marketing. The major ethical aspects of the marketing mix—products, pricing, promotion, and distribution—are summarized in Exhibit A. Marketers need to face ethical questions concerning each element of the marketing mix such as the following (Murphy, et al., 1978):

Product: Are technically superior products withheld from consumers until inventories of the inferior version are depleted?

                                 Are non-functional style changes made only to stimulate repeat sales?

                                 Are packaging variations needlessly proliferated and intentially confusing?

Promotion:	Are advertising claims based on unbiased research results?
	Are certain claims exaggerated or embellished?
	Do salespeople utilize questionable psychological pressure to close a sale?
Pricing:	Has management indirectly cut retail price through unpublicized quality or quantity reduction?
	Are dissimilar prices in different markets attributable to the market being insulated by geography or lack of competition rather than actual costs?
Distribution:	Are channel members frequently threatened or coerced to cooperate?
	Are product exchanges and warranty protection rapidly provided?
	Are repair services and estimates offered in an evasive manner?

In addition, there is concern over the ethics of marketing researchers (Bezilla et al., 1976; Crawford, 1970; Tybout and Zaltman, 1974). Ethical dimensions of research include failure to provide subjects with promised anonymity, deceiving subjects about the real objective of the study, and the failure to preserve the confidentiality of research results.

There is also a growing interest in the ethical practice of international marketing. Events of recent years, particularly the disclosure by scores of U.S. companies of illegal or questionable foreign payments, have intensified concern over the development of international codes of conduct. An excellent review and analysis of international business ethics and codes of conduct are found in Chance (1978).

The ethical level of marketing practice may be raised through government intervention or through marketing self-regulation. In this chapter self-regulation refers to *industrywide* programs of voluntary control in contrast to individual corporate attempts at self-policing. To evaluate government regulation vs. self-regulation of marketing, the benefits as well as the costs of each alternative should be determined. Measuring the costs of regulation is very

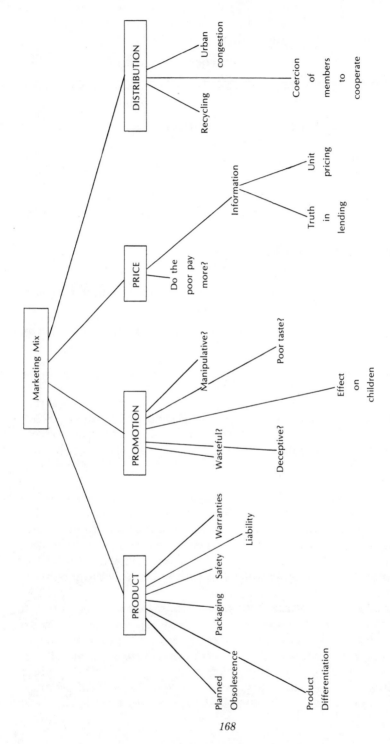

Exhibit A. Ethical dimensions of the marketing mix.

Source: Adapted from Reed Moyer and Michael D. Hutt, *Macro Marketing* (Santa Barbara: John Wiley & Sons, 1978).

complex, but measuring the benefits may be impossible (Hughes et al., 1979). In addition to the usual economic dimensions, the benefits and costs of regulation have social and psychological elements that make their measurement extremely difficult. Despite these problems, an attempt will be made to assess the costs and payoffs of both imposed and voluntary regulation of marketing.

GOVERNMENT REGULATION OF MARKETING

Costs

Since 1962 the volume of federal government regulation of business has grown dramatically. Of a total of 83 federal agencies involved in regulating private business practices in 1977, 34 were created after 1960 and 12 were added between 1970 and 1975 (Schultze, 1977). The cost of operating federal regulatory agencies is increasing faster than the gross national product, population of the country, or federal budget as a whole. In 1979 total federal expenditures for the agencies that regulate business were more than double the amount budgeted as recently as 1974 (Weidenbaum, 1978).

Newer areas of social regulation such as consumer safety and health, job safety, and environment and energy represent the major proportion of regulatory budgets as shown in Exhibit B. Agencies involved in this recent type of regulation include the Consumer Product Safety Commission, the Occupational Safety and Health Administration, Environmental Protection Agency, and the Department of Energy. In contrast to traditional regulatory commissions, which have jurisdiction over individual industries, these agencies cover almost all companies.

The output of government agencies in terms of new regulation is also increasing. During the year 1975 the *Federal Register,* which publishes new and proposed government regulations, contained over 60,000 pages. This represented more than a 200 percent increase since 1970 (Lilley and Miller, 1977).

In 1975 the *Federal Register* included 177 proposed new rules, 2865 proposed amendments to existing rules, 309 final rules, and 7305 final rule amendments. This output represented a 14 percent increase over 1974 (Lilley and Miller, 1978). Furthermore, there are 38 volumes of *The Code of Federal Regulations* that sit on a shelf 15 feet long (Warner and Swasey, 1978).

The paperwork associated with implementing government regu-

Exhibit B. Expenditures on Federal Regulatory Activities (Fiscal years; dollar amounts in millions)

Area of Regulation	1974	1975	1976	1977	1978	1979	Increase (1974-1979) (percent)
Consumer safety and health	$1302	$1463	$1613	$1985	$2582	$2671	105
Job safety and other working conditions	310	379	446	492	562	626	102
Environment and energy	347	527	682	870	989	1116	222
Financial reporting, and other financial	36	45	53	58	70	69	92
Industry-specific regulation	245	269	270	309	340	341	39
Total	2240	2683	3064	3714	4543	4823	115

Source: Center for the Study of American Business, Washington University, St. Louis, Missouri.

Note: Percent distribution of federal regulatory expenditures, fiscal year 1979;

Consumer safety and health	56
Job safety and other working conditions	13
Environment and energy	23
Financial reporting and other financial	1
Industry-specific regulation	7
Total	100

lation is probably the most visible cost. The impact of paperwork on individuals, business enterprises, and the government is dramatic. Over 500 million federal forms are completed each year at a cost of hundreds of millions of hours. According to the Commission on Federal Paperwork, the total cost of federal paperwork is estimated at $100 billion each year or approximately, $500 per person. The federal government incurs expenses of $43 billion and state and local governments $5 to $9 billion, whereas it is estimated that private industry spends $25 to $32 billion for paperwork (Commission on Federal Paperwork, 1977).

These costs, however, represent only the economic costs of paperwork. In addition, there are the psychological costs, which include anxiety and frustration from duplication and overlapping jurisdiction. There are also social costs such as a misallocation of resources to paperwork that could be spent on social output (Hughes et al., 1979).

Several individual business firms have estimated their cost of complying with federal regulation. For example, General Motors estimated that in 1977 it spent $41.6 billion to comply with government regulations in comparison to total corporate earnings that year of $3.3 billion. It took the equivalent effort of 24,500 full-time employees to meet federal regulations (*Wall Street Journal,* 1979). Dow Chemical spent $147 million on regulation in 1975. This corporate classified $87 million as "appropriate regulation," $10 million as "questionable," and $50 million as "excessive" costs beyond those required for good business practices. According to estimates, the pharmaceutical industry spends $650 million on regulation or two-thirds of its annual investment in research and development. A further cost of government regulation is the elimination of small firms that are unable to meet the costs of coping with regulations (Hughes et al., 1979).

An interesting study prepared at the Center for the Study of American Business at Washington University concludes that the total cost of complying with federal regulation was $62.3 billion in 1976 or twenty times the direct cost to the taxpayer of supporting the major regulatory agencies (Weidenbaum, 1978). In this study the more reliable estimates of the costs of specific regulatory programs were culled from the available literature. These estimates were put on a consistent and reliable basis and were aggregated for 1976. Generally, for a given regulatory program where a range of costs was available, the lower end was used and in some cases no costs were available. Therefore, the numbers used in the study are conservative and underestimate the actual costs of federal regulation.

Exhibit C summarizes the findings of this study. In this exhibit regulatory costs include costs incurred by both the federal government and private sectors in response to regulation. Administrative costs, listed in the first category, are the expenditures arising from the operation of regulatory activity by the federal government and include such items as government worker salaries and office supplies. The second category, compliance costs, represents the costs incurred mainly by the private sector (as well as state and local governments) in the process of complying with federal regulation. Unlike the administrative costs, these expenditures do not appear in the federal budget and were estimated.

Government regulation also results in structural changes that have long-run effects. These structural changes reduce the incentives for lowering costs, investing in more productive machinery, and investing in research and development. Hughes et al. (1979) examines the behavior of several regulated industries to illustrate these effects.

Other more subtle costs of government regulation are discussed by Leone (1977). For example, institutional relationships between labor and management may also be altered by regulations. Leone concludes that an increase in employee turnover rates was the result of an agreement between the Equal Employment Opportunity Commission and the steel industry.

In addition, new management skills are required to work with the government. Corporations must develop strategies for public policy such as when to cooperate, when to fight, and when to volun-

Exhibit C. Annual Cost of Federal Regulation, by Area, 1975 (in millions of dollars)

Area	Administrative Cost	Compliance Cost	Total
Consumer safety and health	1516	5094	6610
Job safety and working conditions	483	4015	4498
Energy and the environment	612	7760	8372
Financial regulation	104	1118	1222
Industry specific	474	26,322	26,796
Paperwork	(1)	18,000	18,000
Total	3189	62,309	65,498

Source: Center for the Study of American Business, Washington University, St. Louis, Missouri.

(1) Included in other categories.

teer technical information or remain silent (Leone, 1977). Managers must respond to the changing economies of scale that follow new regulations. Costs are incurred for training or hiring the new skills that are necessary.

Ultimately, the increased costs of business are passed on to the consumer. A rather dramatic example of the direct and visible impact of regulation on the prices charged to consumers is the automobile. As a result of the safety and environmental features the government requires producers to incorporate, the cost increase of these mandated features totals $666.00 per car for the period 1968 to 1978 (Defina, 1977). Aside from increased economic costs, consumers must bear intangible psychological and physical costs. Ross (1978) offers examples of intangible costs to consumers that result from public policy designed to control unethical marketing behavior:

> *Psychological cost:* The (Federal Trade Commission's) substantiation program is directed at improving consumer information. It has been theorized, however, that one by-product of the program might be the "chilling" of advertised speech. That is, advertisers might not make certain claims which are, in fact, true and useful for the consumer to hear about because of fear—misplaced or not—that such claims would result in FTC action, with resultant bad publicity and possibly expensive litigation costs for the firm. Clearly, *decreasing* consumer information is just as much a cost as increasing it is a benefit.

> *Physical cost:* Child-resistant containers are required for most drugs by the United States Consumer Product Safety Commission. These containers are frequently hard to open for average people and occasionally next to impossible for the elderly or infirm. Although exempt containers are available, many of those who need them probably don't have them. If medication cannot be used when needed because an elderly consumer cannot get the regulated container open, there would appear to be a physical cost imposed by the rule.

Brummet (1978) develops a useful framework for assessing the costs of government regulation. This categorization is shown in Exhibit D and serves to summarize much of the foregoing discussion.

Benefits

The potential beneficiaries of government regulation include consumers, labor, industry, regulators, and society in general. Diffi-

Exhibit D. A Framework for Cost Assessment

I. Public sector costs—costs of enactment, enforcement, monitoring, and reenactment of legislation and regulation

II. Private sector costs
   1. Cost of compliance
   2. Cost of compliance assurance

III. Social costs—externalities
   1. Cost of suboptimal resource allocation
   2. Cost of loss of productivity
   3. Cost of decreased capital formation
   4. Cost of dampening of innovation
   5. Cost of developing new required management skills
   6. Cost of suboptimal industry structure through discouraging of smaller firms

---

Source: R. Lee Brummet, "Measuring the Cost of Regulation." In *The Dialogue That Happened,* Proceedings of Workshop on the Private Cost of Regulation, edited by G. David Hughes and E. Cameron Williams, pp. 80–81. Cambridge, Mass.: Marketing Science Institute, August 1979.

culty in measuring the benefits of regulation is compounded by the fact that perceived benefits are related to a person's values. It is therefore necessary to understand the values of all potential beneficiaries of regulation in both the short and long run (Hughes 1979).

To illustrate, each individual probably has his or her own idea of the extent to which the government ought to intervene in market affairs even for the purpose of protecting consumers. For example, some consumers may resent the increased cost and restriction of freedom that accompanies government regulation which makes automobile seatbelts mandatory. In contrast, others may point to the benefit of lives saved as a result of seatbelts.

Some idea about the benefits of government regulation can be gained from an assessment of conditions which lead to enactment of the regulation. For example, the Consumer Product Safety Commission is the outcome of the following circumstances: "Each year 30,000 Americans die from injuries sustained in and around the home: 110,000 are permanently disabled; 585,000 are hospitalized; and more than 20,000 are injured seriously enough to require medical treatment or be disabled for a day or more" (Kimble 1975, p. 1). Through regulation the government has alleviated some of the problems related to unsafe products.

Similarly, there are a number of benefits of government regulation that have protected consumers from other unethical marketing practices. Regulation, for example, has helped to achieve cleaner air; permits consumers to change their minds without penalty up to 72 hours after signing a contract with a door-to-door salesperson; and provides key information necessary for consumers to make a sensible choice between rival brands or to decide whether to buy the product at all. Until the government required or induced disclosure, accurate information was not available in the market concerning the durability of light bulbs, octane ratings for gasoline, tar and nicotine content of cigarettes, mileage per gallon for automobiles, or care labeling of textile wearing apparel (Pitofsky, 1977).

To obtain a fair assessment of the benefits of government regulation, it is necessary to link these benefits to the costs that are borne by consumers. Few studies of the benefits of regulation, however, have done this (Hughes et al., 1979).

Studies have shown that some regulatory programs are ineffective. To date, two major studies of the occupational health and safety program (OSHA) have yielded disappointing findings (Ashford, 1976; Smith, 1976). These studies conclude that OSHA has had little measureable impact in reducing injuries and deaths. Many have criticized OSHA for issuing regulations that have little to do with the important causes of worker illness and industrial accidents. George Steiner (1978) points out that trivial and nonsense regulations are not confined to OSHA. Other regulatory agencies are just as guilty of this shortcoming and further fuel inflation.

An alternative to imposed government regulation is voluntary industrywide control. It has been stated that effective marketing self-regulation may serve as a substitute for government regulation (Kirkpatrick, 1972). According to a national survey, 65 percent of the public agrees and strongly agrees that, in general, self-regulation by business itself is preferable to stricter control of business by the government (Barksdale and Perreault, 1980).

Marketing self-regulation programs have been implemented by trade associations and special industrywide groups. Among the marketing self-regulatory programs that may be undertaken by trade associations are codes of ethical selling and promotion practices, mediation or arbitration mechanisms to resolve consumer complaints, product testing and certification programs, and licensing of industry members. Some of the costs and benefits of self-regulation programs are discussed in the following sections.

MARKETING SELF-REGULATION

Costs

Marketers must pay dues to their trade association or special industry group to support self-regulation programs. Unfortunately, there is a dearth of published statistics on the cost of self-regulation. A study I conducted on advertising self-regulation (La Barbara, 1980a) gives some indication of the budgets that are established for voluntary control programs.

Of 22 self-regulatory groups included in the study, 12 report that the 1980 budget for advertising self-regulation is negligible and 5 groups indicate that advertising self-regulation requires only a few thousand dollars. One trade association has a 1980 self-regulation budget of $25,000. Radio and television broadcasters sponsor an advertising self-regulation program that is supported by a budget of about $1 million. The combined budget of the Council of Better Business Bureaus, which operates the most extensive program of advertising self-regulation that covers all national advertising, has a 1980 budget of approximately $2 million.

Another cost of self-regulation for marketers is the sales or profits that may be reduced as a result of adhering to a code of ethics. An example would be the elimination of tasteless advertising or bait and switch advertising, which may be effective in generating sales. Another cost of universal support of a code of ethics is monitoring other marketers' behavior by observing and acting upon code violations (McKean, 1979).

Brummet's framework (see Exhibit D) is also useful for assessing the costs of voluntary regulation. Private programs of regulation would entail the costs of enactment, enforcement, and monitoring of the voluntary guidelines as well as the social costs that Brummet lists. However, the private sector costs of compliance and compliance assurance that involve costly paperwork are largely eliminated with self-regulation.

There is the potential for an additional cost of self-regulation, however, which is not included in Brummet's classification of government regulation costs. Voluntary guidelines and codes of ethics may be used as vehicles to reduce competition within an industry. For example, the provision prohibiting advertising, which was included in the legal and medical codes of ethics, actually discouraged price competition. Such actions result in higher prices for consumers.

But when self-regulation is designed to be in the consumer's interest it can represent cost advantages when compared to government regulation. Self-regulation has at least two economic advantages over government regulation. First, self-regulation involves a minimum of paperwork. Only those marketers who are alleged to violate the code of ethics must get involved with paperwork to support their position. In contrast to government agency requirements, marketers do not need to complete forms demonstrating that they have complied with voluntary standards. Second, marketers need to deal with only one self-regulatory body rather than a plethora of federal, state, and municipal government agencies.

Business may also be better equipped than the government to regulate itself efficiently. According to one top executive, "The bureaucrat is, by background, single-purposed (usually self-perpetuation). He does not present his wares in a competitive environment. He is not accustomed to measuring results of his work" (Eagle, 1973). On the other hand, the marketer is goal-oriented, is knowledgeable about consumer testing and research, and is experienced with problem solving.

In addition, government regulators may not understand the total inflationary impact of their actions. For example, one member of the Consumer Product Safety Commission has stated: "When it involves a product that is unsafe, I don't care how much it costs the company to correct the problem" (Weidenbaum, 1975). Such an attitude can certainly lead to accelerating costs for industry and to solutions that are not the most economical for the businesses involved. One offending company, for instance, did not include a statement mandated by regulation on its labels. Rather than requiring the company to relabel the packages, the government forced it to destroy the products.

Members of government have also stated their frank beliefs concerning the economies of regulation. For example, the former commissioner of the Federal Trade Commission (FTC), Mary Gardiner Jones, states: "I am struck by the potential advantages and economies which could result from the FTC's enforcement efforts if it could find the means by which to encourage and strengthen industry self-regulation programs" (Jones, 1969).

Benefits

As with government regulation, the potential beneficiaries of self-regulation are consumers, industry, government, and society. And like government regulation, meritorious programs of self-regulation result in more and better consumer information and safer products.

Since executives have the best understanding of their industry's problems, they can develop standards that are the most effective in protecting the public interest. Business members have the greatest knowledge of the decisionmaking processes and special needs of their target markets, the complexities of their products, and the dynamics of their competitive environments. The standards developed by marketers reflect a consideration of these realities and interactions. In my study I found that industry groups are active in updating and revising their advertising codes to reflect new products and to keep them relevant to the environment (LaBarbera, 1980a).

In addition, resolving consumer problems through self-regulation is relatively fast compared to government regulation. For example, advertising complaints are resolved by self-regulators in a matter of weeks or months in contrast to government action, which is normally far slower. A major advertising self-regulation program has examined and resolved nearly 1700 cases in eight years (LaBarbera 1980b). Industry members as well as consumers benefit from continuous monitoring and quick resolution of complaints. Marketers who did not foresee any negative impact on consumers wish to be informed of complaints quickly so that practices can be corrected before widespread damage is done. In addition, when marketers have complaints about competitors, self-regulation provides them with an expeditious alternative to a lengthy and costly legal procedure.

In addition, a program of self-regulation is a continuous educational process for members of an industry. Marketers participate in creating as well as revising, monitoring, and enforcing ethical codes. This process serves to educate them about acceptable marketing practices and increases their ethical consciousness. As a result, the number of complaints about marketing practices from the public should be reduced.

Marketers are also willing to cooperate with peers in a self-regulation program to achieve ethical objectives. In my study I found that advertisers do not view self-regulators to be as much of an adversary as the government. If enforced, government regulation may reduce illegal behavior, but marketers try to skirt the legislation and violate the spirit of the law. Since marketers participate in creating or revising self-regulation programs, or both, they are involved personally and probably want to have successful programs.

For members of an industry there are several qualitative and quantitative benefits from adhering to self-regulation. Qualitative factors include positive feelings and attitudes held by the marketers in the industry (LaBarbera, 1980c). For example, one benefit is the self-respect the marketer derives from abiding by the code and monitoring other marketers' adherence to the code.

An additional benefit to marketers is the approval they receive from consumer activists, customers, and government members for adhering to the code and monitoring other marketers' behavior. This approval can translate into a reduction in the costs for the marketers of government regulation and litigation.

Another quantitative benefit to marketers is any increased effectiveness of advertising value attributable to their own and others' adherence to guidelines concerning truthful advertising. Surveys show that a large percentage of consumers believe that much of advertising is misleading (Sentry Insurance, 1976; Barksdale and Perreault, 1980).

Although in many cases the pragmatic effect of self-regulation may be the same as government action, marketers prefer private regulation for psychological as well as economic reasons. Psychologically, marketers feel that if they must be regulated, they prefer to be regulated by peers who know the business. Executives do not wish to be told how to operate their businesses by outsiders, particularly nonelected members of government agencies.

It is important to note, however, that there are some major limitations in self-regulation. First, the enforcement powers of self-regulators are limited. The antitrust laws guard against restraint of competition resulting from self-regulation. Thus, the only legal means of enforcement of ethical codes is through moral suasion, threat of expulsion from an association, or public disclosure (La Barbera, 1980d). The fringe marketers in an industry are unconcerned when such measures are directed against them.

In addition, self-regulation is inappropriate for situations that call for strict enforcement of rules. Self-regulators cannot jail or fine marketers as can the government. Therefore, in areas where the health and safety of consumers are concerned code violations would be intolerable and government regulation is necessary. Practices involving mostly the fringe marketers in an industry who ignore self-regulation also require government action.

Furthermore, although self-regulation may be the philosophically and economically superior means of achieving ethical marketing practice, it is difficult to raise money for marketing self-regulation. Marketers want maximum creative and competitive freedom. Defending the need for regulation beyond what is required by the government can be a difficult task. Self-regulators are essentially a police force responsible for questioning the conduct of marketers. Some marketers do not wish to contribute a large sum for what they view to be a negative function.

In view of this situation, how can the motivation for marketing self-regulation and the desire to engage in ethical practices be increased? Some possible approaches include business education and seminars, the use of ethical consultants, and greater marketing professionalism. The possibilities of these alternatives are explored in the next section.

APPROACHES TO THE VOLUNTARY IMPROVEMENT OF MARKETING ETHICS

Business Education and Seminars

Frazer (1979) is critical of advertising professors for their lack of emphasis on ethical issues in advertising courses. He believes that it is crucial for students, especially graduate business students, to give thoughtful attention to the ethical questions that advertising raises and to develop ethical positions. The criticism expressed by Frazer may be extended to the marketing discipline in general. But will classroom discussions dealing with the ethical dimensions of marketing prove to be valuable for individuals when they become practitioners?

An interesting longitudinal study designed to answer this question was undertaken by Theodore Purcell (1977). Purcell surveyed his graduate students who were taking a seminar in management ethics with him at Dartmouth in 1961 and again in 1971 when they were businessmen. The majority of his respondents indicated that they often encountered ethical problems in their business decision-making that placed them in conflict situations. Most of the respondents believed that the ethics seminar helped to sharpen ethical training, which had come in their early family life, and which was useful in assisting them with practical decisionmaking in business. Moreover, some of the subjects stated that a refresher business ethics course would be of value after college.

Purcell notes that although some believe that business ethics and values cannot be taught, the work of researchers such as Jean Piaget and Lawrence Kohlberg indicates that ethics can be learned. Based on his research, Kohlberg suggests that individuals can be taught to move from his first stage (merely responding to rewards and punishments) to his sixth stage (acting on principle at any cost). Kohlberg admits that some individuals never move beyond the fourth stage (the realization that there must be law and order to live in society). However, he believes that it is vital to reinforce childhood values and to clarify them in terms of our complex economic, social, and technological environment. It appears that discussions of ethics in both the classroom and seminars with practitioners are valuable.

Ethical Consultants

Another approach to raising the ethical consciousness and behavior of marketers is through the use of ethical consultants. Purcell (1975) proposed the use of ethical consultants, and Steiner (1976) has summarized the arguments for and against their use. Ethical consultants would be available to interact with operating managers, to raise ethical questions concerning proposed marketing actions, and to offer their perspectives on morally difficult issues. A few companies have implemented Purcell's suggestion. For example, Cummins Engine Company employs an ethical consultant and Monsanto has named a director to scrutinize moral issues.

Professionalism

Marketing executives have not historically been viewed as highly professional individuals. In fact today many would argue against classifying marketing as a profession. Some feel that marketing will never be a pure profession since it does not meet all the conditions generally mentioned as necessary, such as a unique theory (Murphy et al., 1978). This is in contrast to the general acceptance of accounting, engineering, law, and other business functions as professions.

Regardless of whether or not marketing can ever become a profession, few would argue that marketers should not strive to become more professional. In any definition of professionalism, the need for a code of ethics is underscored. Such a code must also be enforced (Keane, 1974), and peer pressure should consistently encourage high levels of ethics and actively discourage shortcomings.

A major function that a trade association can perform for its members is the adoption of a code of ethics. Because it represents an entire industry, an association has a responsibility, if not a duty, to encourage and help to implement ethical conduct. Two examples of effective marketing self-regulation through trade associations are the subject of the final section of this chapter.

EXAMPLES OF SUCCESSFUL MARKETING SELF-REGULATION

Complaint Handling in the Appliance Industry

In 1968 appliance problems were the leading source of complaints submitted to the White House Office of Consumer Affairs and government regulation appeared imminent. The appliance industry responded in 1970 by creating the Major Appliance Consumer Action Panel (MACAP). This independent complaint appeal mechanism was established by the joint efforts of the Association of Home Appliance Manufacturers, the Gas Appliance Manufacturers Association, and the National Retail Merchants Association. MACAP is the mechanism through which consumers can resolve their major appliance complaints if they cannot receive satisfaction from local dealers or the manufacturer. This self-policing body investigates complaints and mediates between top corporate executives and consumers to achieve satisfactory solutions.

To assure independence from the industry, the nine MACAP panelists themselves nominate any succeeding members. From the list of nominees the sponsoring associations select panel members who serve three-year terms. Criteria for selection of panel members require that they be professionals with experience and noted ability in some consumer-related field, that they have exemplified leadership on behalf of consumers, and that they be independent of the appliance industry.

MACAP has received thousands of consumer complaints since its creation and has brought the overwhelming majority of them to a satisfactory conclusion (Baumgart, 1974). This voluntary complaint mechanism has received several awards from consumer groups and has served as a model for other industries to study for subsequent adaptation.

Advertising Self-Regulation

During the late 1960s and early 1970s when consumer activists were lobbying federal, state, and local regulatory bodies, all aspects of advertising received particularly harsh criticism. "The advertising business feared the hasty passage of laws that would severely limit its ability to perform effectively as a vital part of the marketing process" (Cox, 1978). Advertisers and their trade associations began to give serious attention to the establishment of a business-sponsored mechanism for the continuous review and policing of advertising.

The result was two groups created in 1971 by the American Advertising Federation, the Association of National Advertisers, the American Association of Advertising Agencies, and the Council of Better Business Bureaus. The National Advertising Division (NAD) of the Council of Better Business Bureaus was to serve as a consumer's complaint bureau and the National Advertising Review Board (NARB) was to be an appeals board if NAD's findings were unsatisfactory to either party involved in the advertising complaint. Twenty percent of NARB panel members are representatives of the public. If an adverse decision is made by NARB, the panel requests that the advertiser either discontinue the advertising or change it to remove the factors found to be misleading. If an advertiser refuses to comply, NARB will send the file to the appropriate government enforcement agency for further action. Thus far, advertisers have accepted NARB decisions in every case. Since its creation in 1971 the NAD/NARB system has resolved almost 1700 complaints concerning national advertisements, and it is considered to be a success by members of both government and industry (LaBarbera, 1980c).

CONCLUSION

This chapter has been concerned with the alternatives of government regulation and industrywide self-regulation for the achievement of a higher level of ethical marketing practice. The quantitative and qualitative costs and benefits of imposed and voluntary controls were explored. Effectively implemented self-regulation has the potential to be the more efficient alternative. However, the need for government regulation will probably always exist. The threat of imposed control is necessary to motivate marketers to self-regulate. In addition, government regulation backed by legal enforcement is needed to control marketers who refuse to cooperate with voluntary controls.

REFERENCES

Ashford, Nicholas A. (1976). *Crisis in the Workplace: Occupational Disease and Injury.* Cambridge, Mass.: MIT Press.

Barksdale, Hiram, G., and William D. Perreault (1980). "Can Consumers Be Satisfied? *MSU Business Topics,* 28 (Spring): 19–30.

Baumgart, Guenter (1974). "Industrywide Cooperation for Consumer Affairs." *California Management Review,* 16 (Spring): 56.

Bezilla, R.; J. B. Haynes; and C. Elliot (1976). "Ethics in Market Research." *Business Horizons* (April): 83–86.

Bowen, Howard R. (1953). *Social Responsibilities of the Businessman.* New York: Harper & Brothers.

Brummet, R. Lee (1979). "Measuring the Cost of Regulation." In *The Dialogue That Happened,* Proceedings of Workshop on the Private Costs of Regulation, G. David Hughes and E. Cameron Williams (eds.). Cambridge, Mass.: Marketing Science Institute (August), pp. 80–85.

Commission on Federal Paperwork (1977). *Final Summary Report* Y3, P19:1/977. Washington, D.C.: Government Printing Office (October 3).

"Complying with Government Regulations Can Be Costly, Corporations Find" (1979). *Wall Street Journal* (March 29).

Cox, Kenneth A. (1978). *A Review and Perspective on Advertising Industry Self-Regulation 1971–77.* New York: National Advertising Review Board.

Crawford, C. Merle (1970). "Attitudes of Marketing Executives Toward Ethics in Marketing Research." *Journal of Marketing* (April): 46.

Defina, Robert (1977). "Public and Private Expenditures for Federal Regulation of Business." St. Louis: Washington University Center for the Study of American Business, Working Paper No. 22 (November).

Eagle, Herbert D. (1973). "Marketer Best Suited to Solve Society's Ills." *Marketing News* (January 15): 3.

Frazer, Charles F. (1979). "Advertising Ethics: The Role of the Educator." *Journal of Advertising,* 8 (Winter): 430–446.

Hughes, G. David (1979). "The Benefits of Rule-Making." In *The Dialogue That Happened,* pp. 86–91.

Hughes, G. David; Paul Verkuil; and E. Cameron Williams (1979). "The Mounting Private Costs of Public Policies in Marketing." In *The Dialogue That Happened,* pp. 4–34.

Jones, Mary Gardiner (1969). "Industry Should Back Self-Policing Programs." *Advertising Age,* 40 (June 2): 2.

Keane, John G. (1974). "On Professionalism in Advertising." *Journal of Advertising,* 3 (Fall): 6–12.

Kimble, William (1975). *Federal Consumer Product Safety Act.* St. Paul: West Publishing Company.

Kirkpatrick, Miles W. (1972). "Advertising and the Federal Trade Commission." *Journal of Advertising,* 1, 10–12.

LaBarbera, Priscilla A. (1980a). "Analyzing and Advancing the State of the Art of Advertising Self-Regulation." New York University Graduate School of Business Administration, Working Paper #80–49 (April).

———— (1980b). "Advertising Self-Regulation: An Evaluation." New York University Graduate School of Business Administration, Working Paper #79–69 (August).

———— (1980c). "Toward the Theoretical Development of Advertising Self-Regulation." In *Conceptual and Theoretical Developments in Marketing,* Vol. 2, edited by O. C. Ferrell, Stephen W. Brown, and Charles Lamb, Jr., Chicago: American Marketing Association.

———— (1980d). "The Antitrust Shadow Over Advertising Self-Regulation." New York University Graduate School of Business Administration, Working Paper #80–04.

Lazer, William, and Priscilla A. LaBarbera (1975). "Business and Self-Regulation." In *Public Policy Issues in Marketing,* edited by O. C. Ferrell and Raymond La Garce. Lexington, Mass.: D. C. Heath and Co., pp. 105–125.

Leone, Robert A. (1977). "The Real Costs of Regulation." *Harvard Business Review* (November/December): 57–55.

Lilley, William III, and James C. Miller (1977). "The New Social Regulation." *Public Interest,* 45 (Spring): 5–51.

McKean, Roland, N. (1979). "Some Economic Aspects of Ethical-Behavioral Codes." *Political Studies,* 27 (June): 251–265.

Murphy, Patrick E.; Gene R. Laczniak; and Robert F. Lusch (1978). "Ethical Guidelines for Business and Social Marketing." *Journal of the Academy of Marketing Science,* 6 (Summer): 195–205.

Pitofsky, Robert (1977). "Beyond Nader: Consumer Protection and the Regulation of Advertising." *Harvard Law Review,* 90 (February): 661–701.

Purcell, Theodore V. (1975). "A Practical Guide to Ethics in Business." *Business and Society Review* (Spring): 43–50.

_____ (1977). "Do Courses in Business Ethics Pay Off?" *California Management Review,* 19 (Summer): 50–58.

Ross, Richard B. (1979). "Some Difficulties in Measuring the Costs and Benefits of Regulation." In *The Dialogue That Happened,* pp. 56–70.

Schultze, Charles L. (1977). *The Public Use of Private Interest.* Washington, D.C.: The Brookings Institution.

Sentry Insurance and Marketing Science Institute (1977). *Consumerism at the Crossroads,* A National Opinion Research Survey of Public, Activist, Business and Regulator Attitudes Toward the Consumer Movement.

Smith, Robert S. (1976). "The Occupational Safety and Health Act." Washington, D.C.: American Enterprise Institute.

Steiner, George A. (1978). "New Patterns in Government Regulation of Business." *MSU Business Topics* (Autumn).

Steiner, John F. (1976). "The Prospect of Ethical Advisors for Business Corporations." *Business and Society* (Spring).

Tybout, Alice M., and Gerald Zaltman (1974). "Ethics in Marketing Research: Their Practical Relevance." *Journal of Marketing Research* (November): 357–368.

Warner and Swasey (1978). Advertisement in *Across the Board* (January): 1.

Weidenbaum, Murray L. (1975). "The Case for Economizing on Government Controls." *Journal of Economic Issues,* 11 (June).

_____ (1978). *The Costs of Government Regulation of Business.* Study submitted to the Subcommittee on Economic Growth and Stabilization (April).

Chapter 10

Management Development: A Practical Ethical Method and a Case

Theodore V. Purcell, S.J.

Management decisions regularly involve knowledge of economics, law, finance, public relations, and so forth. In this process applied ethics can also be integrated with these disciplines, and more readily than is commonly thought. Ethics is neither fuzzy nor merely personal taste.[1]

Let me propose a practical threefold ethical process that managers can introduce into their decisionmaking.[2] This process calls for (1) the examination and support of general ethical principles; (2) the examination and support of middle-level ethical principles; and (3) in-depth study of cases and classes of similar cases.

These three tools are interactive and must be used simultaneously, each reinforcing or clarifying the other.

The First Tool: General Ethical Principles. Ethical inquiry can yield valid and basic principles such as the following:

1. People should do good and avoid evil.
2. Human life is more precious than animal life.
3. One's conscience should be influenced by the fact that basic needs have priority over luxury wants.
4. Persons and institutions should be just and honest.

I believe that most managers would agree with these general principles. They might want to add others. These principles are important because they are absolutely fundamental, the foundation on which ethics is built. But being general, they have little *practical* value until they are *specified* by middle principles and case analyses. On the other hand, judging cases has no ethical meaning unless judgments are based on fundamental ethical principles. This is where the *simultaneity* comes in.

The Second Tool: Applied or "Middle" Ethical Principles.
1. *Greater social power requires greater social responsibility.* This was dramatically brought out a few years ago in the hearings for the confirmation of Nelson Rockefeller as Vice President.
2. *The rule of law is central, but unjust laws can exist; and there are times when a higher moral cause may justify breaking the law, provided the violator is willing to accept the consequences.* The civil disobedience of the Montgomery, Alabama, bus riders is an example of this principle.
3. *Property connotes a vital private right, but it has a social aspect.* The statement "I may not build any kind of building I want regardless of my neighbors" demonstrates this principle.
4. *Private power need not always be based on property ownership to be legitimate.* Take the power of union leaders and corporate managers, for example. *But such power, and indeed all private power, carries the obligation of public accountability.*
5. *The firm does not exist solely for its own corporate prosperity or even survival; it also has social responsibilities to its various publics or stakeholders.* Witness the growth of public interest organizations.

There are two other kinds of middle principles more logical in character that can guide us applying the other five:
6. *There is a difference between a precept or commandment, saying what must be done, and a counsel, recommending the better or more saintly action.* The statement "I must fulfill a contract; I may give half my income to the poor" illustrates this principle.
7. *When a (good) action has both a good effect and a bad effect (a common situation), one may morally perform the action provided (a) he does not directly intend the bad effect; (b) the bad effect is not a means to the good end, but is simply a side effect; and (c) the good effect sufficiently outweighs the bad.* An example is a pharmaceutical company marketing a needed

drug (that might in some cases have harmful side effects) provided the good and bad effects are carefully weighed and consumers are encouraged to take all reasonable precautions. One consideration for the company: Is there another drug that would achieve the same benefits with less risk? Another example would be cigarettes.

I call these ethical principles "middle" because they are *in between* the more general principles and specific cases. They stem from a study of general principles and from a study of specific case situations. Therefore, practical experience is important in formulating them. They should be held firmly as long as they promote justice; some should be modified when new situations demand it. Managers will need to spend more time on these principles, developing and clarifying them. They may also wish to derive new principles—briefly stated—relevant to the particular cases their companies face.

Most of the thirty articles of the United Nations' *Universal Declaration of Human Rights* are middle ethical principles.[3] For example, Article 3: "Everyone has the right to life, liberty and security of person"; Article 23 (1): "Everyone has the right to work, to just and favorable conditions of work and to protection against unemployment"; Article 23 (2): "Everyone, without any discrimination, has the right to equal pay for equal work."

The Third Tool: Specific Case Analysis. While essential to the process of ethical reasoning, these middle-level principles are not fully usable unless the manager applies them to specific cases.

Take the middle principle just cited: "The rule of law is central but unjust laws can exist and there are times when a higher moral cause may justify breaking the law." Immediately one must ask: When does individual conscience justify violating the law? Who has the right to determine when a law is "unjust"? What about laws that grant rights to people to take actions that others consider immoral? Specific case analyses should help to answer these questions.

Another example: "Property is a vital private right, but it has a social aspect." One practical issue related to this principle is covering over strip mines for the benefit of the people in Kentucky and West Virginia versus the resulting higher cost in electric power and perhaps fewer urban jobs in Chicago or Pittsburgh. Who is right? The tough tradeoff questions between different groups in our society cannot be solved by principles alone but must also involve the continuous and careful analysis of cases and classes of cases along with the principles.

Managers may wish to consult a specialist in ethics but they will also need to study the findings of economists, lawyers, sociologists, psychologists, engineers, and others to weigh the benefits and the costs.

One class of cases is the "acceleration-preferential practice" for hiring and promoting minorities and women. In my judgment, such practices are morally justified to correct the injustices in our society if certain provisos are met. I shall present a case on this issue.

Another set of cases involves an employee's obligations of loyalty and confidentiality toward his or her employer versus the conflicting right and obligation to "blow the whistle" and reveal (leak) to the public the misconduct of this employer if the employee feels this is the only way to correct abuses. Philip Blumberg treats these cases very well in terms of law.[4] Much of his reasoning can guide the student of ethics. Management needs to provide its employees with a reasonable right of dissent. At the heart of the matter is the balancing of the ethical rights of the individual and the ethical rights of the organization.

Still another case class involves multinational corporations bribing foreign officials or making political contributions abroad. Official bribery in many countries is often a way of life. Going along with bribery to meet competition downgrades the business climate for everybody. But first we must determine whether such actions are in fact bribery, middlemen's commissions, public relations according to local custom, or sheer extortion. Only a careful study of each case and of classes of cases, along with principles, will give valid ethical answers here. You can start from what is legal in the host country, while recognizing that there is a moral minimum across all cultures not to injure or to harm people, even when honesty is not valued by those cultures.

By using these three tools with simultaneous interaction, and with study, discussion, and consultation, if necessary, managers have at their disposal a practical process for ethical decisionmaking. Applying ethics to complex business decisions will sometimes be difficult. At times, differences of opinion may be due to ethical pluralism. But more often I think differences will be due to the complexity or ambiguity of the facts in specific cases.

We all know that two honest and ethical persons sometimes take opposite sides on an issue. In such cases I would advise a manager— both as an individual and as a member of a management team—to follow his or her own conscience with both prudence and courage.

Now let me apply this ethical process to a specific case involving reverse discrimination versus affirmative action.

THE McALEER v. A.T.&T. CASE[5]

Daniel McAleer was a $10,500 per year service representative at A.T.&T.'s Washington, D.C., Long Lines Division. In 1974 he put in for a promotion, which he did not receive. Instead, the promotion was given to a woman, Sharon Hulvey, who was qualified for the job, but less qualified than McAleer and who had less seniority with the company.

McAleer claimed that he was unjustly discriminated against solely because of his sex. He brought a lawsuit against A.T.&T., seeking the $135 per week difference in salary between his present job and the job he sought, plus $100,000 damages for the opportunities for further promotion he claims to have lost.

Some Background Information

In November 1970, A.T.&T., the largest private employer in the world, filed with the Federal Communications Commission (FCC) a proposed tariff that would increase interstate telephone rates. Before the filing was acted upon, the EEOC filed with the FCC a petition requesting that the increase be denied because A.T.&T.'s operating companies were engaged in systemwide discrimination against women and minorities. The FCC initiated a special proceeding to consider the charges, holding 60 days of hearings in 1971 and 1972. A number of organizations intervened in support of the EEOC. While the hearings progressed, settlement negotiations took place between A.T.&T. and the government parties, which eventually led to the termination of the FCC special proceeding, and the entry of the consent decree finally approved by the Philadelphia U.S. District Court on January 18, 1973, to last until January 1979. Note that this decree did not contain any admission by A.T.&T. of past discrimination.

The consent decree directed the Bell System Companies to establish goals and intermediate targets to promote the full utilization of all job classifications. The intermediate targets, set annually, were to reflect the representation of such groups in the external labor market. When any Bell Company was unable to achieve its intermediate target by applying normal selection standards, it was required by the decree to depart from those standards.

The A.T.&T.–C.W.A. union contract said that seniority would be given "full consideration" for promotions but would not be the "governing factor." Rather, ability and qualifications would govern. However, the consent decree explicitly called for an "affirmative action override," bypassing the promotion clause of the union contract when it was necessary to do so to achieve the targets set. Thus a basically qualified person might pass over another person who had more seniority or ability. Incidentally (and importantly), the affirmative action override applied only to *promotions* and not to layoffs or rehires, in which cases seniority continued to prevail.

How would you decide this case, reasoning not from the law but from ethics?

IS IT AFFIRMATIVE ACTION OR REVERSE DISCRIMINATION?

First we need to examine some relevant socioeconomic and legal data that will give us background for arriving at an ethical decision. By the end of the 1960s, it was clear that merely opening doors to minorities and women, while good, was not enough. There were many encrusted, stereotyped traditions and practices that obstructed change. Minorities need affirmative action, outreach, special help. Without this, equitable participation of minorities and women at all levels of the modern corporation would take decades.

Black Projection Statistics

I give data here for only one minority group: black Americans.[6] But similar projection statistics can be supplied for women. How many years would it take for black Americans to hold a fair proportion of jobs at every step of the ladder in American industry and business? Ten percent seems a desirable proportion, say at the levels of officials and managers, professionals, technicians, sales, and craftsmen. I am not arguing for precise or rigid statistical parity, but the *opportunity* to achieve statistical parity. Making projections for a cross section of American manufacturing, let us estimate the number of years it will take blacks to achieve 10 percent in each of the nine levels specified by the EEOC. Blacks already comprise more than 10 percent of unskilled and semiskilled workers. But their progress in craft jobs and especially in white-collar jobs will be much slower. My base years are the rate of change from 1966 to 1969, the end of the most affluent decade in the history of this country. If that rate continued, it would take 9 years for blacks to reach 10 percent in clerical positions, 14 years for craft jobs, 55 years for officials and managers, and 86 years for professionals!

These figures should not be construed as exact predictions; they are projections of what could very well happen. Several forces could make them go faster or slower. First, the business cycle: The recession of 1973–1979 cut down many of the gains of the late 1960s, and the present recession is repeating those losses. Ironically, wars would help. Education will be a major factor, also civil rights laws, white backlash and urban segregation, and unemployment resulting from the flight of whites and jobs from central cities. The figures predicting the progress of blacks in employment could well be much longer unless reasonable but strong affirmative action is taken by *all* segments of our society.

Will blacks and other minorities have the patience to wait? Does American industry have the time?

A self-made vice president of a major agricultural chemical firm in Houston said on hearing these figures: "My father was born as an immigrant from central Europe in 1890. He was on relief. I was born in 1932, one of seven children. In 1957 I graduated from the University of Texas. It took 66 years (from 1890 to 1956) for my *white* family to become 'professionals'." But the forefathers of the blacks now working for this man's company were unwilling immigrants to this country 200 or 300 years ago and not one black employee is close to becoming vice president of that company today.

As a Sears executive put it, "We do not have the time to wait. We will not achieve these changes unless we make a special extra effort. We must work a tradeoff between the color-blind test and 'institutionalized change creations' methods." Projections like these lead us to the consideration of acceleration–preferential practices for minorities and women.

The Law and the Executive Orders on Reverse Discrimination

The Civil Rights Act of 1964 neither requires nor forbids preferential treatment. But Revised Orders 4 and 14 of the OFCCP (Office of Federal Contract Compliance Programs, 1978) and practices from the EEOC do call for preferential practices. *Some companies have unabashedly worked these practices into their affirmative action plans, for example, Sears, Kaiser, and GE.*

As for the courts, the *Bakke* decision[7] clearly did not settle the matter. A more important decision is the *Weber* v. *Kaiser Aluminum* case.[8] In the *Kaiser* case, the company and the union, the United Steelworkers, in a 1974 collective bargaining agreement, decided that entrance into Kaiser's skilled crafts training program would be based on seniority, but from two lists, one for whites and one for minorities. Thus, minorities would comprise 50 percent of the program until the percentage of minorities in the craft would approximate their percentage in the area surrounding each Kaiser plant. This seems to be a rigid quota. But in 1979 the Supreme Court decided in a five-to-two decision that voluntary affirmative action plans, even those containing numerical quotas, do not automatically violate the Civil Rights Act of 1964. The Court said:

> It is not necessary in this case to define the line of demarcation between permissible and impermissible affirmative action plans; it suffices to hold that the challenged Kaiser–USWA plan falls on the permissible side of the line.... At the same time, the plan does not unnecessarily trammel the interests of white employees, neither requiring the discharge of white workers and their replacement with new black hirees, nor creating an absolute bar to the advancement of white employees since half of those trained in the program will be white. Moreover, the plan is a temporary measure, not intended to maintain racial balance, but simply to eliminate a manifest racial imbalance.

But other cases are also pending, and the courts will not finish clarifying this matter for years to come.[9]

ETHICAL GUIDELINES

Let me present my own theory and policy proposal. The minority person should be either qualified (or qualifiable in a reasonable time) for the job or promotion, according to a *single* standard of minimum qualifications for performing that job applicable to everyone. Unqualified people should not be accepted. Standards should not be lowered, but they should be clearly job related.

Each case or class of cases should be considered in an *ad hoc* manner with targets and goals, but *not* with rigid quotas. If both a minority and a majority person are clearly qualified but the majority person is more qualified in job-related abilities, then these two variables must be carefully analyzed and considered simultaneously.

The Strategic Importance of the Job. When the job is less sensitive or important regarding the safety and efficiency of the company or the welfare of fellow workers or customers, I suggest picking the qualified minority person. But as the job becomes more important, or is actually a pass-through position to a higher job demanding greater qualifications, I suggest picking the *better*-qualified person—in this case, the majority person. An example: When choosing between applicants for an airline pilot's job, one would more readily consider merit over preference than when choosing between applicants for a flight attendant's job. At the lower end of the spectrum, minority preference is desirable. At the upper end of the spectrum, greater merit should take precedence, if the qualifications gap *also* becomes larger. However, the strategic sensitivity or importance of the job should not be *exaggerated* when qualified minorities or women apply for such jobs.

The Qualifications Gap. Suppose a very small but perceptible gap appears, with the majority person being more qualified, and at the same time the strategic job importance is low. Then I still suggest that the minority person be given preference. An example: A combination of test scores plus subjective judgments might put a majority person at 87 on a scale of 1 to 100 and a minority person at 86—a slight difference. As the qualifications gap widens, greater merit should take precedence, if the job importance also becomes greater.

Preferring the qualified, but less qualified, minority person when both the job importance and qualifications gap are *high* would be reverse discrimination. Not preferring the qualified, but lesser qualified minority person, when both the job importance and qualifications gap are *low* would be unaffirmative action, or reverse affirmative action.

One might take a cost–benefit approach in the problem of drawing the line between reverse discrimination and reverse affirmative action. If preference would probably lead to alarmingly high potential *costs* to the firm and to society as a whole (the case of the airline pilot), this would surely outweigh the benefits society also needs to provide for minorities and women. Obviously the Equal Employment Opportunity specialist needs both prudent and human wisdom plus good faith to make these decisions when judging the strategic job importance and the qualifications gap, for these factors cannot be perfectly quantified or mechanically evaluated.

Preference is not necessarily reverse discrimination. Neither the qualified majority nor the qualified minority person has an unqualified right in either distributive or commutative justice to a *specific* job or promotion. Fair consideration does not always require the employer to hire or promote the more qualified persons. *If the employer has a good and valid reason, called for by the common good, for employing the qualified, but less qualified person, this does not violate the rights in justice of the person passed over.*

If the employer passes over the more qualified majority person—a white male, for example—for some frivolous reason (say only because the employer does not like white males and not because the employer is trying to fulfill legitimate and important goals), this would be reverse discrimination.

Finally, preferential practice in employment has time limitations. It is not a practice necessary forever. But it will probably be necessary for the groups now protected at least until the year 2000.

Here is my general reasoning: Because a person is a social being shaped by social and economic structures, social justice is not achieved simply by ensuring the rights of persons as individuals standing alone. When the rights of individuals are violated, *precisely because these persons are members of certain specially deprived groups,* society's remedy must also take account of the fact that these individual persons belong to such groups.

Social justice requires just socioeconomic structures and institutions. When encrusted patterns of education, housing, and employment put individuals of certain *groups* at a special disadvantage just because they are members of such groups, it is within the context of social justice to give acceleration–preferential aid in employment to those individuals (if they are otherwise qualified) *precisely because* of their group membership.

Nathan Glazer thinks that taking account of an individual's group affiliation means "that we abandon the first principle of a liberal society, that the individual and the individual's interests and good and welfare are the test of a good society.... It is now our task... to reestablish this simple and clear understanding, that rights attach to the individual, not the group, and that the public policy must be exercised without distinction of race, color, or national origin."[10]

I agree with Glazer that not *every* group needs or should get preference. To ascribe "groupness" to every individual employee would lead to chaos in hiring and promotion. I do believe that the five groups designated by the EEOC, namely, blacks, Hispanics, American Indians, Asians, and women, are groups in singular need of help in America. This is supported by clear sociological data. These groups more than others are at a disadvantage. Not all, but most, individuals from these groups are disadvantaged regarding employment at this time. (A talented black would not need or want preference. He might get the promotion on greater merit. But conceivably a slightly less talented Hispanic might be chosen over him if the targets called for that.) Taking account of their group affiliation is, in my judgment, an ethical pursuit of the common good.

TWO LEGAL SOLUTIONS FOR THE McALEER v. A.T.&T. CASE

Federal Judge Gerhard A. Gesell ruled that Daniel McAleer was a "faultless employee" and a "blameless third party,"[11] and that A.T.&T.'s action presented "a classic case of sex discrimination" under Title VII of the Civil Rights Act of 1964. Judge Gesell ordered A.T.&T. to pay damages to McAleer.

Paradoxically, however, the judge did *not* rule that McAleer should be given the promotion, because granting the promotion "might well perpetuate and prolong the effects of the discrimination" that the A.T.&T. consent decree "was designed to eliminate."[12] He stated that his court (Washington, D.C.) had "no jurisdiction to pass on the validity of the consent decree or amend its terms" since this decree had been approved by the Philadelphia District Court.

The Philadelphia Federal Judge, A. Leon Higginbotham, in another case the same year, rejected the Communications Workers' petition to remove the affirmative action override from the A.T.&T. consent decree, stating:

> With all due respect to Judge Gesell, I believe that case to be wrongly decided. Title VII recognizes a narrow but nevertheless real and complete immunity for employer conduct undertaken in good faith reliance on a written interpretation or opinion of the EEOC.[13]

After Higginbotham's decision, the *McAleer* v. *A.T.&T.* case was settled out of court. McAleer received $7500 for himself and $6500 for his attorney.

In an ideal world (in which minorities and women would be fairly represented at the various levels of supervision and expertise in the modern corporation), the rights of a majority person to hiring and promotion would not be qualified by the needs of others to achieve the common good goal of fair representation. Therefore, preferring a minority person then would indeed be an invasion of the rights of the majority person. It would be a "moral harm."

But in the real world of America in the 1980s, such a situation does not obtain.

However, I fully agree with Judge Gesell's opinion that McAleer was a "faultless employee" and a "blameless third party." In no way is McAleer personally to blame for the deficiency at A.T.&T. (My argument is not a reparations agrument.) But I argue that McAleer's right to the promotion is not an absolute right. It is rather a *qualified* right. McAleer does not have an unqualified right to the promotion merely on the basis of merit or seniority under all circumstances. When both the qualifications gap is low or indistinct and when the strategic job importance is at the lower end of the spectrum in relation to a minority person or a woman, McAleer's qualified right becomes inoperative. The right of society to seek the common good by correcting the deficiencies prevails. McAleer suffers no unjust moral harm.

McAleer's possible resentment is understandable, and the situation must be explained to him. If he can accept the situation, so much the better. If he does not, the fault is his, not that of society.

To give my own solution, first let us consider the qualifications gap. A.T.&T. has annual performance appraisals made by supervisors after consultation with their peers. Thirty "points," as they are called, is generally the top grade. This grade is computed on a maximum of six points for five "indicators" covering education, job knowledge, skills, responsibility, quantity and quality of work, cooperation, and so on. There are also "surplus points" above 30.

When there is a job opening, the application of a formula sets the cutoff level. For example, candidates with scores of 30, 29, 28, and perhaps 27, might all be considered. Aside from the affirmative action override, A.T.&T. normally promoted the person with the highest number of points. If two persons were tied, the person with the longest seniority would automatically get the promotion.

Daniel McAleer was in Title Grade V and he had surplus points with a rating of 34. Sharon Hulvey was in a *higher* Title Grade VI. She had the normal maximum of 30 points.

A.T.&T. placed both Title V and Title VI in one promotion pool for certain purposes of convenience. Technically, McAleer had more points, 34 as opposed to 30. But as A.T.&T. attorney Robert W. Jeffrey (who handled this case) admitted: "You could argue that comparing those points was like comparing apples and oranges. Had McAleer been rated in the higher grade [VI], he might well have had less than 34 points, even 29."

Be that as it may, technically McAleer had more points, 34 over 30. In addition, he had slightly more seniority, November 24, 1969, as opposed to Hulvey's July 6, 1970.

The main point here is that the qualifications gap was very small.

Next let us consider the strategic job importance variable. The job in question was called ST-I Staff and Technical, Grade I. It was a newly created job, nonsupervisory, within the company–union bargaining unit. The job description called for "making conference arrangements" for executive management: luncheons, transportation, accommodations for guests, and so forth. It called for tact, a pleasant manner, some humility, and practical competence. It was well paid, but not a sensitive or highly important job. Thus, on my scale, we can rate this ST-I job relatively low on strategic job importance.

In a word, the qualifications gap and the strategic job importance were both low. Therefore, I would put the variable "ethical importance of preference for the minority or female person" as high.

My own solution to the case is that Sharon Hulvey was justly given the promotion and that A.T.&T. was not obligated to pay any back pay or front pay damages whatsoever to Daniel McAleer. Failure to do this would have been unaffirmative action or reverse affirmative action.

* * *

Some Middle Principles Applicable to This Case

1. People should not be hired or promoted unless they are basically qualified for the job.
2. Using the principle of the double effect, we find two effects in this case. The good effect is the faster promotion of women and minorities to correct the gross imbalances at A.T.&T. The bad effect is passing over a more qualified and more senior male. The bad effect is not strictly a *means* to the good effect. (I reason that the end does not justify the means.) The mere nonpromotion of McAleer does not in itself strictly *cause* the promotion of the woman. It merely *permits* it. Both are fully qualified. Were there more openings, *both* could have been promoted. Furthermore, analysis shows the good effect to outweigh the bad effect, for the present time. Therefore, the evil may justly be *permitted* in this case.
3. For hiring and promotions, to take account of the group relatedness of individuals from the most seriously disadvantaged groups in our society is ethically justifiable, at least for a limited time, while these groups are still seriously disadvantaged.
4. Merit should take precedence over group preference when there is considerable economic risk or cost, or danger to others, or when there is a *great* difference in the qualifications of the persons involved.
5. Though everyone should get fair *consideration,* a person does not have an unqualified right in either distributive or commutative justice to be hired or promoted for a *specific* job.

Some Relevant Comments from the Supreme Court in the Weber v. Kaiser Case (June 27, 1979)

Congress' primary concern in enacting the prohibition against racial discrimination in Title VII was the plight of the Negro in our economy,... [substitute women, also] opening opportunities for Negroes in occupations which have been *traditionally* [emphasis mine] closed to them.... The [Kaiser] plan does not unnecessarily trammel the interests of white employees, neither requiring the discharge of white workers or their replacement with new black hirees.... Moreover the plan is a temporary measure.[14]

Two Obvious Psychological Problems

Some persons passed over will be resentful. One can only ask them to try to accept the common good reasons for the bypass. Daniel McAleer is described by one A.T.&T. manager as a "nice kid, not vindictive." He apparently felt little resentment. Actually he was, in a sense, acting as a test case for the union. He is now in the Washington area in a supervisory position, overseeing chauffeuring for executive management.

Some persons receiving preference will be sensitive, believing that they are not being recognized for their own abilities but are being promoted *only* because of their minority or female status. One can only ask them to try to accept the common good reasons for their advancement. One can also remind them of their valid and basic qualifications. Sharon Hulvey was somewhat mortified and embarrassed by her experience, for she was being talked about. Actually, it seems she did not feel she was being promoted merely because she was a woman, apart from her abilities. On the contrary, she felt that she was not less qualified but quite deserving of the promotion. She is still with A.T.&T. And after a stint in Philadelphia she is in a marketing position with the Long Lines Division in Washington, D.C.

EPILOGUE

Since the consent decree expired in January 1979, A.T.&T. cannot use the affirmative action override. It must promote the senior, best qualified person. Otherwise the CWA would have a grievance over the contract. However, Chairman John de Butts made this statement in 1979: "I know this: we will continue our affirmative action programs just as urgently after the consent decree as now."[15]

A.T.&T. was apprehensive at the termination of the consent decree about fulfilling its targets and goals. Today Long Lines anticipates no problems. According to one of its top attorneys, A.T.&T. learned a lot in the six years of the consent decree about managing affirmative action. The EEOC often boasts about A.T.&T.'s performance.

One final point: Did A.T.&T.'s productivity fall as a result of its very extensive affirmative and preferential activities for minorities and women? The company has made no formal productivity studies. Admittedly, it took women time to learn some of the nontraditional jobs. But those who stayed apparently became good workers. The company's answer is simply to point to its excellent profit situation and its continuing reputation for efficiency.

WHAT DID WE LEARN?

Ethics can be a practical aid in management decisionmaking. Moral reasoning, by the threefold process described, gives usable guidelines for solving such complex issues as affirmative action versus reverse discrimination. Other issues can be approached by this process. Applied ethics is a new and useful tool for the manager.

NOTES

1. See, for example, Theodore V. Purcell, S.J., "Institutionalizing Ethics on Corporate Boards," *Review of Social Economy* 36, 1 (April 1978): 41-54.
2. Managers, of course, could also explicitly study and use ethical theories such as utilitarianism justice, rights, natural law.
3. *Everyman's UN Handbook,* 8th ed. (New York: United Nations, 1961).
4. Philip I. Blumberg, "Corporate Responsibility and the Employee's Duty of Loyalty and Obedience: A Preliminary Inquiry," *Oklahoma Law Review* 24, 3 (August 1971).
5. *McAleer* v. *A.T.&T. Co.,* 12 FEP Cases, 1473-1478. This case is not a major or Supreme Court case, contributing to precedent, such as *Weber* v. *Kaiser.* Rather, *McAleer* is important because it throws light on the ethical arguments for and against preference.
6. For these data and the following treatment, see: Theodore V. Purcell, S.J., and Gerald F. Cavanagh, S.J., "Equal Versus Preferential Practice," Chapter 10 in *Blacks in the Industrial World* (New York: The Free Press, 1973). Also see T. V. Pursell, S.J., "Case of the Borderline Black," *Harvard Business Review* (November-December 1971); T. B. Blodgett, "Borderline Black Revisited," *Harvard Business Review* (March-April 1972); Theodore V. Purcell, S.J., "Management and Affirmative Action in the Late Seventies," in *Equal Rights and Industrial Relations* (Madison, Wis.: Industrial Relations Research Association Series, 1977);

and "Policies on Minority Employment: A Psychologist's View," *Professional Psychology* (June 1980).

7. *U.S. Law Week* 46 (1978).
8. *U.S. Law Week* 47 (1979).
9. For a legal analysis, see the Equal Employment Advisory Council's *Preferential Treatment in Employment,* by Kenneth C. McGuiness (Washington, D.C., 1977). For books of readings on the topic, see William T. Blackstone and Robert D. Heslep, eds., *Social Justice and Preferential Treatment* (Athens: University of Georgia Press, 1977); Barry R. Gross, ed., *Reverse Discrimination* (Buffalo, N.Y.: Prometheus Books, 1977); and Marshall Cohen, Thomas Nagel, and Thomas Scanlon, eds., *Equality and Preferential Treatment* (Princeton, N.J.: Princeton University Press, 1977). Note that all the above antedate the U.S. Supreme Court's *Weber* decision in 1979.
10. Nathan Glazer, *Affirmative Discrimination, Ethnic Inequality and Public Policy* (New York: Basic Books, 1975).
11. *McAleer* v. *A.T.&T. Co.,* 12 FEP Cases, 1473–1478.
12. Ibid.
13. *Equal Employment Opportunity Commission v. A.T.&T. Co., et al.,* Bureau of National Affairs (No. 1012), September 3, 1976, p. C16.
14. *U.S. Law Week* 47 (1979): 4851.
15. Carol J. Loomis, "A.T.&T. in the Throes of 'Equal Employment,'" *Fortune* (January 15, 1979), p. 57.

Select Bibliography

BUSINESS ETHICS: GENERAL

Books

Armerding, George D., and Phil Landrum. *The Dollars and Sense of Honesty: Stories from the Business World.* New York: Harper & Row, 1979.

Barry, Vincent. *Moral Issues in Business.* Belmont, Calif.: Wadsworth Publishing Co., 1979.

Baum, Robert, and J. Randell. *Ethical Arguments for Analysis.* New York: Holt, Rinehart, and Winston, 1976.

Beauchamp, Tom L., and Norman E. Bowie, eds. *Ethical Theory and Business.* Englewood Cliffs, N.J.: Prentice-Hall, 1979.

Bergier, Jacques. *Secret Armies: The Growth of Corporate Industrial Espionage.* Indianapolis: Bobbs-Merrill Co., 1976.

Bowie, Norman E. *Business Ethics.* Englewood Cliffs, N.J.: Prentice-Hall, 1982.

Brown, Courtney C. *Beyond the Bottom Line.* New York: Macmillan, 1979.

Callis, Robert, ed. *Ethical Standards Casebook.* Falls Church, Va.: American Personnel and Guidance Association, 1976.

Clinard, Marshall B., and Peter C. Yeager. *Corporate Crime.* New York: The Free Press, 1980.

Dam, Cees van, and Laud M. Stallaert, eds. *Trends in Business Ethics: Implications for Decision Making.* Boston: Kluwer, 1978.

D'Aprix, Roger M. *In Search of a Corporate Soul.* New York: American Management Association, 1976.

Danner, Peter L. *An Ethics for the Affluent.* Washington, D.C.: University Press of America, 1980.

Davids, Lewis E. *What Every Director Should Know About Corporate Ethics.* St. Louis: Director Publications, 1978.

DeGeorge, Richard T., and Joseph A. Pichler, eds. *Ethics, Free Enterprise, and Public Policy: Original Essays on Moral Issues in Business.* New York: Oxford University Press, 1978.

DeMente, Boye. *Japanese Manners and Ethics in Business.* Paradise Valley, Ariz.: Phoenix Books, 1976.

Donaldson, Thomas. *Corporations and Morality.* Englewood Cliffs, N.J.: Prentice-Hall, 1982.

Dworkin, Gerald; Gordon Beemanto; and Peter G. Brown, eds. *Markets and Morals.* Washington, D.C.: Hemisphere Publishing Corp., 1977.

Englebourg, Saul. *Power and Morality: American Business Ethics, 1840–1914*. Westport, Conn.: Greenwood Press, 1980.

Epstein, Edwin, and Dow Votow, eds. *Legitimacy, Responsibility, and Rationality*. Santa Monica, Calif.: Goodyear, 1978.

Evans, William A. *Management Ethics: An Intercultural Perspective*. Boston: Martinus Nijhoff, 1981.

Geis, Gilbert, and Robert S. Meier. *White Collar Crime: Offenses in Business, Politics, and Professions*. New York: The Free Press, 1977.

Gelinier, Octave. *The Enterprise Ethic*. Central Islip, N.Y.: Transatlantic, 1980.

Hess, J. Daniel. *Ethics in Business and Labor*. Scottsdale, Penn.: Herald Press, 1977.

Hill, Ivan, ed. *The Ethical Basis of Economic Freedom*. Chapel Hill, N.C.: American Viewpoint, 1976.

Hoffman, W. Michael, ed. *Proceedings of the First National Conference on Business Ethics*. Waltham, Mass.: Center for Business Ethics at Bentley College, 1977.

————. *Proceedings of the 2nd National Conference on Business Ethics*. Wolfe City, Tex.: University Press of America, 1979.

Jones, Donald G. *A Bibliography of Business Ethics: 1971–1975*. Charlottesville: University Press of Virginia, 1977.

————. *A Bibliography of Business Ethics: 1976–1980*. Charlottesville: University Press of Virginia, 1982.

Jones, Donald G., ed. *Business, Religion, and Ethics*. Cambridge, Mass.: Oelgeschlager, Gunn & Hain, 1982.

Kaufman, Andrew L. *Problems in Professional Responsibility*. Boston: Little, Brown, and Company, 1976.

Kinter, Earl W. *A Primer on the Law of Deceptive Practices: A Guide For Business*. New York: Macmillan, 1978.

Kranzberg, Melvin, ed. *Ethics in an Age of Pervasive Technology*. Boulder, Colo.: Westview, 1980.

Kugel, Yerachmiel, and Gladys W. Gruenberg, eds. *Ethical Perspectives on Business and Society*. Lexington, Mass.: D. C. Heath Co., 1977.

LaCroiz, W. L. *Principles for Ethics in Business*. Washington, D.C.: University Press of America, 1979.

Litschert, Robert J., et al. *The Corporate Role and Ethical Behavior: Concepts and Cases*. New York: Van Nostrand Rheinhold Co., 1977.

Moffitt, Donald, ed. *Swindled! Classic Business Frauds of the Seventies*. Princeton, N.J.: Dow Jones Books, 1976.

Moskowitz, Milton; Michael Katz; and Robert Levering, eds. *Everybody's Business: An Almanac*. New York: Harper and Row, 1980.

Parker, Donn B., ed. *Ethical Conflicts in Computer Science and Technology*. Menlo Park, Calif.: Stanford Research Institute, 1978.

Purcell, Theodore V., and James Weber, S.J. *Institutionalizing Corporate Ethics: A Case History*. New York: The Presidents Association, 1979.

Robinson, Henry Mauris. *Relativity in Business Morals*. New York: Houghton Mifflin Co., 1978.

Rohr, John A. *Ethics for Bureaucrats: An Essay on Law and Values.* Park Forest South, Ill.: Governors State University, 1978.
Selekman, Sylvia Kopald, and Benjamin M. Selekman. *Power and Morality in a Business Society.* Westport, Conn.: Greenwood Press, 1978.
Simon, William E. *A Time for Truth.* New York: McGraw-Hill, 1978.
Sobel, Lester A., ed. *Corruption in Business.* New York: Facts on File, Inc., 1977.
Southard, Samuel. *Ethics for Executives.* New York: Cornerstone, 1977.
Stevens, Edward. *Business Ethics.* New York: Paulist Press, 1979.
Sufrin, Sidney C. *Management of Business Ethics.* Port Washington, N.Y.: Kennikat Press, 1980.
Twentieth Air Force Academy Assembly. *The Ethics of Corporate Conduct.* Englewood Cliffs, N.J.: Prentice-Hall, 1978.
Uris, Auren. *The Blue Book of Broadminded Business Behavior.* New York: Harper and Row, 1977.
Velasquez, Manuel G. *Business Ethics: Concepts and Cases.* Englewood Cliffs, N.J.: Prentice-Hall, 1982.
Veri, Anthony. *The New Moral Code of Action for the Large Corporation's Executive.* Albuquerque, N.M.: American Classical Collegiate Press, 1977.
Walton, Clarence C., ed. *The Ethics of Corporate Conduct.* Englewood Cliffs, N.J.: Prentice-Hall, 1977.
Wheatley, Edward W. *Values in Conflict.* Miami: Banyan Books, 1976.
Whiteside, Thomas. *Computer Capers: Tales of Electronic Thievery, Embezzlement, and Fraud.* New York: Thomas Y. Crowell Co., 1978.

TEACHING AND TRAINING IN BUSINESS ETHICS

Books

Baum, Robert J. *Ethics and Engineering Curricula.* Hastings-on-Hudson, N.Y.: The Hastings Center, 1980.
Bowie, Norman E. *Teaching Business Ethics.* Hyde Park, N.Y.: Helvetia Press, 1979. (Booklet), 18 pp.
Callahan, Daniel, and Sissela Bok, eds. *Ethics Teaching in Higher Education.* New York: Plenum, 1980.
DeGeorge, Richard T. *Moral Issues in Business: An Outline of a Course in Business Ethics.* Lawrence: The Committee on Business and the Humanities, The University of Kansas, 1979.
Dill, David; Thomas Donaldson; Kenneth Goodpaster; and William May. *Syllabi for the Teaching of Management Ethics.* New Haven, Conn.: Society for Values in High Education, 1979.
Fleishman, Joel L., and Bruce L. Payne. *Ethical Dilemmas and the Education of Policymakers.* Hastings-on-Hudson, N.Y.: The Hastings Center, 1980.

Hall, Robert T. *Moral Education: A Handbook for Teachers*. Minneapolis: Winston Press, 1979.

Huber, C. E. *The Promise and Perils of Business Ethics: A Resource for Curriculum Development*. Washington, D.C.: Association of American Colleges, 1979. (Booklet)

Kelly, Michael J. *Legal Ethics and Legal Education*. Hastings-on-Hudson, N.Y.: The Hastings Center, 1980.

Ladenson, Robert F., et al., compilers. *A Selected Annotated Bibliography of Professional Ethics and Social Responsibility in Engineering*. Chicago: Center for the Study of Ethics in the Professions, Illinois Institute of Technology, 1980.

Powers, Charles W., and David Vogel. *Ethics and the Education of Business Managers*. Hastings-on-Hudson, N.Y.: Institute of Society, Ethics, and the Life Sciences, The Hastings Center, 1980.

Report of the Committee for Education in Business Ethics (sponsored by NEH). Skokie, Ill.: Fel-Pro, Inc., 1980.

Warwick, Donald P. *The Teaching of Ethics and the Social Sciences*. Hastings-on-Hudson, N.Y.: The Hastings Center, 1980.

Articles

Arledge, Elizabeth. "How Do You Pass a Course in Corporate Ethics?" *Rolling Stone* (October 1, 1981): 43.

Arlow, Peter, and Thomas A. Ulrich. "Business Ethics, Social Responsibility and Business Students: An Empirical Comparison of Clark's Study." *Akron Business and Economic Review* 11 (Fall 1980): 17–22.

Biegler, John C. "Ethics and Education: A Value Judgment." *Price Waterhouse Review* 21, 3 (1976): 2–3.

Bok, Derek C. "Can Ethics Be Taught?" *Change* (October 1976): 26–30.

Camenisch, Paul F. "Business Ethics: On Getting to the Heart of the Matter." *Business and Professional Ethics Journal* 1 (Fall 1981): 59–69.

DeGeorge, Richard T. "Ethical Responsibilities of Engineers in Large Organizations: The Pinto Case." *Business and Professional Ethics Journal* 1 (Fall 1981): 1–14.

Donaldson, Thomas. "Ethics in the Business Schools." *National Forum* 58 (Summer 1978): 11–14.

Eger, Martin. "The Conflict in Moral Education: An Informal Case Study." *The Public Interest* 63 (Spring 1981): 62–80.

Faber, Nancy. "Arjay Miller Thinks Business Schools Should Stress Ethics, but the Bottom Line Isn't Bad: His Grads Start at $27,500." *People* 11 (June 25, 1979): 65.

Goodpastor, Kenneth, and John B. Matthews, Jr. "Can a Corporation Have a Conscience?" *Harvard Business Review* (January–February 1982): 132–141.

Hamilton, Patricia. "Teaching Business Ethics." *D & B Reports* (July/August 1981): 38–41.

Hofstede, Geert. "Businessmen and Business School Faculty: A Comparison of Value Systems." *Journal of Management Studies* 15 (February 1978): 77–87.

Horwitt, Liz. "Corporate Ethics 101." *American Way* (September, 1981): 29–32.

"How Ethical Are You?" *Training* 14/12 (December 1977): 46–47.

Johnson, Harold L. "Adam Smith and Business Education." *AACSB Bulletin* 13 (October 1976).

Jones, Donald G. "Teaching Business Ethics: State of the Art and Normative Critique." *Selected Papers, Annual Meeting of the Society of Christian Ethics* (1981): 185–215.

Kirk, Russell. "Ethics in the Academy." *National Review* 29 (June 24, 1977): 726.

Konrad, A. Richard. "Are Business Ethics Worth Studying?" *Business and Society Review* 27 (Fall 1978): 54–57.

Kramer, Otto P. "Ethics Programs Can Help Companies Set Standards of Conduct." *Administrative Management* 38 (January 1977): 46–49.

Langholm, Odd, and J. Lundi. "Empirical Methods for Business Ethics Research." *Review of Social Economy* 35 (October 1977): 133–142.

Larwood, Laurie; Marion M. Wood; and Sheila David Inderlied. "Training Women for Management: New Problems, New Solutions." *Academy of Management Review* 3 (July 1978): 584–593.

Levy, Robert. "Business' Big Morality Play." *Dons Review* (August 1980): 56–61.

"Managers 0, Students 1 in an Ethics Contest." *Management Review* 67 (June 1978): 58.

McMahon, Thomas F. "Will Corporate Responsibility Flunk Out of College?" *Business and Society Review* 28 (Winter 1978–1979): 50–53.

Miller, Mary Susan, and A. Edward Miller. "It's Too Late for Ethics Courses in Business Schools." *Business and Society Review* 17 (Spring 1976): 39–42.

"Morality via the Classroom." *Management Review* 67 (May 1978): 54.

Nash, Laura. "Ethics Without the Sermon." *Harvard Business Review* (November–December 1981): 78–90. (Reprinted in this book as Chapter 6.)

Ottoson, Gerald O. "A Business Ethics Seminar for Corporate Executives." *The Lamplighter* (a publication of the American Society for Training and Development) 11 (January 1980): 6–7.

Purcell, Theodore V. "Do Courses in Business Ethics Pay Off?" *California Management Review* 19 (Summer 1977): 50–58.

Rachels, James. "Can Ethics Provide Answers?" *The Hastings Center Report* 10 (June 1980): 32–40.

Rohr, John A. "Ethics for the Senior Executive Service: Suggestions for Management Training." *Administration and Society* 12 (August 1980): 203–216.

Seligmann, J., and P. Malamud. "Game of Lying? Wall Street Journal Story on Harvard's Alleged Teaching of Unethical Business Behavior." *Newsweek* 93 (February 26, 1979): 57.

Simon, William E. "The Great American Challenges: Education and Ethics." *Financial Executive* 45 (April 1977): 34-39.

Steiner, John F. "The Prospect of Ethical Advisors for Business Corporations." *Business and Society* 16 (Spring 1976): 5-10.

Stone, Marvin. "Let's Teach Ethics." *Conservative Digest* (April 1979): 44.

Streeter, Deborah. "Doing Ethics as a Career: Answers and Questions." *Ethics and Policy* (Summer 1979): 9.

Thomas, Kenneth W. "Toward Multi-Dimensional Values in Teaching— The Example of Conflict Behaviors." *Academy of Management Review* 2 (July 1977): 484-490.

Vaccaro, Vincent T. "Philosophers and Business and Professional Ethics." *Business and Professional Ethics* 3 (Summer-Fall 1980): 2-4.

Vidali, Joseph J., and Douglas N. Behrman. "Collegiate Education in Business Administration: How Important a Role in Student Judgments of Ethical Business Practices?" *AACSB Bulletin* 13 (Spring 1977): 7-10.

Walton, C. C. "To Break the Pentameter—Ethics Courses?" *AACBS Bulletin* (Proceedings, Annual Meeting 1979): 31-60.

———. "Business Ethics: The Present and the Future." *The Hastings Center Report* 10 (October 1980): 16-20.

Walzer, Michael. "Teaching Morality." *The New Republic* (June 1978): 12-14.

Index

A

Acceleration-preferential practices. *See also* Affirmative action; Reverse discrimination
argument for, 192-193, 198
groups designated for, 196
guidelines on, 194-196, 198-199
law on, 193-194
McAleer v. *A.T.&T.* case, 191-192, 197-201
psychological problems in, 198, 200-201
vs. reverse discrimination, 195, 196
Acton, Lord John, 78
Advertising. *See also* Promotion
industry self-regulation of, 182-183
in personal-integrity example, 12
Affirmative action. *See also* Acceleration-preferential practices; Equal Employment Opportunity; Reverse discrimination
in business-ethics teaching, 149
groups designated for, 196
law on, 193-194

Affirmative moral responsibility (obligation), 35, 38-39, 40t
Age discrimination, in Sun Co. survey, 88
Allied Corporation
description of, 3-4
Kepone pollution by, 6, 17, 19n-20n
policy of, 7-8, 15-16
social commitment of, 4, 15-16
Allied Corporation Seminar
and anticipatory ethics, 17-18
benefits of, 18-19
content of, 10-11, 21-25
corporate-policy understanding in, 15-16
ethical decisionmaking in, 13-15, 24-25
genesis of, 4-8
importance of, 3
methods in, 9
objectives of, 10, 11-18
and organizational change, 16-17
participants in, 3, 8
problem analysis in, 11-13
Alternatives, in moral choice, 51

About the Editor
and Contributors

Donald G. Jones is a professor of social ethics at Drew University, where he teaches in the college and the graduate school. He has been a consultant to Allied Corporation in the area of management development training in ethics. He has taught a Business Ethics Seminar at Allied for eight years and has conducted numerous other management ethics training programs for major corporations. In addition, he has been a visiting Research Professor and Business Ethics at the Darden Graduate School of Business, University of Virginia and has participated in curriculum development programs at other universities in the field of business ethics.

Professor Jones is the author of two volumes of *A Bibliography of Business Ethics* (1976, 1982) and of *The Sectional Crisis* and *Northern Methodism* (1979); editor of *Private and Public Ethics* (1978) and of *Religion, Ethics, and Business* (1982); and coeditor of *American Civil Religion* (1974).

Robert C. Batchelder	Manager, Communications and Frequency Lockheed–California
Janet Dudrow	Social Policy and Programs Officer Northwestern National Bank, Minneapolis

Priscilla A. LaBarbara   Associate Professor of Marketing
New York University Graduate
School of Business

Laura L. Nash   Assistant Professor
Harvard Business School

Gerald E. Ottoson   Managing Human Resources
Consultant
Other Resources, Summit, N.J.

Theodore V. Purcell, S.J.   Professor of Business Ethics
Georgetown University

Michael R. Rion   Corporate Responsibility Director
Cummins Engine Company

Douglas Sturm   Professor of Social Ethics
Bucknell University;
Consultant to Sun Company

Douglas Wallace   Vice President, Social Policy and
Programs
Northwestern National Bank,
Minneapolis

Manuel Velasquez, S.J.   Professor of Business Policy
School of Business, University of
Santa Clara